Multilingual
Phrase Book

PASSPORT BOOKS
NTC/Contemporary Publishing Group

The publishers would like to thank the various national tourist offices for their
help during the preparation of this book

This edition first published in 1984 by Passport Books,
a division of NTC/Contemporary Publishing Group, Inc.,
4255 West Touhy Avenue, Lincolnwood, Illinois 60712-1975 U.S.A.
Originally published by Pan Books,

9 0 1 2 3 4 5 6 7 8 VP 9 8 7 6

Contents

Using the phrase book and a note on the pronunciation system

- This phrase book is designed to help you get by in eight languages, to get what you want or need. It concentrates on the simplest but most effective way you can express these needs in an unfamiliar language.

- The CONTENTS for each different language section gives you a good idea of which pages to consult for the phrase you need.

- The INDEX at the end of each language section gives more detailed information about where to look for your phrase. When you have found the right page you will be given:

  either – the exact phrase
  or – help in making up a suitable sentence
  and – help in getting the pronunciation right

- The English sentences in **bold type** will be useful for you in a variety of different situations, so they are worth learning by heart.

- In some cases you will find help in understanding what people say to *you*, in reply to your questions.

- Note especially these two sections:
  Everyday expressions
  Shop talk
  You are sure to want to refer to them most frequently.

- When you arrive in the foreign country make good use of the tourist information offices.

- The pronunciation system in this book is founded on three assumptions: firstly, that it is not possible to describe in print the sounds of a foreign language in such a way that the English speaker with no phonetic training will produce them accurately, or even intelligibly; secondly, that perfect pronunciation is not essential for communication; and lastly that the average visitor abroad is more interested in achieving successful communication than in learning how to pronounce new speech sounds. Observation and experience have shown these assumptions to be justified. The most important characteristic of the present system, therefore, is that it makes no attempt whatsoever to teach the sounds of the other language, but uses instead the nearest English sounds to them. The sentences transcribed for pronunciation are designed to be read as naturally as possible, as if they were ordinary English and with no attempt to make the words sound 'foreign'. In this way you will still sound quite American or English but you will at the same time be understood. Practice always helps performance and it is a good idea to rehearse out loud any of the sentences you know you are going to need. When you come to the point of using them, say them with conviction.

Dutch

D. L. Ellis, D. van der Luit

Pronunciation **Dr J. Baldwin**

Useful addresses

Netherlands Tourist Office
576 5th Ave.
New York, NY 10036

Belgium National Tourist Office
745 5th Ave.
New York, NY 10020

Contents

Pronunciation hints

In Dutch it is important to stress or emphasize the syllables in italics, just as you would if we were to take as an English example: *Li*ttle *Jack* *Hor*ner *sat* in the *cor*ner. Here we have ten syllables but only four stresses.
Succes!

Everyday expressions

[See also 'Shop talk', p. 23]

- Although you will find the correct greetings listed below, the Dutch commonly use **daag** (duk) to express all of these.

Hello	**Hallo**
	hullo
Good morning	**Goede morgen**
	hoo-der mor-hen
Good afternoon	**Goede middag**
	hoo-der mid-duk
Good day	**Goede dag**
	hoo-der duk
Good evening	**Goede avond**
	hoo-der ah-vent
Good night	**Goede nacht**
	hoo-der nukt
Goodbye	**Tot ziens**
	tot zeens
Yes	**Ja**
	yah
Please	**Alstublieft**
	uls-too-bleeft
Thank you	**Dank u**
	dunk oo
Thank you very much	**Dank u wel**
	dunk oo wel
That's right	**Precies**
	prer-sees
No	**Nee**
	nay
No, thank you	**Nee, dank u**
	nay dunk oo
I disagree	**Ik ben het er niet mee eens**
	ik ben et er neet may ayns
Excuse me	**Pardon**
	par-don
Don't mention it	**Geen dank**
	hain dunk

It doesn't matter

Het geeft niet
et ha*y*ft neet

Where's the toilet please?

Waar is het toilet, alstublieft?
wahr is et twah-let uls-too-bl*ee*ft

Do you speak English?

Spreekt u engels?
spr*ay*kt oo *e*ng-els

What's your name?

Hoe heet u?
hoo hate oo

My name is . . .

Ik heet . . .
ik hate . . .

Asking the way

ESSENTIAL INFORMATION

- Keep a look out for all these place names as you will find them on shops, maps and notices.

WHAT TO SAY

Excuse me, please

Neem me niet kwalijk . . .
name mer neet kw*a*h-lek . . .

How do I get . . .

Hoe kom ik naar . . .
hoo kom ik nar . . .

to the airport?

het vliegveld?
et vl*ee*k-velt

to Amsterdam?

Amsterdam?
umster-d*u*m

to the beach?

het strand?
et strunt

to the bus station?

het bus station?
et b*u*s st*a*ts-see-on

to the Centraal hotel?

het Centraal Hotel?
et cen-tr*a*hl hotel

to the Concertgebouw?

het Concertgebouw?
et con-s*ai*rt-her-ba-oo

to the Delta Works?

de Delta Werken?
der d*e*lta w*ai*rken

How do I get . . .

    to the market?

    to the police station?

    to the post office?

    to the railway station?

    to the Rijksmuseum?

    to the Rokin?

    to the sports stadium?

    to the tourist information
       office?

    to Utrecht?

Is there . . . near by?

    a baker's

    a bank

    a bar

    a bus stop

    a butcher's

    a café

    a cake shop

    a campsite

    a car park

    a change bureau

Hoe kom ik naar . . .
hoo kom ik nar

de markt?
der markt

het politiebureau?
et poh-*lee*-tsee-boo-r*o*

het postkantoor?
et p*o*sst-kun-tor

het spoorwegstation?
et sp*o*r-wek-st*a*ts-see-on

het Rijksmuseum?
et r*ey*ks-moo-sayem

het Rokin?
et r*o*k-kin

het stadion?
et st*a*h-dee-on

het VVV kantoor?
et vay-vay-vay kun-t*o*r

Utrecht?
oo-trekt

Is hier in de buurt . . .
is here in der boort . . .

een bakker?
en b*u*kker

een bank?
en bunk

een bar?
en bar

een bushalte?
en b*u*s-hulter

een slager?
en sl*a*h-her

een café
en cuf-f*ay*

een banketwinkel?
en bunk*et*-winkel

een camping?
en camping

een parkeerterrein?
en par-k*ai*r-terreyn

een wissel kantoor?
en w*i*ssel kun-t*o*r

a chemist's	**een drogist?**
	en dro-*hist*
a delicatessen	**een delicatessen winkel?**
	en day-lee-kah-*tes*-sen w*i*nkel
a dentist's	**een tandarts?**
	en t*u*nt-arts
a department store	**een warenhuis?**
	en w*a*h-ren-ho-ees
a disco	**een disco**
	en dis-ko
a doctor's surgery	**een dokter?**
	en d*o*k-ter
a dry-cleaner's	**een stomerij?**
	een stomer-r*e*y
a fishmonger's	**een viswinkel?**
	en v*i*s-winkel
a garage (for repairs)	**een garage?**
	en hah-r*a*h-zher
a hairdresser's	**een kapper?**
	en k*u*pper
a greengrocer's	**een groentewinkel?**
	en hroonter-w*i*nkel
a grocer's	**een kruidenierswinkel?**
	en kro-ee-der-n*ee*rs-winkel
a Health and Social Security Office	**een Kantoor Gezondheids en Sociale Zorg Dienst?**
	en kun-t*o*r her-z*o*nt-heyts en soh-see-*ah*-ler z*o*rk deenst
a hospital	**een ziekenhuis?**
	en z*ee*ken-ho-ees
a hotel	**een hotel?**
	en ho-t*e*l
an ice-cream parlour	**een ijs-salon?**
	en *e*ys-sah-lon
a laundry	**een wasserij?**
	en wusser-r*e*y
a night club	**een nacht club?**
	en n*u*kt cloop
a park	**een park?**
	en park
a petrol station	**een benzinepompstation?**
	en ben-zee-ner-p*o*mp-stats-see-on

Is there . . . near by?	**Is hier in de buurt . . .**
	is here in der boort . . .
a post box	**een brievenbus?**
	en br*ee*ven-bus
a public toilet	**een openbaar toilet?**
	en open-bar twah-l*e*t
a restaurant	**een restaurant?**
	en res-to-r*a*n
a supermarket	**een supermarkt?**
	en s*oo*per-markt
a telephone (booth)	**een telefoon cel?**
	en telef*o*ne cel
a tobacconist's	**een sigarenwinkel?**
	en see-h*a*hren winkel
a travel agent's	**een reisbureau?**
	en reys-boo-r*o*
a youth hostel	**een jeugdherberg?**
	en y*e*rkt-hair-bairk

DIRECTIONS

- Asking where a place is, or if a place is near by, is one thing; making sense of the answer is another.

- Here are some of the most important key directions and replies.

Left	**Links**
	links
Right	**Rechts**
	rekts
Straight on	**Rechtdoor**
	rekt-dor
There	**Daar**
	dar
First left/right	**Eerste links/rechts**
	*ai*r-ster links/rekts

Accommodation

ESSENTIAL INFORMATION
Hotel

- If you want hotel-type accommodation, all the following words in capital letters are worth looking for on signs:
  HOTEL MOTEL
  PENSION (boarding house)
  JEUGDHERBERG (youth hostel)
- A list of hotels in the town or district can usually be obtained at the local tourist office.
- All hotels are listed, the cheaper ones having no star rating, while the more luxurious and expensive having proportionally more stars.
- The cost is displayed in the room itself, so you can check it when having a look round before agreeing to stay.
- The displayed cost is for the room itself, per night and not per person. Breakfast is extra and therefore optional.
- Service and VAT (**BTW**) is always included in the cost of the room, so tipping is voluntary.
- Not all hotels provide meals, apart from breakfast. A breakfast will consist of coffee/tea, bread (usually rolls), cold meats, cheese, jam and fruit.
- An identity document is requested when registering at a hotel and will normally be kept overnight.

WHAT TO SAY

I have a booking	**Ik heb een gereserveerde kamer** ik hep en her-ray-ser-vair-der kah-mer
Have you any vacancies, please?	**Heeft u nog kamers?** hayft oo nok kah-mers
Can I book a room?	**Kan ik een kamer reserveren?** kun ik en kah-mer ray-ser-vairen
It's for . . .	**Het is voor . . .** et is vor . . .
one adult/person	**één volwassene/persoon** ayn vol-wusserner/pair-sohn

It's for . . .	**Het is voor . . .**
	et is vor . . .
two adults/people	**twee volwassenen/personen**
	tway vol-w*u*ssernen/pair-s*o*h-nen
and one child	**en één kind**
	en ayn kint
and two children	**en twee kinderen**
	en tway k*i*n-der-en
It's for . . .	**Het is voor . . .**
	et is vor . . .
one night	**één nacht**
	ayn nukt
two nights	**twee nachten**
	tway nukten
one week	**één week**
	ayn wake
two weeks	**twee weken**
	tway w*a*ken
I would like . . .	**Ik zou graag . . .**
	ik zow hrahk . . .
a room	**een kamer**
	en k*a*h-mer
two rooms	**twee kamers**
	tway k*a*hmers
with a single bed	**met een één-persoonsbed**
	met en *a*yn-pair-sohns-bet
with two single beds	**met twee één-persoonsbedden**
	met tway *a*yn-pair-sohns-bed-den
with a double bed	**met een tweepersoonsbed**
	met en tway-pair-sohns-bet
with a toilet	**met toilet**
	met twah-l*e*t
with a bathroom	**met badkamer**
	met b*u*t-kah-mer
with a shower	**met douche**
	met doosh
with a cot	**met een wieg**
	met en week
I'd like . . .	**Ik wil het graag met . . . hebben**
	ik wil et hrahk met . . . h*e*bben
full board	**vol pension**
	vol pun-see-*o*n

half board	**half (demi) pension**
	hulf (d*a*y-mee) pun-see-*o*n
Do you serve meals?	**Kunnen we hier eten?**
	koonnen wer here *a*y-ten
Can I look at the room?	**Kan ik de kamer zien?**
	kun ik der k*a*h-mer zeen
OK, I'll take it	**Goed, ik neem het**
	hoot ik name et
No thanks, I won't take it	**Nee dank u, deze niet**
	nay dunk oo d*a*zer neet
The bill, please	**De rekening, alstublieft**
	der r*a*yker-ning uls-too-bl*ee*ft
Is service included?	**Is het inclusief bediening?**
	is et in-cloo-seef ber-d*ee*-ning
I think this is wrong	**Ik denk dat dit verkeerd is**
	ik denk dut dit ver-k*ai*rt is
May I have a receipt?	**Mag ik een kwitantie hebben?**
	muk ik en kwee-t*u*n-tsee hebben

Camping

- Look for the words **CAMPING** or **KAMPEERTERREIN**.
- Be prepared to have to pay:
  per person
  for the car
  for the tent or for trailer space
  for electricity
  for hot showers
- You must provide proof of identity, such as your passport.
- Officially recognized campsites have a star rating: the more stars, the better equipped.
- Camping is regulated by local and provincial by-laws. Lists are available from the VVV.
- Off-site camping is not permitted.

Youth hostels

- Look for the word: **JEUGDHERBERG**
- You must have a YHA card.
- The charge for the night is the same for all ages, but some hostels are more expensive than others.

- You must bring your own sleeping bag lining.
- Accommodation is usually provided in small dormitories.
- Food and cooking facilities vary from place to place and you may also have to help with jobs.

WHAT TO SAY

Have you any vacancies? **Heeft u nog iets vrij?**
hayft oo nok eets vrey

How much is it . . . **Hoeveel is het . . .**
h*oo*-vale is et . . .

  for the tent? **voor de tent?**
vor der tent

  for the caravan? **voor de caravan?**
vor der c*a*ravan

  for the car? **voor de auto?**
vor der *ow*to

  for the electricity? **voor de elektriciteit?**
vor der ay-lek-tree-see-t*ai*t

  per person? **per persoon?**
pair pair-s*oh*n

  per day/night? **per dag/nacht?**
pair duk/nukt

May I look round? **Mag ik even rondkijken?**
muk ik *ay*-ven rond-kaiken

Do you provide anything . . . **Serveert u iets . . .**
s*ai*r-v*ai*rt oo eets . . .

  to eat? **te eten?**
ter *ay*-ten

  to drink? **te drinken?**
ter dr*i*nken

Do you have . . . **Heeft u . . .**
hayft oo . . .

  a bar? **een bar?**
en bar

  hot showers? **warme douches?**
w*a*rmer dooshes

  a kitchen? **een keuken?**
en k*e*rken

  a laundry? **een wasserij?**
en wusser-r*ey*

  a restaurant? **een restaurant?**
en res-to-r*a*n

a shop?	**een winkel?**
	en winkel
a swimming pool?	**een zwembad?**
	en zwem-but

[*For food shopping, see p. 26, and for eating and drinking out, see p. 36*]

Problems

The toilet	**Het toilet**
	et twah-let
The shower	**De douche**
	der doosh
The tap	**De kraan**
	der krahn
The razor point	**Het scheer-contact**
	et skair-contuct
The light	**Het licht**
	et likt
. . . is not working	**. . . werkt niet**
	. . . wairkt neet
My camping gas has run out	**Ik heb geen kampgas meer**
	ik hep hane kump-hus mair

LIKELY REACTIONS

Have you an identity document?	**Heeft u een identiteitsbewijs?**
	hayft oo en ee-den-tee-taits-ber-weys
Your membership card, please	**Uw lidmaatschap-kaart, alstublieft**
	oo lit-maht-skup-kart uls-too-bleeft
What's your name?	**Wat is uw naam?**
[*see p. 11*]	wut is oo nahm
Sorry, we're full	**Het spijt me, we zijn vol**
	et spate mer wer zane vol
How many people is it for?	**Voor hoeveel personen is het?**
	vor hoo-vale pair-soh-nen is et
How many nights is it for?	**Voor hoeveel nachten is het?**
	vor hoo-vale nukten is et
It's (12) guilders . . .	**Het is (twaalf) gulden . . .**
	et is (twahlf) hool-den . . .
per day/night	**per dag/nacht**
[*For numbers, see p. 54*]	pair duk/nukt

I haven't any rooms left	**Ik heb geen kamers meer**
	ik hep hane k*ah*-mers mair
Do you want to have a look?	**Wilt u even kijken?**
	wilt oo *ay*-ven kai-ken

General shopping

The drugstore/The chemist's

ESSENTIAL INFORMATION

- Look for the words
  APOTHEEK and **DROGIST**.
  You may also see the following
  signs: a serpent on a staff denotes
  an **apotheek** and a bust of a **gaper**
  (yawner) a **drogist**.
- Medicines (drugs) are available
  only at the **apotheek**.
- Some non-drugs can be bought
  at the **drogist**, at department
  stores or supermarkets.
- Drugstores are open
  Monday to Friday
  8.00 a.m. – 5.30 p.m.
  Drugstores take turns
  staying open over the
  weekend and at night.
- Some toiletries can also be
  bought at a **PARFUMERIE** and at hairdressing salons.

WHAT TO SAY

I'd like . . .	**Ik zou graag . . . hebben**
	ik zow hrahk . . . h*e*bben
some Alka Seltzer	**wat Alka Seltzer**
	wut alka seltzer

some antiseptic	**een antiseptisch middel**
	en *u*ntee-septees middel
some aspirin	**wat aspirine**
	wut uspee-r*ee*ner
some baby food	**wat baby voeding**
	wut b*a*by v*oo*ding
some contraceptives	**wat voorbehoedsmiddelen**
	wut v*o*r-ber-hoots-m*i*ddelen
some cotton	**wat watten**
	wut w*u*tten
some disposable diapers	**wat weggooi luiers**
	wut w*e*k-hoy lo-ee-ers
some eye drops	**wat oogdruppels**
	wut *oa*k-druppels
some inhalant	**een inhaleermiddel**
	en in-hah-l*ai*r-middel
some insect repellent	**een insecten afweermiddel**
	een insecten *u*f-wair-middel
some paper tissues	**wat papieren tissues**
	wut pah-p*ee*-ren t*i*s-sues
some sanitary napkins	**wat damesverband**
	wut d*a*h-mer-ver-b*u*nt
some sticking plaster	**wat pleisters**
	wut pl*e*y-sters
some suntan oil/lotion	**wat zonnebrand olie/creme**
	wut z*o*nner-brunt *o*h-lee/crem
some Tampax	**wat Tampax**
	wut t*u*mpux
some throat lozenges	**wat keelpastilles**
	wut k*a*le-pus-til-yes
some (soft) toilet paper	**wat (zacht) toiletpapier**
	wut (zukt) twah-let-pah-peer
I'd like something for . . .	**Ik zou graag iets hebben voor . . .**
	ik zow hrahk eets h*e*bben vor . . .
bites	**beten**
	b*a*yten
burns	**brandwonden**
	br*u*nt-wonden
a cold	**verkoudheid**
	ver-k*o*wt-hate
constipation	**constipatie**
	con-stee-p*a*h-tsee

I'd like something for . . .	Ik zou graag iets hebben voor . . .
	ik zow hrahk eets hebben vor . . .
a cough	**hoest**
	hoost
diarrhea	**diarree**
	dee-ar-ray
earache	**oorpijn**
	or-pain
flu	**griep**
	hreep
sore gums	**zeer tandvlees**
	zair tunt-vlays
stings	**steken**
	stayken
sunburn	**zonnebrand**
	zonner-brunt
travel sickness	**reis ziekte**
	reys zeek-ter

[*For other essential expressions, see 'Shop talk', p. 23*]

Holiday items

ESSENTIAL INFORMATION

- Places to shop at and signs to look for:
  BOEKWINKEL (bookshop/stationery shop)
  FOTOGRAFIE
  and of course department stores such as: **DE BIJENKORF**
  HEMA **VROOM EN DREESMANN**

WHAT TO SAY

I'd like . . .	Ik zou graag . . .
	ik zow hrahk . . .
a bag	**een tas**
	en tus

a beach ball	**een strandbal**
	en str*u*nt-bul
a bucket	**een emmer**
	en *e*mmer
an English newspaper	**een engelse krant**
	en eng-el-ser krunt
some envelopes	**wat enveloppen**
	wut enver-loppen
a guide book	**een reisgids**
	en r*ey*s-hits
a map (of the area)	**een kaart (van de omgeving)**
	en kart (vun der om-h*a*yving)
some postcards	**wat ansichtkaarten**
	wut uns*i*kt-karten
a spade	**een schop**
	en skop
a straw hat	**een stroohoed**
	en str*o*h-hoot
some sunglasses	**een zonnebril**
	en z*o*nner-bril
some writing paper	**wat schrijfpapier**
	wut skr*ey*f-pah-peer
a roll of color film	**een kleurenfilm**
[*show camera*]	en kler-ren-film
a roll of black and white film	**een zwart-wit film**
	en zwart-wit film

Shop talk

ESSENTIAL INFORMATION

- Know how to say the important weights and measures. You will hear grams, ounces, kilos and pounds used in shops and markets. The metric Dutch pound **pond** (pont) is ten per cent more than the U.S. pound and there are exactly **2 pond** in 1 kilo. The metric

Dutch ounce **ons** (ons) is equivalent to 100 grams. Throughout the book you will find that we have used the colloquial Dutch expressions (i.e. ½ oz, 1 oz, 1 lb) to translate grams and kilograms, as they are both more widely used and simpler to say.
[*For numbers, see p. 54*]

50 grams/½ oz	**vijftig gram/een half ons** v*ey*ftik hrum/en hulf ons
100 grams/1 oz	**honderd gram/één ons** h*o*ndert hrum/ayn ons
200 grams/2 oz	**tweehonderd gram/twee ons** tw*ay*-hondert hrum/tway ons
250 grams/½ lb	**tweehonderdvijftig gram/een half pond** tw*ay*-hondert-v*ey*ftik hrum/en hulf pont
½ kilo/1 lb	**een halve kilo/één pond** en h*u*lver kilo/ayn pont
1 kilo/2 lbs	**één kilo/twee pond** ayn kilo/tway pont
2 kilos	**twee kilo** tway kilo
½ litre	**een halve liter** een h*u*lver l*ee*ter
1 litre	**één liter** ayn l*ee*ter
2 litres	**twee liter** tway l*ee*ter

- In small shops don't be surprised if customers, as well as the shop assistant say 'hello' and 'goodbye' to you.

CUSTOMER

I'm just looking	**Ik kijk even** ik keyk *ay*-ven
How much is this/that?	**Hoeveel is dit/dat?** h*oo*-vale is dit/dut
What's that?	**Wat is dat?** wut is dut
What are those?	**Wat zijn dat?** wut zane dut
Is there a discount?	**Is er korting op?** is er korting op

I'd like that, please	**Ik wil dat graag hebben, alstublieft**
	ik wil dut hrahk hebben uls-too-bleeft
Not that	**Dat niet**
	dut neet
Like that	**Zoals dat**
	zo-uls dut
That's enough, thank you	**Dat is genoeg, dank u**
	dut is her-nook dunk oo
More please	**Wat meer alstublieft**
	wut mair uls-too-bleeft
Less please	**Wat minder alstublieft**
	wut min-der uls-too-bleeft
That's fine	**Dat is fijn**
	dut is fane
OK	**Ok**
	okay
I won't take it, thank you	**Ik neem het niet, dank u**
	ik name et neet dunk oo
It's not right	**Het is niet goed**
	et is neet hoot
Have you got something . . .	**Heeft u iets . . .**
	heyft oo eets . . .
better?	**beters?**
	bayters
cheaper?	**goedkopers?**
	hoot-kopers
different?	**anders?**
	unders
larger?	**groters?**
	hroh-ters
smaller?	**kleiners?**
	kleyners
Can I have a bag, please?	**Mag ik een zak, alstublieft?**
	muk ik en zuk uls-too-bleeft
Can I have a receipt?	**Mag ik een kwitantie?**
	muk ik en kwee-tun-tsee
Do you take . . .	**Neemt u . . . aan?**
	naymt oo . . . ahn
English/American money?	**engels/amerikaans geld**
	eng-els/ah-may-ree-kahns helt

Do you take . . .	**Neemt u . . . aan?**
	naymt oo . . . ahn
travellers' cheques?	**reischeques**
	reys-sheks
credit cards?	**credietkaarten**
	credeet-karten

SHOP ASSISTANT

Can I help you?	**Kan ik u helpen?**
	kun ik oo helpen
What would you like?	**Wat wilt u hebben?**
	wut wilt oo hebben
Will that be all?	**Is dat alles?**
	is dut ul-les
Anything else?	**Iets anders?**
	eets unders
Would you like it wrapped?	**Wilt u het ingepakt hebben?**
	wilt oo et in-her-pukt hebben
Sorry, none left	**Tot mijn spijt, uitverkocht**
	tot mane spate o-eet-ver-kokt
I haven't got any	**Ik heb geen**
	ik heb hane
I haven't got any more	**Ik heb geen meer**
	ik hep hane mair
How many do you want? ⌉ How much do you want? ⌋	**Hoeveel wenst u?**
	hoo-vale wenst oo
Is this enough?	**Is dit genoeg?**
	is dit her-nook

Shopping for food

Bread

ESSENTIAL INFORMATION

• Key words to look for:
  BAKKERIJ (bakery)
  BAKKER (baker)
  BROOD (bread)

- Supermarkets of any size and general stores nearly always sell bread.
- Opening times are usually 8.30 a.m. – 5.30 p.m.; early closing time varies slightly locally.
- The most characteristic type of loaf is the 'French stick', which comes in two sizes: large and small.
- Most bread is sold unsliced in both bakeries and supermarkets. However, if you prefer your bread sliced **gesneden** (her-snayden), hand the loaf to the assistant and she will slice it for you. You will have to pay a small charge for this service.

WHAT TO SAY

A loaf (like that)	**Een brood (zoals dat)**
	en brote (zo-uls dut)
A white loaf	**Een wit brood**
	en wit brote
A wholemeal loaf	**Een tarwe brood**
	en tar-wer brote
A packet of pumpernickel	**Een pakje roggebrood**
	en puk-yer rok-her-brote
A bread roll	**Een broodje**
	een brote-yer
A currant bun	**Een krentenbol**
	en krenter-bol
Two loaves	**Twee broden**
	tway broden
A French stick	**Een stokbrood**
	en stok-brote

[*For other essential expressions, see 'Shop talk' p. 23*]

Cakes and ice cream

ESSENTIAL INFORMATION

- Key words to look for:
  BANKETBAKKERIJ (cake shop)
  BANKETBAKKER (cake/pastry maker)

> **GEBAK** (pastries/cakes)
> **IJS** (ice cream)
> **IJS-SALON** (ice cream parlor)
> **BONBONS en CHOCOLADE** (chocolates)
> **SUIKERWERKEN** (candy shop)

- **THEE-SALON**: a place to buy cakes and have a drink, usually in the afternoon. See also p. 36 'Ordering a drink and a snack'.

WHAT TO SAY

The type of cakes you find in the shops may vary from region to region but the following are the most common; cake is *not* bought per slice.

een cake en cake	a plain butter cake; size about 300–700 grams
een rozijnen cake en roh-*zey*nen cake	a raisin cake
een citroen cake en cit*roo*n cake	a lemon cake
een appeltaart en *u*ppel-tart	an apple tart
een slagroomtaart en sl*u*k-rome-tart	a cream tart
een vruchtentaart en vr*u*kten-tart	a fruit tart
een kwarktaart en kwark-tart	a cheese (cream) cake
roomsoezen r*o*me-soozen	éclairs
slagroomgebakjes sl*u*k-rome-her-b*u*k-yers	cream pastries
vruchtengebakjes vr*u*kten-her-buk-yers	fruit pastries
amandelbroodjes um-m*u*ndel-brote-yers	almond rolls

A . . . ice cream, please	**Een . . . ijsje, alstublieft** en . . . *eys*-yer uls-too-bl*ee*ft
banana	**bananen** bah-n*ah*-nen
chocolate	**chocolade** shocol*ah*-der

mocha	**mokka**
	mokka
pistachio	**pistache**
	peestush
strawberry	**aardbeien**
	ard-bey-yen
vanilla	**vanille**
	vun-il-yer
One cone	**Eén van**
	ayn vun
Two cones	**Twee van**
	tway vun

Picnic food

ESSENTIAL INFORMATION

● Key words to look for:
DELICATESSEN ⎤
VLEESWAREN ⎦ delicatessen

WHAT TO SAY

Two slices of . . .	**Twee plakken . . .**
	tway plakken . . .
roast beef	**rosbief**
	ros-beef
roast pork	**varkens rollade**
	var-kens rollah-der
tongue	**tong**
	tong
ham	**ham**
	hum
liver sausage	**leverworst**
	layver-worst
garlic sausage	**knoflook worst**
	knof-loke worst
salami	**salami**
	sah-lah-mee

You might also like to try some of these:

een stuk rookworst	a piece of smoked sausage (best
en sterk roke-worst	eaten hot)
een zoute nieuwe haring	a salted fresh herring
en zowter nee-wer hahring	
en gerookte paling	a smoked eel
en her-roke-ter pah-ling	
een Frankfurter	a Frankfurter sausage
en frunk-foorter	
een stuk boterhammenworst	some luncheon meat
en sterk boter-hummer-worst	
wat rookvlees	some smoked beef (thin, salty
wut roke-vlays	slices)
wat gerookte makreel	some smoked mackerel
wut her-roke-ter mah-krayl	
wat zult	some brawn: pork (boar's flesh)
wut zult	pickled in vinegar
wat vis-sla	some fish salad
wut vis-slah	
wat champignon-sla	some mushroom salad
wut shum-peen-yon-slah	
wat gehakt	cold, spicy minced meat (pork or
wut her-hukt	beef)
wat kippesla	some chicken salad
wut kipper-slah	
wat worstsla	some sausage salad
wut worst-slah	
wat kaassla	some cheese salad
wut kahs-slah	
Goudse kaas (belegen)	Gouda cheese (mature)
howtser kahs (berlay-hen)	
Edammer kaas	Edam cheese
ay-dummer kahs	
Leidse kaas	Leiden cheese (cumin seed cheese)
leyt-ser kahs	
nagelkaas	clove cheese
nah-hel kahs	
Limburgse kaas	Limburger (piquant) cheese
limburg-ser kahs	

Fruit and vegetables

ESSENTIAL INFORMATION

- Key words to look for:
  FRUIT
  FRUITHANDELAAR (fruit seller)
  GROENTEN (vegetables)
- It is customary for you to choose your own fruit and vegetables at
  the market and for the vendor to weigh and price them. You must
  take your own shopping bag as paper and plastic bags are not
  normally provided.
  [*For further details on Dutch weights, see 'Shop talk', p. 23*]

WHAT TO SAY

1 kilo of . . .	Eén kilo . . .
	ayn *ki*lo . . .
apples	**appels**
	*u*ppels
apricots	**abrikozen**
	ah-bree-k*o*zen
bananas	**bananen**
	bah-n*ah*-nen
bilberries	**bosbessen**
	b*o*s-bessen
cherries	**kersen**
	k*air*sen
grapes (white/black)	**druiven (witte/zwarte)**
	dr*o*-ee-ven (witter/zw*ar*ter)
greengages	**reine claudes**
	reyner-cl*ow*des
mulberries	**moerbeien**
	m*oo*r-bey-en
oranges	**sinaasappels**
	s*ee*-nahs-uppels
pears	**peren**
	p*ay*ren
peaches	**perziken**
	p*air*zi-ken

1 kilo of . . .	**Eén kilo . . .**
	ayn *ki*lo . . .
plums	**pruimen**
	pr*o*-ee-men
raspberries	**frambozen**
	frum-b*o*zen
strawberries	**aardbeien**
	*a*rd-bey-yen
A pineapple, please	**Een ananas, alstublieft**
	en *u*n-ah-nus uls-too-bl*ee*ft
A grapefruit	**Een grapefruit**
	en grape-fruit
A melon	**Een meloen**
	en mer-l*oo*n
A water melon	**Een watermeloen**
	en w*a*h-ter-mer-loon
½ kilo of . . .	**Eén pond . . .**
	ayn pont . . .
aubergines	**aubergines**
	*o*h-ber-sheens
broad beans	**tuinbonen**
	t*o*-een-bonen
carrots	**wortels**
	w*o*r-tels
green beans	**slabonen**
	sl*a*h-bonen
leeks	**prei**
	prey
mushrooms	**champignons**
	shum-peen-y*o*ns
onions	**uien**
	*o*we-yen
peas	**doperwten**
	dop*air*-ten
podded peas	**peultjes**
	p*e*rlt-yers
potatoes	**aardappels**
	*a*r-duppels
red cabbage	**rode kool**
	roder kohl
shallots	**sjalotten**
	shah-l*o*t-ten

spinach	**spinazie**
	spee-nah-zee
tomatoes	**tomaten**
	toh-mah-ten
A bunch of . . .	**Een bosje . . .**
	en bos-yer . . .
parsley	**peterselie**
	pa-ter-saylee
radishes	**radijs**
	rah-deys
A garlic	**Een knoflook**
	en knof-loke
A lettuce	**Een krop sla**
	en krop slah
A stick of celery	**Een bleekselderij**
	en blake-sel-der-ray
A cucumber	**Een komkommer**
	en kom-kommer
A turnip	**Een witte raap**
	en witter rahp
Like that, please	**Zoals dat, alstublieft**
	zo-uls dut uls-too-bleeft

[*For other essential expressions, see 'Shop talk' p. 23*]

Meat and fish

ESSENTIAL INFORMATION

- Key words to look for:
  SLAGERIJ (butcher shop)
  SLAGER (butcher)
  VISWINKEL (fish store)
- Lamb and mutton are expensive in Holland.
- Markets and large supermarkets usually have fresh-fish counters.

WHAT TO SAY

For roasts, choose the type of meat and then say how many people it is
for:

Some beef, please	**Wat rundvlees, alstublieft** wut r*u*nt-vlays uls-too-bl*ee*ft
Some lamb	**Wat lamsvlees** wut l*u*ms-vlays
Some mutton	**Wat schapevlees** wut sk*a*h-per-vlays
Some pork	**Wat varkensvlees** wut v*a*rkens-vlays
Some veal	**Wat kalfsvlees** wut k*u*lfs-vlays
A roast . . .	**Groot stuk vlees . . .** hrote sterk vlays . . .
for two people	**voor twee personen** vor tway pair-s*o*hnen
for four people	**voor vier personen** vor veer pair-s*o*hnen
for six people	**voor zes personen** vor zes pair-s*o*hnen

For steak, liver and kidneys do as above:

Some steak, please	**Wat biefstuk, alstublieft** wut b*ee*f-sterk uls-too-bl*ee*ft
Some liver	**Wat lever** wut l*a*yver
Some kidneys	**Wat nieren** wut n*ee*-ren
Some sausages	**Wat worst** wut worst
for three people	**voor drie personen** vor dree pair-s*o*hnen
Two veal scallops	**Twee kalfsoesters** tway k*u*lfs-oosters
Three pork chops	**Drie varkenskarbonaden** dree v*a*rkens-karboh-n*a*hden

Four mutton chops	**Vier schaapskarbonaden**
	veer sk*a*hps-karboh-nahden
Five lamb chops	**Vijf lamskarbonaden**
	veyf l*u*ms-karboh-nahden
A chicken	**Een kip**
	en kip
A rabbit	**Een konijn**
	en koh-n*ey*n
A tongue	**Een tong**
	en tong

Purchase large fish and small shellfish by weight:

½ kilo of . . .	**Eén pond . . .**
	ayn pont . . .
cod	**kabeljauw**
	kahbel-y*o*w
eel	**paling**
	p*a*hling
haddock	**schelvis**
	sk*e*lvis
herring	**haring**
	h*a*h-ring
pike	**snoek**
	snook
plaice	**schol**
	skol
turbot	**tarbot**
	tarbot
mussels	**mosselen**
	m*o*ssel-en
prawns	**garnalen**
	har-n*a*hlen
shrimps	**kleine garnalen**
	kl*ey*ner har-n*a*hlen
salmon	**zalm**
	zulm
tuna	**tonijn**
	toh-n*ey*n

For some shellfish and 'frying pan' fish specify the number
you want:

A crab, please	**Een krab, alstublieft**
	en krup uls-too-bleeft
A lobster	**Een zeekreeft**
	en zay-krayft
A scallop	**Een kammossel**
	en kum-mossel
A whiting	**Een wijting**
	en waiting
A trout	**Een forel**
	en foh-rel
A sole	**Een tong**
	en tong
A mackerel	**Een makreel**
	en mah-krayl

Eating and drinking out

Ordering a drink and a snack

ESSENTIAL INFORMATION

- The places to ask for
  CAFÉ SNELBUFFET CAFETARIA
- By law, the price list of drinks (**TARIEF**) must be displayed
  outside or in the window.
- There is waiter service in all cafés, but you can drink at the bar
  or counter if you wish.
- When the bill is presented, the amount will be inclusive of service
  and VAT (**BTW**). Tipping: some additional small change is often
  given.
- Cafés serve both non-alcoholic drinks and alcoholic drinks and
  are normally open all day. Cream/milk is always served separately when ordering coffee or tea.
- Children are allowed into bars.

- If you want a sandwich lunch, look out for **KOFFIETAFEL**. You will be served a variety of breads, cold meats, cheeses – possibly a hot dish – and a bowl of soup or a salad. Coffee, milk or tea are also usually included.

WHAT TO SAY

I'll have . . . please	**Ik wil graag . . . alstublieft** ik wil hrahk . . . uls-too-bleeft
a cup of coffee	**een kop koffie** en kop koffee
a cup of tea	**een kop thee** en kop tay
with milk/lemon	**met melk/citroen** met melk/citroon
a glass of milk	**een glas melk** en hlus melk
a hot chocolate	**een kop chocolade** en kop shocolah-der
a chilled chocolate	**een glas chocomel** en hlus shoco-mel
a mineral water	**een mineral water** en mee-ne-rahl wah-ter
a lemonade	**een citroen limonade** en citroon leemo-nah-der
an orangeade	**een sinaasappel limonade** en seenahs-uppel leemo-nah-der
a Coca-Cola	**een Coca-Cola** en coca-cola
a fresh orange juice	**een sinaasappelsap** en seenahs-uppel-sup
a blackcurrant drink	**een cassis** en cussis
an apple juice	**een appelsap** en uppel-sup
a Pilsener beer (light ale)	**een Pils** en pils
a brown ale	**een donker bier** en donker beer
a bitter	**een bitter** en bitter
a draught beer	**een bier van het vat** en beer vun et vut

I'll have . . . please	**Ik zou graag . . . hebben**
	ik zow hrahk . . . hebben
a cheese roll	**een broodje kaas**
	en brote-yer kahs
a ham roll	**een broodje ham**
	en brote-yer hum
a hamburger	**een hamburger**
	en humbur-her
an omelet	**een omelet**
	en omerlet
with mushrooms	**met champignons**
	met shum-peen-yons
with ham	**met ham**
	met hum
with cheese	**met kaas**
	met kahs

These are some other snacks you might like to try:

een boterham	an open sandwich
en boter-rum	
een dubbele boterham	a sandwich with two pieces of
en dubay-lee boter-rum	bread, i.e. like our sandwiches
een croquet	a croquette
en croh-ket	
een fricandel	a minced meat roll
en free-cun-del	
een saté	cubed meat (mostly pork or
en sateh	chicken) on skewers with a spicy
	peanut sauce
een pannekoek	a pancake
en punner-kook	
een saucijze broodje	a sausage roll
en sow-seyzer-brote-yer	
een broodje Tartaar	a minced beef (raw) roll
en brote-yer tar-tar	
een tosti	a toastie (ham and cheese)
en tostee	
een uitsmijter	two slices of bread with ham, roast
en o-eet-smayter	beef or cheese, topped by two or
	three fried eggs
hutspot met klapstuk	carrots mashed with onions and
herts-pot met klup-sterk	potatoes, cooked with rib of
	pork

een kop erwtensoep	a cup of pea soup
en kop airten-soop	
een kop tomatensoep	a cup of tomato soup
en kop toh-m*a*hten-soop	
een kop groentesoep	a cup of vegetable soup
en kop hr*oo*nter-soop	

In a restaurant

ESSENTIAL INFORMATION

- You can eat at the following places:
  RESTAURANT
  HOTEL-RESTAURANT
  STATIONS-RESTAURATIE
  MOTEL
  CAFÉ-RESTAURANT
- By law, the menus must be displayed outside or in the window – and that is the *only* way to judge if a place is right for your needs.
- Self-service restaurants are not unknown, but most places have waiter service.
- A service charge is always added to the bill. Tipping is therefore optional.
- Most restaurants have children's portions.
- Some 700 restaurants offer a *tourist menu* (three courses) at a set price throughout the Netherlands although the courses themselves will differ from region to region. Restaurants participating in this scheme display a sign with the words 'tourist menu'.
- Hot meals are served from 12.00 p.m. – 2.00 p.m. at lunchtime and from 6.00 p.m. – 9.00/10.00 p.m. at night. After that many restaurants offer snacks for latecomers (soups, sausages, salads etc.). Many cities have Indonesian restaurants, where you will find the best *rijsttafel* (lit. 'rice table') outside Indonesia. This speciality consists of nine to ten varying dishes of meats, vegetables, fruits.

WHAT TO SAY

May I book a table?	**Kan ik een tafel reserveren?**
	kun ik en t*ah*-fel ray-ser-v*ai*ren
I have booked a table	**Ik heb een tafel gereserveerd**
	ik hep en t*ah*-fel he-ray-ser-v*ai*rt
A table . . .	**Een tafel . . .**
	en t*ah*-fel . . .
for one	**voor één persoon**
	vor ayn pair-s*oh*n
for three	**voor drie personen**
	vor dree pair-s*oh*nen
The à la carte menu, please	**Het à la carte menu, alstublieft**
	et ah la cart mer-n*oo* uls-too-bl*ee*ft
The fixed-price menu	**Het vastgestelde menu**
	et v*u*st-her-stelder mer-n*oo*
Today's special menu	**Het menu van de dag**
	et mer-n*oo* vun der duk
The tourist menu	**Het touristen menu**
	et too-r*i*sten mer-n*oo*
What is this, please?	**Wat is dit, alstublieft?**
[*point to menu*]	wut is dit uls-too-bl*ee*ft
The wine list	**De wijnlijst**
	der weyn-leyst
A glass of wine	**Een glas wijn**
	en hlus weyn
A half-bottle	**Een halve fles**
	en h*u*lver fles
A bottle	**Een fles**
	en fles
Red/white/rosé/house wine	**Rode/witte/rosé/huis wijn**
	r*o*der/w*i*tter/roh-s*ay*/h*o*-ees weyn
Some more bread, please	**Nog wat brood, alstublieft**
	nok wut brote uls-too-bl*ee*ft
Some more wine	**Nog wat wijn**
	nok wut weyn
Some oil	**Een beetje olie**
	en b*ay*t-yer *o*lee
Some vinegar	**Een beetje azijn**
	en b*ay*t-yer ah-z*ey*n
Some salt/pepper	**Een beetje zout/peper**
	en b*ay*t-yer zowt/p*a*per

Some water	**Een beetje water**
	en b*a*yt-yer w*a*h-ter
With/without garlic	**Met/zonder knoflook**
	met/z*o*nder kn*o*f-loke
How much does that come to?	**Hoeveel is dat?**
	h*oo*-vale is dut
Is service included?	**Is het inclusief bediening?**
	is et *i*n-cloo-seef ber-d*ee*ning
Where is the toilet?	**Waar is het toilet?**
	w*a*hr is et tw*a*h-l*e*t
Miss! [*This does not sound abrupt in Dutch*[	**Juffrouw!**
	yer-fr*ow*
Waiter!	**Ober!**
	*o*ber
The bill, please	**De rekening, alstublieft**
	der r*a*yker-ning uls-too-bl*ee*ft

Key words for courses, as seen on some menus

[*Only ask this question if you want the waiter to remind you of the choice*]

What have you got in the way of . . .	**Wat voor . . . heeft u?**
	wut vor . . . h*a*yft oo
STARTERS?	**VOORGERECHTEN**
	vor-her-rekten
SOUP?	**SOEP**
	soop
EGG DISHES?	**EIERGERECHTEN**
	ey-er-her-rekten
FISH?	**VIS**
	vis
MEAT?	**VLEES**
	vlays
GAME?	**WILD**
	wilt
FOWL?	**GEVOGELTE**
	her-v*o*h-helter
VEGETABLES?	**GROENTE**
	hr*oo*nter
CHEESE?	**KAAS**
	kahs
FRUIT?	**FRUIT**
	fr*o*-eet

What have you got in the way of . . .	Wat voor . . . heeft u?
	wut vor . . . hayft oo
ICE-CREAM?	**IJS**
	eys
DESSERT?	**DESSERT**
	des-*sair*t

UNDERSTANDING THE MENU

- You will find the names of the principal ingredients of most dishes on these pages:

Starters p. 29	Fruit p. 31
Meat p. 33	Cheese p. 30
Fish p. 35	Ice-cream p. 28
Vegetables p. 32	Dessert p. 28

  Used together with the following lists of cooking and menu terms, they should help you decode the menu.
- These cooking and menu terms are for understanding – not for speaking.

Cooking and menu terms

aangemaakt	dressed
aspic	aspic
bouillon	broth, clear soup
doorgebakken	well-done
gebakken	fried, baked
gebraden	roasted
gefileerd	filleted
gegarneerd	garnished
geglazeerd	glazed
gegratineerd	au gratin
gegrilleerd	grilled
gekookt	boiled
gekruid	spiced
gelardeerd	larded
gemarineerd	marinated
gemengd	mixed
gepaneerd	dressed with eggs and breadcrumbs
gepocheerd	poached
geraapt	grated
gerookt	smoked

geroosterd	toasted
gesmoord	braised
gestoomd	steamed
gevulde	filled
gezouten	salted
in gelei	jellied
jus	gravy
kaasgerechten	cheese dishes
koude schotels	cold dishes
pikant	savoury
puree	mashed
ragout	ragout
rauw	raw
room	cream
salade/sla	salad
saté/sateh	meat cubes on sticks with peanut sauce
slagroom	whipped cream (with sugar)
soufflé	soufflé
wild en gevogelte	game and poultry
zoet	sweet
zuur	sour

Further words to help you understand the menu

aalbessen; rode, witte, zwarte	currants; red, white, black
aalbessen gelei	currant jelly
artisjok	artichoke
asperge	asparagus
augurken	pickled gherkins
bami	Indonesian noodle dish with diced pork and often shrimps
blinde vinken	veal fillet, filled with spiced minced veal, fried in butter
bloemkool	cauliflower
boerenkool (stamppot)	kale (hotchpotch)
borst	breast
bruine bonensoep	brown bean soup
brussels lof met ham en kaas	chicory with ham and cheese (oven dish)
chantilly crème met kastanje puree	whipped cream with chestnut purée

chinese kool	chinese cabbage
compote	stewed fruit
doperwten	peas
duitse biefstuk	hamburger steak
eend	duck
fazant	pheasant
flensjes	very thin pancakes
fondue	fondue
gebakken aardappels	fried potatoes
gebakken ananas	fried pineapple
gehakt	minced meat
gewelde boter	creamed butter
haantje	young cock
haas	hare
hachee	braised steak with onions, spices and vinegar
jachtschotel	hot-pot
kalfsvlees	veal
kappertjes saus	caper sauce
kapucijners	marrowfat peas
karbonade	chops
kervel	chervil
kip (gebraden)	chicken (roasted)
kotelet	cutlet
koude schotels	cold dishes
leverworst	liver sausage
loempia	Indonesian deep-fried pancake, filled with bamboo shoots, meat and vegetables
nasi goreng	Indonesian spicy rice dish
ossestaart soep	oxtail soup
paprika (gevulde)	green/red peppers (stuffed)
peterselie	parsley
prei	leeks
reebout	haunch of venison
roerei	scrambled egg
rolmop	rolled-up pickled herring filled with onion
russische eieren	hard boiled eggs with mayonnaise and caper sauce
schildpadsoep	turtle soup

snijbonen	green beans
sperciebonen	french beans
spruitjes	sprouts
taugé soup	bean sprouts soup
tonijn	tuna fish
zuukool met spek	sauerkraut with boiled bacon

Health

ESSENTIAL INFORMATION

- Be sure to have medical insurance.
- For minor disorders and treatment at a drugstore, see p. 20.
- For finding your own way to a doctor, dentist, pharmacist or Health and Social Security Office, see p. 13.
- The cost of the medical care of the tourist must be settled directly with the doctor, pharmacist, dentist, hospital, etc.
- The name of the medical practitioner on duty on weekends and nights can be found in the local papers.

What's the matter?

I have a pain here [*point*]	**Ik heb hier pijn**
	ik hep here pain
I have toothache	**Ik heb kiespijn**
	ik hep kees-pain
I have broken . . .	**Ik heb . . . gebroken**
	ik hep . . . herbroken
my dentures	**mijn kunstgebit**
	mane koonst-her-bit
my glasses	**mijn bril**
	mane bril

I have lost . . .	**Ik heb . . . verloren**
	ik hep . . . ver-loren
my contact lenses	**mijn contact lenzen**
	mane contuct lenzen
a filling	**een vulling**
	en verling
My child is ill	**Mijn kind is ziek**
	mane kint is zeek

Already under treatment for something else?

I take . . . regularly [*show*]	**Ik neem geregeld . . .**
	ik name her-ray-helt . . .
this medicine	**dit medicijn**
	dit may-dee-seyn
these pills	**deze pillen**
	dazer pillen
I have . . .	**Ik heb . . .**
	ik hep . . .
a heart condition	**een hart conditie**
	en hart con-dee-tsee
haemorrhoids	**aambeien**
	ahm-bey-yen
rheumatism	**reumatiek**
	rer-mah-teek
I think I have . . .	**Ik geloof dak ik . . . heb**
	ik her-lohf dut ik . . . hep
food poisoning	**voedselvergiftiging**
	vootsel-ver-hiftee-hing
sunstroke	**een zonnesteak**
	en zonner-stake
I'm . . .	**Ik lijd aan . . .**
	ik leyt ahn . . .
diabetic	**diabetes**
	dee-ah-bay-tes
asthmatic	**asthma**
	ust-mah
I'm pregnant	**Ik ben zwanger**
	ik ben zwung-er
I'm allergic to penicillin	**Ik ben gevoelig voor penicilline**
	ik ben her-voolik vor penicilleener

Problems: loss, theft

ESSENTIAL INFORMATION

- If worse comes to worst, find a police station. To ask the way, see p. 12.
- Look for: **POLITIE**
- If you lose your passport report the loss to the nearest police station and go to the U.S. consulate.

LOSS
[*See also 'Theft' below: the lists are interchangeable*]

I have lost . . .	**Ik heb . . . verloren** ik hep . . . verloren
my camera	**mijn camera** mane cahmer-rah
my car keys	**mijn autosleutels** mane owto-slertels
my car registration	**mijn auto papieren** mane owto pah-pee-ren
my driver's license	**mijn rijbewijs** mane rey-ber-weys
my insurance certificate	**mijn verzekeringsbewijs** mane ver-zaykerrings-ber-weys

THEFT
[*See also 'Loss' above: the lists are interchangeable*]

Someone has stolen . . .	**Iemand heeft . . . gestolen** ee-munt hayft . . . her-stolen
my car	**mijn auto** mane ow-to
my money	**mijn geld** mane helt
my purse	**mijn portemonnaie** mane porter-monay
my tickets	**mijn kaartjes** mane kart-yers

Someone has stolen . . .	**Iemand heeft . . . gestolen**
	ee-munt hayft . . . her-st*o*len
my travellers' cheques	**mijn reischeques**
	mane r*e*ys-sheks
my wallet	**mijn portefeuille**
	mane porter-f*o*y-yer
my luggage	**mijn bagage**
	maine bah-h*a*h-sher

The post office and phoning home

ESSENTIAL INFORMATION

- Key words to look for:
  POSTKANTOOR
  POSTERIJEN
  POST EN SPAARBANK
- Look for the following sign:
- For stamps look for the word **POSTZEGELS** on a machine, or **ZEGELVERKOOP** or **FRANKEERZEGELS** at a post office counter.
- Stamps may be obtained at a stationery shop, provided postcards are also bought there.
- Unless you read and speak Dutch well, it is best not to make phone calls by yourself. Go to a post office and write the town and number you want on a piece of paper.
- The code for the UK is 0944, and for the USA 091; then dial the number you want (less any initial 0).

WHAT TO SAY

To England, please	**Naar Engeland, alstublieft**
	nar *e*ng-er-lunt uls-too-bl*ee*ft
[Hand letters, cards or parcels over the counter]	
To Australia	**Naar Australië**
	nar ah-oostr*a*h-lee-yer

To the United States	**Naar de Verenigde Staten**
	nar der very-*ay*-nik-der st*ah*-ten
I'd like to send a telegram	**Ik zou graag een telegram sturen**
	ik zow hrahk en telehr*u*m st*oo*-ren
Where can I make a telephone call?	**Waar kan ik telefoneren?**
	wahr kun ik telefon*ay*-ren
Local/abroad	**Lokaal/buitenland**
	lokahl/b*o*-ee-ten-lunt
I'd like this number . . .	**Ik wou dit nummer : . . .**
[*show number*]	ik wow dit n*oo*mmer . . .
in England	**in Engeland**
	in *e*ng-er-lunt
in Canada	**in Canada**
	in *ca*hnada
Can you dial it for me, please?	**Kunt u het voor me draaien, alstublieft?**
	koont oo et vor mer dr*ah*-yen uls-too-bl*ee*ft

Cashing checks and changing money

ESSENTIAL INFORMATION

- Look for these words on buildings:
  BANK
  GRENSWISSELKANTOREN NV
  (more commonly given as **GWK**: these are to be found in stations and at the borders only)
  BUREAU DE CHANGE
- Banks are open weekdays 9.00 a.m. – 4.00 p.m. The exchange offices (**WISSELKANTOREN**) are open Monday to Saturday and often in the evenings and on Sundays.
- To cash checks, exactly as at home, use your bank card where you see the Eurocheque sign. Write in English.
- Have your passport ready.

WHAT TO SAY

I'd like to cash . . .	**Ik wou . . . wisselen** ik wow . . . wisselen
this travellers' cheque	**deze reischeque** dazer reys-shek
these travellers' cheques	**deze reischeques** dazer reys-sheks
this cheque	**deze cheque** dazer shek
I'd like to change this . . .	**Ik wou dit graag omwisselen . . .** ik wow dit hrahk om-wisselen . . .
into guilders	**in guldens** in hooldens
into Belgian francs	**in belgische franken** in bel-hee-ser frunken
into French francs	**in franse franken** in frun-ser frunken
into German marks	**in duitse marken** in do-eet-ser marken
What is the rate of exchange?	**Wat is de koers?** wut is der koors

---

Car travel

ESSENTIAL INFORMATION

- Is it a self-service station? Look out for: **ZELFBEDIENING**
  Grades of gasoline:
  NORMAAL (regular)
  SUPER (premium)
  DIESEL OLIE (diesel)
- 1 gallon is about 3¾ liters.
- The minimum sale is often 5 litres (less at self-service pumps).
- Filling stations may be able to deal with minor mechanical problems during the day only. For major repairs you have to go to a garage.

- All main roads are patrolled by the yellow cars of the Royal Dutch Touring Club (**ANWB**) between 7.00 a.m. and 12.00 p.m. Telephones have been installed along Holland's main roads to be used to obtain information from the local **ANWB** station. They will assist tourists whose cars break down. If you are not a member of an automobile club affiliated with the **AIT**, roadside service will be available if you become a temporary member of the **ANWB**.

WHAT TO SAY

[*For numbers, see p. 54*]

(Nine) litres of . . .	**(Negen) liter . . .** (*na*yhen) *lee*ter . . .
(20) guilders of . . .	**Voor (twintig) gulden . . .** vor (*twi*ntik) *hoo*lden . . .
Fill it up, please	**Vol alstublieft** vol uls-too-bl*ee*ft
standard/premium/diesel	**normaal/super/diesel** norm*ah*l/*soo*per/diesel
Will you check . . .	**Wilt u . . . nakijken?** wilt oo . . . *na*h-kayken
the oil?	**de olie** der *o*lee
the battery?	**de accu** der *u*ccoo
the radiator?	**de radiator** der rah-d*ee*-ah-tor
the tires?	**de banden** der b*u*nden
I have run out of petrol	**Ik zit zonder benzine** ik zit z*o*nder ben-z*ee*ner
Can you help me, please?	**Kunt u me helpen, alstublieft?** koont oo mer h*e*lpen uls-too-bl*ee*ft
Do you do repairs?	**Doet u reparaties?** doot oo ray-pah-r*ah*tsees
I have a puncture	**Ik heb een lekke band** ik hep en l*e*kker b*u*nt
I have a broken windscreen	**Ik heb een kapotte voorruit** ik hep en kah-p*o*tter vor-ro-eet

I think the problem is here . . . [*point*]	**Ik denk dat het probleem hier is . . .** ik denk dut et pro-blame here is . . .

LIKELY REACTIONS

I don't do repairs	**Ik repareer niet** ik ray-pah-*rair* neet
Where is your car?	**Waar is uw auto?** wahr is oo *ow*to
What make is it?	**Welk merk is het?** welk mairk is et
Come back tomorrow/on Wednesday [*For days of the week, see p. 56*]	**Kom morgen/woensdag terug** kom mor-hen/woons-duk ter-rerk

Public transport

ESSENTIAL INFORMATION

* Key words on signs:
  TREINKAARTJES (tickets)
  LOKET (ticket office)
  INGANG (entrance)
  UITGANG (exit)
  VERBODEN (forbidden)
  PERRON (platform)
  DOORGAAND VERKEER (transit passengers)
  WACHTKAMER (waiting room)
  INLICHTINGEN (information)
  BAGAGE DEPOT (left luggage)
  AANKOMST (arrivals)
  VERTREK (departures)
  NS (initials of Dutch railways)
  BUSHALTE (bus stop)
  DIENSTREGELING (timetable)

- Buying a ticket: train tickets are available at the station ticket office, in some main post offices and in some tobacco shops.
- When travelling by bus or tram you usually pay as you enter. A bus and tram **STRIPPENKAART** can be bought at post offices.
- There is a 'rover ticket' allowing unlimited travel through Holland for 3–7 days.
- A **GROEP KAART** permits unlimited travel by train for 2–6 persons for one day at a reduced rate.
- In some towns you can purchase a tram ticket which allows you to make transfers between trams going in one direction.

WHAT TO SAY

Where does the train for (Rotterdam) leave from?	**Van waar vertrekt de trein naar (Rotterdam)?**
	vun wahr ver-trekt der train nar (rotter-dum)
Is this the train for (Rotterdam)?	**Is dit de trein naar (Rotterdam)?**
	is dit der train nar (rotter-dum)
Where does the bus for (Edam) leave from?	**Van waar vertrekt de bus naar (Edam)?**
	vun wahr ver-trekt der bus nar (ay-dum)
Is this the bus for (Edam)?	**Is dit de bus naar (Edam)?**
	is dit der bus nar (ay-dum)
Do I have to change?	**Moet ik overstappen?**
	moot ik over-stuppen
Can you put me off at the right stop, please?	**Kunt u mij op de juiste plaats afzetten, alstublieft?**
	koont oo mey op der yo-ees-ter plahts uf-zetten uls-too-bleeft
Where can I get a taxi?	**Waar kan ik een taxi krijgen?**
	wahr kun ik en tuk-see kray-hen
Can I book a seat?	**Kan ik een plaats bespreken?**
	kun ik en plahts ber-sprayken
A single	**Een enkele**
	en enkerler
A return	**Een retour**
	en rer-toor
First class	**Eerste klas**
	airster klus
Second class	**Tweede klas**
	tway-der klus

One adult	**Eén volwassene**
	ayn vol-wusserner
Two adults	**Twee volwassenen**
	tway vol-wussernen
and one child	**en één kind**
	en ayn kint
and two children	**en twee kinderen**
	en tway kin-der-ren
How much is it?	**Hoeveel is het?**
	hoo-vale is et

Reference

NUMBERS

0	**nul**	nerl
1	**één**	ayn
2	**twee**	tway
3	**drie**	dree
4	**vier**	veer
5	**vijf**	veyf
6	**zes**	zes
7	**zeven**	zayven
8	**acht**	ukt
9	**negen**	nayhen
10	**tien**	teen
11	**elf**	elf
12	**twaalf**	twahlf
13	**dertien**	dairteen
14	**veertien**	vairteen
15	**vijftien**	veyfteen
16	**zestien**	zesteen
17	**zeventien**	zayventeen
18	**achttien**	ukteen
19	**negentien**	nayhenteen
20	**twintig**	twintik

21	**ééNentwintig**	*a*yn-en-tw*i*ntik
22	**tweeëntwintig**	tw*a*y-en-tw*i*ntik
23	**drieëntwintig**	dr*ee*-en-tw*i*ntik
24	**vierentwintig**	v*ee*r-en-tw*i*ntik
25	**vijfentwintig**	v*e*yf-en-tw*i*ntik
26	**zesentwintig**	z*e*s-en-tw*i*ntik
27	**zevenentwintig**	z*a*yven-en-tw*i*ntik
28	**achtentwintig**	*u*kt-en-tw*i*ntik
29	**negenentwintig**	n*a*yhen-en-tw*i*ntik
30	**dertig**	d*a*irtik
31	**ééNendertig**	ayn-en-d*a*irtik
35	**vijfendertig**	v*e*yf-en-d*a*irtik
40	**veertig**	v*a*irtik
41	**ééNenveertig**	*a*yn-en-v*a*irtik
50	**vijftig**	v*e*yftik
51	**ééNenvijftig**	*a*yn-en-v*e*yftik
60	**zestig**	z*e*stik
70	**zeventig**	z*a*yventik
80	**tachtig**	t*u*ktik
81	**ééNentachtig**	*a*yn-en-t*u*ktik
90	**negentig**	n*a*yhentik
95	**vijfennegentig**	v*e*yf-en-n*a*yhentik
100	**honderd**	h*o*nd*e*rt
101	**honderdééN**	h*o*ndert-*a*yn
102	**honderdtwee**	h*o*ndert-tw*a*y
125	**hondervijfentwintig**	h*o*ndert-v*e*yf-en-tw*i*ntik
150	**honderdvijftig**	h*o*ndert-v*e*yftik
175	**honderdvijfenzeventig**	h*o*ndert-v*e*yf-en-z*a*yventik
200	**tweehonderd**	tw*a*y-hondert
300	**driehonderd**	dr*ee*hondert
400	**vierhonderd**	v*ee*r-hondert
500	**vijfhonderd**	v*e*yf-hondert
1000	**duizend**	d*o*-ee-zent
1100	**elfhonderd**	*e*lf-hondert
3000	**drieduizend**	dr*ee*-do-ee-zent
5000	**vijfduizend**	v*e*yf-do-ee-zent
10,000	**tienduizend**	t*ee*n-do-ee-zent
100,000	**honderdduizend**	h*o*ndert-do-ee-zent
1,000,000	**ééN miljoen**	*a*yn mil-y*o*on

TIME

What time is it?	**Hoe laat is het?**
	hoo laht is et
It's . . .	**Het is . . .**
	et is . . .
one o'clock	**één uur**
	ayn oor
two o'clock	**twee uur**
	tway oor
three o'clock	**drie uhr**
	dree oor
four o'clock	**vier uur**
	veer oor
noon	**middag**
	mid-duk
midnight	**middernacht**
	midder-nukt
a quarter past five	**kwart over vijf**
	kwart over veyf
half past five	**half zes**
	hulf zes
a quarter to six	**kwart vóór zes**
	kwart vor zes

DAYS AND MONTHS

Monday	**maandag**
	mahn-duk
Tuesday	**dinsdag**
	dins-duk
Wednesday	**woensdag**
	woons-duk
Thursday	**donderdag**
	donder-duk
Friday	**vrijdag**
	vrey-duk
Sunday	**zondag**
	zon-duk
January	**januari**
	yun-oo-ah-ree

February	**februari**
	fay-broo-*ah*-ree
March	**maart**
	mart
April	**april**
	ah-pr*i*l
May	**mei**
	may
June	**juni**
	y*oo*-nee
July	**juli**
	y*oo*-lee
August	**augustus**
	ow-h*e*rs-tes
September	**september**
	sept*e*mber
October	**oktober**
	okt*o*ber
November	**november**
	nov*e*mber
December	**december**
	day-s*e*mber

Public holidays

- Shops, schools and offices are closed on the following dates:

1 January	**Nieuwjaarsdag**	New Year's Day
	Paasmaandag	Easter Monday
	Pinkstermaandag	Whitsun Monday
	Hemelvaartsdag	Ascension Day
30 April	**Koninginnedag**	The Queen's birthday
25 December	**Eerste Kerstdag**	Christmas Day
26 December	**Tweede Kerstdag**	Boxing Day
5 May	**Bevrijdingsdag**	Liberation Day (once every 5 years)

Index

French

D. L. Ellis, F. Clark

Pronunciation **Dr J. Baldwin**

Useful addresses

French Government Tourist Office
610 5th Ave.
New York, NY 10020

Swiss National Tourist Office
608 5th Ave.
New York, NY 10020

Canadian Government Office of Tourism
1251 Avenue of the Americas
Rm. 1030
New York, NY 10020

Contents

Pronunciation hints

In French it is important to read each syllable with equal emphasis.
For instance, in the following English example we have ten syllables
and ten stresses: Little Jack Horner sat in the corner. Though this
will probably sound rather mechanical to an English ear, it will help
the French speaker to understand you.
Bon courage!

Everyday expressions

[See also 'Shop talk' p. 77]

Hello ⎤	**Bonjour**
Good morning ⎟	bonshoor
Good day ⎟	**Salut** (friends only)
Good afternoon ⎦	saloo
Good evening	**Bonsoir**
	bonswah
Good night	**Bonne nuit**
	bon nwee
Goodbye	**Au revoir**
	o-revwah
Yes	**Oui**
	wee
Please	**S'il vous plaît**
	sil voo pleh
Yes, please	**Oui, s'il vous plaît**
	wee sil voo pleh
Thank you	**Merci**
	mair-see
Thank you very much	**Merci beaucoup**
	mair-see bo-coo
That's right	**C'est exact**
	set exah
No	**Non**
	non
No, thank you	**Non, merci**
	non mair-see
('Merci' by itself can also mean 'No thank you.')	
I disagree	**Je ne suis pas d'accord**
	sher ner swee pah dah-cor
Excuse me ⎤	**Pardon**
Sorry ⎦	par-don
Don't mention it ⎤	**De rien**
That's OK ⎦	der ree-an
It doesn't matter	**Ça ne fait rien**
	sah ner feh ree-an
Where's the toilet, please?	**Où sont les WC, s'il vous plaît?**
	oo son leh veh-seh sil voo pleh

Do you speak English?	**Parlez-vous anglais?** parleh-voo ahngleh
What is your name?	**Comment vous appelez-vous?** commahn vooz appleh-voo
My name is . . .	**Je m'appelle . . .** shmappel . . .

Asking the way

ESSENTIAL INFORMATION

- Keep a look out for all these place names as you will find them on shops, maps and notices.

WHAT TO SAY

Excuse me, please	**Pardonnez-moi, s'il vous plaît** par-do-neh mwah sil voo pleh
How do I get . . .	**Pour aller . . .** poor alleh . . .
to Paris?	**à Paris?** ah pahree
to rue St Pierre?	**à la rue Saint-Pierre?** ah lah roo san-pee-air
to the hotel Metropole?	**à l'hôtel Métropole?** ah lotel meh-tro-pol
to the airport?	**à l'aéroport?** ah lah-eh-ropor
to the beach?	**à la plage?** ah lah plash
to the bus station?	**à la gare d'autobus?** ah lah gar dotoboos
to the market?	**au marché?** o marsheh
to the police station?	**au commissariat?** o commissaree-ah

to the port?	**au port?**
	o por
to the post office?	**à la poste?**
	ah lah post
to the railway station?	**à la gare?**
	ah lah gar
to the sports stadium?	**au stade?**
	o stad
to the tourist information office?	**au syndicat d'initiative?**
	o sandeecah dinisee-ativ
to the town centre?	**au centre de la ville?**
	o sahnt der lah veel
to the town hall?	**à la mairie?**
	ah lah mai-ree
Excuse me, please	**Pardonnez-moi, s'il vous plaît**
	par-do-neh mwah sil voo pleh
Is there . . . near by?	**Est-ce qu'il y a . . . près d'ici?**
	eskil yah . . . preh dee-see
a baker's	**une boulangerie**
	oon boolahn-shree
a bank	**une banque**
	oon bahnk
a bar	**un bar**
	an bar
a bus stop	**un arrêt d'autobus**
	an ahreh dotoboos
a butcher's	**une boucherie**
	oon booshree
a café	**un café**
	an cahfeh
a campsite	**un camping**
	an camping
a car park	**un parking**
	an parking
a change bureau	**un bureau de change**
	an buro der shahnsh
a chemist's	**une pharmacie**
	oon pharmacy
a delicatessen	**une charcuterie**
	oon sharcootree
a dentist's	**un dentiste**
	an dahnteest

Is there . . . near by?

Est-ce qu'il y a . . . près d'ici?
eskil yah . . . preh dee-see

a department store **un grand magasin**
an grahn mahgahzan

a disco **une discothèque**
oon discotek

a doctor's surgery **un docteur**
an doc-ter

a dry cleaner's **un pressing**
an pressing

a fishmonger's **une poissonnerie**
oon pwah-son-ree

a garage (for repairs) **un garage**
an gahrash

a hairdresser's **un coiffeur**
an kwah-fer

a greengrocer's **un marchand de légumes**
an marshahn der lehgoom

a grocer's **une épicerie**
oon ehpeess-ree

a Health and Social **un bureau de la Sécurité Sociale**
Security Office an buro der lah sehcooreeteh
sossee-al

a hospital **un hôpital**
an opeetal

a hotel **un hôtel**
an otel

a hypermarket **un hypermarché**
an eepair-marsheh

a laundry **une laverie**
oon lav-ree

a newsagent's **un marchand de journaux**
an marshahn der shoorno

a night club **une boîte de nuit**
oon bwaht der nwee

a petrol station **une station service**
oon stah-see-on sairvees

a post box **une boîte à lettres**
oon bwaht ah let

a public telephone **un téléphone**
an telefon

a public toilet	**des WC publics**
	deh veh-seh poobleek
a restaurant	**un restaurant**
	an restorahn
a supermarket	**un supermarché**
	an soopair-marsheh
a taxi stand	**une station de taxis**
	oon stah-see-on der taxee
a tobacconist's	**un bureau de tabac**
	an buro der tahbah
a travel agent's	**une agence de voyage**
	oon ashahns der vwah-yash
a youth hostel	**une auberge de jeunesse**
	oon obairsh der sher-ness

DIRECTIONS

- Asking where a place is, or if a place is nearby, is one thing; making sense of the answer is another.
- Here are some of the most important key directions and replies.

Left	**Gauche**
	goshe
Right	**Droite**
	drwaht
Straight on	**Tout droit**
	too drwah
There	**Là**
	lah
First left/right	**La première rue à gauche/droite**
	lah prem-yair roo ah goshe/drwaht
Second left/right	**La deuxième rue à gauche/droite**
	lah der-zee-em roo ah goshe/ drwaht

Accommodation

ESSENTIAL INFORMATION
Hotel

- If you want hotel-type accommodation, all the following words in capital letters are worth looking for on signs:
  HÔTEL
  MOTEL
  PENSION (a small, privately run hotel)
  AUBERGE (often picturesque type of hotel situated in the countryside)
- Lists of hotels and **pensions** can be obtained from local tourist offices or government tourist offices in New York, p. 60.
- The cost is displayed in the room itself, so you can check it when having a look around before agreeing to stay.
- The displayed cost is for the room itself, per night and not per person. Breakfast is extra, and therefore optional.
- Not all hotels provide meals, apart from breakfast. A **pension** always provides meals. Breakfast is continental style: coffee or tea with rolls/croissants, butter and jam.
- An identity document is requested when registering at a hotel and will normally be kept overnight. Passports or driver's licenses are accepted.
- Tipping: Look for the words **service compris/non compris** (service included/not included) on your bill. Tip porters.

WHAT TO SAY

I have a booking	**J'ai une réservation**
	sheh oon rehzairvah-see-on
Have you any vacancies, please?	**Avez-vous des chambres libres, s'il vous plaît**
	ahveh-voo deh shahmb leeb sil voo pleh
Can I book a room?	**Puis-je réserver une chambre?**
	pweesh rehzairveh oon shahmb
It's for . . .	**C'est pour . . .**
	seh poor . . .
one adult/one person	**un adulte/une personne**
	an ahdoolt/oon pairson

two adults/two people	**deux adultes/deux personnes** der zahdoolt/der pairson
and one child	**et un enfant** eh an ahnfahn
and two children	**et deux enfants** eh der zahnfahn

[*For numbers, see p. 106*]

It's for . . .	**C'est pour . . .** seh poor . . .
one night	**une nuit** oon nwee
two nights	**deux nuits** der nwee
one week/two weeks	**une semaine/deux semaines** oon ser-men/der ser-men
I would like . . .	**Je voudrais . . .** sher voodreh . . .
a (quiet) room	**une chambre (tranquille)** oon shahmb (trahnkeel)
two rooms	**deux chambres** der shahmb
with a single bed	**à un lit** ah an lee
with two single beds	**à deux lits** ah der lee
with a double bed	**avec un grand lit** ahvec an grahn lee
with a toilet	**avec WC** ahvec veh-seh
with a bathroom	**avec salle de bains** ahvec sal der ban
with a shower	**avec douche** ahvec doosh
with a cot	**avec un lit d'enfant** ahvec an lee dahnfahn
with a balcony	**avec balcon** ahvec bal-con
I would like . . .	**Je voudrais . . .** sher voodreh
full board	**pension complète** pahn-see-on complet

I would like . . .	**Je voudrais . . .** sher voodreh . . .
half board	**demi-pension** der-me pahn-see-on
bed and breakfast [*see essential information*]	**chambre et petit déjeuner** shahmb eh ptee desh-neh
Do you serve meals?	**Est-ce que vous faites restaurant?** esk voo fet restorahn
Can I look at the room?	**Puis-je voir la chambre?** pweesh vwah lah shahmb
OK, I'll take it	**D'accord, je la prends** daccor sher lah prahn
No thanks, I won't take it	**Non merci, je ne la prends pas** non mair-see sher ner lah prahn pah
The bill, please	**La note, s'il vous plaît** lah not sil voo pleh
Is service included?	**Est-ce que le service est compris?** esk ler sairvees eh compree
I think this is wrong	**Je crois qu'il y a une erreur** sher crwah kil yah oon error
May I have a receipt?	**Puis-je avoir un reçu?** pweesh ahvwah oon rer-soo

Camping

- Look for the word **CAMPING**
- Be prepared to have to pay:
  per person
  for the car (if applicable)
  for the tent or for trailer space
  for electricity
  for hot showers
- You must provide proof of identity such as your passport.
- You can obtain lists of campsites from local tourist offices or from the French Government Tourist Office in New York.
- Some campsites offer discounts to campers with the International Camping Carnet and some offer weekly, fortnightly or monthly rates.
- Officially recognized campsites have a star rating (like hotels).

- City-run campsites are often reasonably priced and well-run.
- Off-site camping (**le camping sauvage**) is prohibited in many areas. As a rule it is better and safer to use recognized sites.

Youth hostels

- Look for the words: **AUBERGE DE JEUNESSE**.
- You will be asked for a YHA card and your passport on arrival.
- Food and cooking facilities vary from hostel to hostel and you may have to help with the domestic chores.
- You must take your own sleeping bag lining but sheets can usually be rented on arrival.
- In the high season it is advisable to book beds in advance, and your stay will be limited to a maximum of three consecutive nights per hostel.
- Apply to the French Government Tourist Office in New York or local tourist offices in France for lists of youth hostels and details of regulations for hostellers.

WHAT TO SAY

I have a booking	**J'ai une réservation**
	sheh oon rehzairvah-see-on
Have you any vacancies?	**Avez-vous de la place?**
	ahveh-voo der lah plass
How much is it . . .	**C'est combien . . .**
	seh combee-an . . .
for the tent?	**pour la tente?**
	poor lah tahnt
for the caravan?	**pour la caravane?**
	poor lah caravan
for the car '	**pour la voiture?**
	poor lah vwah-toor
for the electricity?	**pour l'électricité?**
	poor leh-lectriciteh
per person?	**par personne?**
	par pairson
per day/night?	**par jour/nuit?**
	par shoor/nwee
May I look round?	**Puis-je voir?**
	pweesh vwah

Do you provide anything . . .	**Est-ce qu'on peut avoir . . .**
	eskon per ahvwah . . .
to eat?	**de la nourriture?**
	der lah nooreetoor
to drink?	**des boissons?**
	deh bwah-son
Is there/are there . . .	**Est-ce qu'il y a . . .**
	eskil yah . . .
a bar?	**un bar?**
	an bar
hot showers?	**des douches chaudes?**
	deh doosh shod
a kitchen?	**une cuisine?**
	oon kweezeen
a laundry?	**une laverie?**
	oon lav-ree
a restaurant?	**un restaurant?**
	an restorahn
a shop?	**un magasin?**
	an mahgah-zan
a swimming pool?	**une piscine?**
	oon pee-seen
a takeaway?	**des plats à emporter?**
	deh plah ah ahmporteh

[*For food shopping, see p. 80, and for eating and drinking out, see p. 90.*]

I would like a counter for the shower	**Je voudrais un jeton pour la douche**
	sher voodreh an sher-ton poor lah doosh

Problems

The toilet	**Le WC**
	ler veh-seh
The shower	**La douche**
	lah doosh
The tap	**Le robinet**
	ler robbeeneh
The razor point	**La prise pour le rasoir**
	lah preez poor ler rah-zwah

The light	**La lumière**
	lah loom-yair
. . . is not working	**. . . ne marche pas**
	. . . ner marsh pah
My camping gas has run out	**Je n'ai plus de gaz**
	sher neh ploo der gaz

LIKELY REACTIONS

Have you an identity document?	**Avez-vous une pièce d'identité?**
	ahveh-voo oon pee-ess deedahnteeteh
Your membership card, please	**Votre carte, s'il vous plaît**
	vot cart sil voo pleh
What's your name?	**Votre nom, s'il vous plaît**
	vot nom sil voo pleh
Sorry, we're full	**Je regrette, c'est complet**
	sher rer-gret seh compleh
How many people is it for?	**C'est pour combien de personnes?**
	seh poor combee-an der pairson
I haven't any rooms left	**Je n'ai plus de chambres**
	sher neh ploo der shahmb
Do you want to have a look?	**Vous voulez voir?**
	voo vooleh vwah
How many nights is it for?	**C'est pour combien de nuits?**
	seh poor combee-an der nwee
It's (5) francs . . .	**C'est (cinq) francs . . .**
	seh (san) frahn . . .
per day/per night	**par jour/par nuit**
	par shoor/par nwee

[*For numbers, see p. 106*]

General shopping

ESSENTIAL INFORMATION
The drugstore/The chemist's

- Look for the word **PHARMACIE.**
- Medicines (drugs) are only available at a drugstore.

- Some non-drugs can be bought at a supermarket or department store.
- Try a pharmacist *before* going to a doctor: they are usually qualified to treat minor injuries.
- To claim money back on prescriptions, remove price labels from medicines, and stick them on the prescription sheet.
- Drugstores take turns staying open all night and on Sundays. A notice on the door headed **PHARMACIE DE GARDE** or **PHARMACIE DE SERVICE** gives the address of the nearest pharmacist on duty.
- Some toiletries can also be bought at a **PARFUMERIE** but these will be more expensive.
- Finding a drugstore, see p. 65.

WHAT TO SAY

I'd like . . .	**Je voudrais . . .** sher voodreh . . .
some Alka Seltzer	**de l'Alka Seltzer** der lalka seltzer
some antiseptic	**un antiseptique** an anti-septeek
some aspirin	**de l'aspirine** der laspeereen
some baby food	**de la nourriture pour bébés** der lah nooreetoor poor behbeh
some contraceptives	**des contraceptifs** deh contraceptif
some cotton	**du coton** doo cotton
some deodorant	**un déodorant** an deh-odorahn
some disposable diapers	**des couches en cellulose** deh coosh ahn celluloz
some handcream	**de la crème pour les mains** der lah crem poor leh man
some eye drops	**des gouttes pour les yeux** deh goot poor leh zee-er
some inhalant	**un inhalateur** an eenahlah-ter
some insect repellent	**une crème anti-moustiques** oon crem anti-moosteek

some lipstick	**du rouge à lèvres**
	doo roosh ah lev
some make-up remover	**un démaquillant**
	an dehmahkee-yahn
some paper tissues	**des Kleenex**
	deh kleenex
some razor blades	**des lames de rasoir**
	deh lam der rahzwah
some safety pins	**des épingles de sûreté**
	dez ehpang der soor-teh
some sanitary napkins	**des serviettes périodiques**
	deh sairv-yet pehree-odeek
some shaving cream	**de la crème à raser**
	der lah crem ah rahzeh
some soap	**du savon**
	doo sav-on
some suntan lotion/oil	**une crème/huile solaire**
	oon crem/weel solair
some toilet paper	**du papier hygiénique**
	doo pap-yeh eeshee-ehneek
I'd like something for . . .	**Je voudrais un produit pour . . .**
	sher voodreh an prodwee poor . . .
bites/stings (insect)	**les piqûres (d'insectes)**
	leh peek-oor (dan-sect)
burns/scalds	**les brûlures**
	leh brool-yoor
a cold	**le rhume**
	ler room
constipation	**la constipation**
	lah consteepah-see-on
a cough	**la toux**
	lah too
diarrhea	**la diarrhée**
	lah dee-ah-reh
earache	**le mal d'oreille**
	ler mal doray
flu	**la grippe**
	lah greep
sore gums	**la gingivite**
	lah shanshee-veet
sunburn	**les coups de soleil**
	leh coo der solay

I'd like something for . . .	**Je voudrais un produit pour . . .**
	sher voodreh an prodwee poor . . .
travel sickness	**le mal de mer**
	ler mal der mair

[*For other essential expressions, see 'Shop Talk', opposite.*]

Holiday items

ESSENTIAL INFORMATION

- Places to shop at and signs to look for:
  LIBRAIRIE-PAPETERIE (bookshop/stationery shop)
  BUREAU DE TABAC (tobacco shop)
  CARTES POSTALES – SOUVENIRS (postcards – souvenirs)
  PHOTOGRAPHIE (films and photographic equipment)
- and the main department stores:
  MONOPRIX PRISUNIC INNO

WHAT TO SAY

I'd like . . .	**Je voudrais . . .**
	sher voodreh . . .
a bag	**un sac**
	an sac
a beach ball	**un ballon pour la plage**
	an bah-lon poor lah plash
a bucket	**un seau**
	an so
an English newspaper	**un journal anglais**
	an shoornahl ahngleh
some envelopes	**des enveloppes**
	deh zahnv-lop
a guide book	**un guide**
	an gheed
a map (of the area)	**une carte (de la région)**
	oon cart (der lah resh-yon)

some postcards	**des cartes postales**
	deh cart postahl
a spade	**une pelle**
	oon pel
a straw hat	**un chapeau de paille**
	an shahpo der pie
some sunglasses	**des lunettes de soleil**
	deh loonet der solay
some writing paper	**du papier à lettres**
	doo pap-yeh ah let
a colour film	**un rouleau de pellicules couleur**
[*show camera*]	an roolo der pelleecool cooler
a black and white film	**un rouleau de pellicules noir et blanc**
	an roolo der pelleecool nwah eh blahn

Shop talk

ESSENTIAL INFORMATION

• Know how to say the important weights and measures:

50 grams	**cinquante grammes**
	sankahnt gram
100 grams	**cent grammes**
	sahn gram
200 grams	**deux cents grammes**
	der sahn gram
½ kilo	**un demi-kilo**
	an der-me keelo

1 kilo	**un kilo**
	an keelo
2 kilos	**deux kilos**
	der keelo
½ litre	**un demi-litre**
	an der-me leet
1 litre	**un litre**
	an leet
2 litres	**deux litres**
	der leet

- In small shops don't be surprised if customers, as well as the shop assistant, say 'hello' and 'goodbye' to you.

CUSTOMER

I'm just looking	**Je regarde**
	sher rer-gard
How much is this/that?	**C'est combien ça?**
	seh combee-an sah
What is that/what are those?	**Qu'est-ce que c'est ça?**
	kesk seh sah
Is there a discount?	**Est-ce que vous faites une remise?**
	esk voo fet oon rer-meez
I'd like that, please	**Je voudrais ça, s'il vous plaît**
	sher voodreh sah sil voo pleh
Not that	**Pas ça**
	pah sah
Like that	**Comme ça**
	com sah
That's enough, thank you	**Ça suffit, merci**
	sah soofee mair-see
More please	**Encore un peu, s'il vous plaît**
	ahncor an per sil voo pleh
Less please	**Moins, s'il vous plaît**
	mwen sil voo pleh
That's fine ⎤ OK ⎦	**Ça va**
	sah vah
I won't take it, thank you	**Merci je ne le prends pas**
	mair-see sher ner ler prahn pah
It's not right	**Ça ne va pas**
	sah ner vah pah

Have you got something . . .	**Avez-vous quelque chose . . .**
	ahveh-voo kelk shoz . . .
better?	**de mieux?**
	der me-er
cheaper?	**de moins cher?**
	der mwen shair
different?	**de différent?**
	der dee-fay-rahn
larger?	**de plus grand?**
	der ploo grahn
smaller?	**de plus petit?**
	der ploo ptee
Can I have a bag, please?	**Puis-je avoir un sac, s'il vous plaît?**
	pweesh ahvwah an sac sil voo pleh
Can I have a receipt?	**Puis-je avoir un reçu?**
	pweesh ahvwah an rer-soo
Do you take . . .	**Acceptez-vous . . .**
	accepteh-voo . . .
English/American money?	**l'argent anglais/américain?**
	larshahn ahngleh/american
travellers' cheques?	**les traveller chèques?**
	leh traveller sheck
credit cards?	**la carte bleue?**
	lah cart bler

SHOP ASSISTANT

Can I help you?	**Qu'y a-t-il pour votre service?**
	kee ah-til poor vot sairvees
What would you like?	**Vous désirez?**
	voo dehzeereh
Will that be all?	**Ce sera tout?**
	ser ser-rah too
Is that all?	**C'est tout?**
	seh too
Anything else?	**Vous désirez autre chose?**
	voo dehzeereh ot shoz
Would you like it wrapped?	**Je vous l'enveloppe?**
	sher voo lahnv-lop
Sorry, none left	**Je regrette, il n'y en a plus**
	sher rer-gret il nee ahn-nah ploo

I haven't got any	**Je n'en ai pas** sher nahn-neh pah
I haven't got any more	**Je n'en ai plus** sher nahn-neh ploo
How many do you want? ⎤ How much do you want? ⎦	**Vous en voulez combien?** voo-zahn vooleh combee-an
Is that enough?	**Ça suffit?** sah soofee

Shopping for food

Bread

ESSENTIAL INFORMATION

- Finding a bakery, see p. 65.
- Key words to look for:
  BOULANGERIE (bakery)
  BOULANGER (baker)
  PAIN (bread)
- Small bakers are usually open between 7.30 a.m. and 7/8 p.m. Most close on Mondays and public holidays but open on Sunday mornings.
- For types of loaf other than a 'French stick' say '**un pain**' (an pan) and point.

WHAT TO SAY

Some bread, please	**Du pain, s'il vous plaît** doo pan sil voo pleh
A loaf (like that)	**Un pain (comme ça)** an pan (com sah)
A French stick	**Une baguette** oon bah-get
A large one	**Une grande** oon grahnd
A long, thin one	**Une ficelle** oon feesel

Half a French stick   **Une demi-baguette**
oon der-me bah-get

A brown loaf   **Un pain intégral**
an pan an-tay-gral

A bread roll   **Un petit pain**
an ptee pan

Cakes and ice cream

ESSENTIAL INFORMATION

- Key words to look for:
  PÂTISSERIE (cake shop)
  PÂTISSIER (cake/pastry maker)
  PÂTISSERIES (pastries/cakes)
  GLACES (ice creams)
  GLACES (ice cream)
  GLACIER (ice cream maker/seller)
  CONFISERIE (candy shop)
  CONFISEUR (candy maker/seller)
- **SALON DE THÉ:** a room, usually in a pâtisserie, where customers sit at tables and are served cakes, ices, soft drinks, tea, coffee or chocolate. See p. 90, 'Ordering a drink and a snack'.
- Pâtisseries are open on Sundays, but not on Mondays.

WHAT TO SAY

The types of cakes you find in the shops vary from region to region, but the following are some of the most common.

un éclair an eclair	an éclair
un chou à la crème an shoo ah lah crem	choux pastry filled with vanilla cream
une religieuse oon rer-leeshee-erz	choux pastry in the shape of a small cottage loaf with coffee cream filling (literally: a nun)
un baba au rhum an bahbah o rom	a rum baba

un millefeuille
an meelfey

un chausson aux pommes
an sho-son o pom

un pet de nonne
an peh der non

une tartelette aux pommes
oon tartlet o pom

. . . aux fraises
. . . o frez

. . . aux abricots
. . . o-zahbreeco

alternate layers of puff pastry and
   almond cream

an apple turnover

a doughnut

a small apple tart

. . . strawberry . . .

. . . apricot . . .

A . . . ice cream, please
   Une glace . . . s'il vous plaît
   oon glass . . . sil voo pleh

banana
   à la banane
   ah lah bah-nan

chocolate
   au chocolat
   o shocolah

coffee
   au moka
   o makah

pistachio
   à la pistache
   ah lah pee-stash

raspberry
   à la framboise
   ah lah frahm-bwahz

strawberry
   à la fraise
   ah lah frez

vanilla
   à la vanille
   ah lah vahneel

Two francs worth
   Deux francs
   der frahn

A single cone [*specify flavour, as above*]
   Un cornet simple
   an corneh samp

Picnic food

ESSENTIAL INFORMATION

- Key words to look for:
  CHARCUTERIE (delicatessen)
  TRAITEUR (delicatessen)
  CHARCUTIER (delicatessen owner)
- In these shops you can buy a wide variety of food such as ham, salami, cheese, olives, appetizers, sausages and freshly made take-out dishes. Specialties differ from region to region.

WHAT TO SAY

Two slices of . . .	**Deux tranches de . . .**
	der trahnsh der . . .
garlic sausage	**saucisson à l'ail**
	so-see-son ah lie
ham (cooked)	**jambon cuit**
	shahmbon kwee
ham (cured)	**jambon cru**
	shahmbon croo
pâté	**pâté**
	pahteh
roast beef	**rôti de bœuf**
	rotee der berf
roast pork	**rôti de porc**
	rotee der por
salami	**saucisson**
	so-see-son

You might also like to try some of these:

andouille	tripe sausage
ahn-dooy	
barquette de crevettes	boat-shaped pastry case with
barket der crer-vet	prawn filling
bœuf aux champignons	diced beef cooked with wine and
berf o shahmpeen-yon	mushrooms
. . . aux olives	sliced beef cooked with wine and
. . . o zoleev	olives

. . . en daube . . . ahn dobe	diced beef in a thick wine sauce
bouchée à la reine boo-shay ah lah rain	vol-au-vent case filled with sweet-breads and mushrooms in cream sauce
boudin boo-dain	black pudding
brandade de morue brahn-dad der moroo	salt cod, crushed and mixed with oil, cream and garlic
champignons à la grecque shahmpeen-yon ah lah grec	mushrooms cooked in wine, tomatoes and spices
cœurs d'artichaux ker dar-tee-sho	artichoke hearts
macédoine de légumes masshe-dwan der lehgoom	diced vegetables in mayonnaise
œufs mayonnaise er my-onez	hard boiled eggs with mayonnaise
quiche lorraine keesh lorren	egg and ham/bacon pie
rillettes ree-yet	minced pork (goose or duck) baked in fat
rouleau au fromage roolo o fromash	pastry roll with creamy cheese filling
salade niçoise sal-ad nee-swahz	tomato, potato, egg, anchovy, tunny fish and olive salad in oil and vinegar
saucisse de Strasbourg so-seess der strasboor	frankfurter
saucisson sec so-see-son sec	smoked garlic sausage
tarte à l'oignon tart ah lonion	onion pie
tarte au fromage tart o fromash	cheese pie
tomates farcies tomaht far-see	stuffed tomatoes
Brie bree	creamy white cheese
Camembert cahmahmbair	full fat soft white cheese
Emmental emmentahl	Swiss cheese with big holes

fromage de chèvre	goat's cheese
fromash der shev	
Gruyère	Swiss cheese, rich in flavour,
gru-yair	smooth in texture
Pont l'Évêque	soft, runny cheese with holes,
pon leh-vek	strong flavour
Roquefort	resembles Stilton
rockfor	

[*For other essential expressions, see 'Shop talk', p. 77.*]

Fruit and vegetables

ESSENTIAL INFORMATION

- Key words to look for:
  FRUITS (fruit)
  LÉGUMES (vegetables)
  PRIMEURS (fresh fruit and vegetables)
  FRUITIER (fruit seller)
  MARCHÉ (market)
- It is customary for you to choose your own fruit and vegetables at the market (and in some shops) and for the vendor to weigh and price them. You must take your own shopping bag: paper and plastic bags are not normally provided.

WHAT TO SAY

1 kilo of . . .	**Un kilo de* . . .**
	an keelo der . . .
apples	**pommes**
	pom
bananas	**bananes**
	bah-nan
cherries	**cerises**
	ser-eez
grapes (white/black)	**raisins (blancs/noirs)**
	rehzan (blahn/nwah)

*Use **d'** in front of words beginning with a vowel.

1 kilo of . . .	**Un kilo de* . . .** an keelo der . . .
oranges	**oranges** orahnsh
peaches	**pêches** pesh
pears	**poires** pwah
plums	**prunes** proon
strawberries	**fraises** frez
A grapefruit, please	**Un pamplemousse, s'il vous plaît** an pahmp-mousse sil voo pleh
A melon	**Un melon** an mer-lon
A pineapple	**Un ananas** an ahnahnah
A water melon	**Une pastèque** oon passtek
½ kilo of . . .	**Un demi-kilo de* . . .** an der-me keelo der . . .
asparagus	**asperges** aspersh
carrots	**carottes** car-rot
green beans	**haricots verts** ahreeco vair
leeks	**poireaux** pwah-ro
mushrooms	**champignons** shahmpeen-yon
onions	**oignons** onion
peas	**petits pois** ptee pwah
peppers (green/red)	**poivrons (verts/rouges)** pwah-vron (vair/roosh)
potatoes	**pommes de terre** pom der tair

*Use **d**' in front of words beginning with a vowel.

shallots	**échalotes** eh-shallot
spinach	**épinards** ehpeenar
tomatoes	**tomates** tomaht
A bunch of parsley	**Un bouquet de persil** an bookeh der pair-see
A bunch of radishes	**Une botte de radis** oon bot der rahdee
A head of garlic	**Une tête d'ail** oon tet die
A lettuce	**Une salade** oon sal-ad
A stick of celery	**Un pied de céleri** an pee-eh der seleree
A cucumber	**Un concombre** an concomb
Like that, please	**Comme ça, s'il vous plaît** com sah sil voo pleh

Meat and fish

ESSENTIAL INFORMATION

- Key words to look for:
  BOUCHERIE (butcher shop)
  BOUCHER (butcher)
  UNE POISSONNERIE (fish store)
  FRUITS DE MER (seafood)
- Markets and large supermarkets usually have a fresh fish counter.

WHAT TO SAY

For roasts, choose the type of meat and then say how many people it is for:

Some beef, please	**Du bœuf, s'il vous plaît** doo berf sil voo pleh

Some lamb	**De l'agneau** der lan-yo
Some mutton	**Du mouton** doo mooton
Some pork	**Du porc** doo por
Some veal	**Du veau** doo vo
A roast . . .	**Un rôti . . .** an rotee . . .
for two people	**pour deux personnes** poor der pair-son
for four people	**pour quatre personnes** poor kat pair-son
for six people	**pour six personnes** poor see pair-son
Some steak, please	**Du biftek, s'il vous plaît** doo beeftek sil voo pleh
Some liver	**Du foie** doo fwah
Some kidneys	**Des rognons** deh ron-yon
Some heart	**Du cœur** doo ker
Some sausages	**Des saucisses** deh so-seess
Some mince	**De la viande hachée** der lah vee-ahnd asheh
Two veal scallops	**Deux escalopes de veau** der escalop der vo
Three pork chops	**Trois côtelettes de porc** trwah cotlet der por
Four lamb chops	**Quatre côtelettes d'agneau** kat cotlet dan-yo
Five mutton chops	**Cinq côtelettes de mouton** san cotlet der mooton
A chicken	**Un poulet** an pooleh
A rabbit	**Un lapin** an lah-pan
A tongue	**Une langue** oon lahng

Purchase large fish and small shellfish by weight:

½ kilo of . . .	**Un demi-kilo de*** . . .
	an der-me keelo der . . .
anchovies	**anchois**
	ahn-shwah
cod	**morue**
	moroo
eel	**anguille**
	ahn-gweel
mussels	**moules**
	mool
oysters	**huîtres**
	weet
prawns	**crevettes roses**
	crer-vet rose
red mullet	**rougets**
	roosheh
sardines	**sardines**
	sardeen
shrimps	**crevettes grises**
	crer-vet greez
turbot	**turbot**
	toorbo
whiting	**merlans**
	mairlahn
salmon	**saumon**
	somon
tuna (fresh)	**thon**
	ton

For some shellfish and 'frying pan' fish, specify the number you want:

A crab, please	**Un crabe, s'il vous plaît**
	an crab sil voo pleh
A herring	**Un hareng**
	an ah-rahn
A lobster	**Une langouste/un homard**
	oon lahngoost/an omar
A mackerel	**Un maquereau**
	an mackro

*Use **d'** in front of words beginning with a vowel.

A scallop	**Une coquille de Saint-Jacques**
	oon cokee der san shack
A sole	**Une sole**
	oon sol
A trout	**Une truite**
	oon trweet
A whiting	**Un merlan**
	an mairlahn

Eating and drinking out

Ordering a drink and a snack

ESSENTIAL INFORMATION

- The places to ask for:
  BAR
  CAFÉ
- The price list of drinks (**TARIF DES CONSOMMATIONS**) must, by law, be displayed outside or in the window.
- There is a waiter service in all cafés and bars, but you can drink at the bar or counter if you wish (cheaper).
- Always leave a tip of 10% or 15% of the bill unless you see **SERVICE COMPRIS** or **PRIX NETS** (service included) printed on the bill or on a notice.
- Bars and cafés serve both alcoholic and non-alcoholic drinks. There are no licensing laws and children are allowed in.

WHAT TO SAY

I'd like . . . please	**Je voudrais . . . s'il vous plaît**
	sher voodreh . . . sil voo pleh
a black coffee	**un café nature/un café noir**
	an cahfeh nahtoor/an cahfeh nwah

a coffee with cream	**un café crème** an cahfeh crem
a hot chocolate	**un chocolat chaud** an shocolah sho
a tea	**un thé** an teh
with milk	**au lait** o leh
with lemon	**au citron** o seetron
a Coca-Cola	**un Coca-Cola** an coca-cola
a glass of milk	**un verre de lait** an vair der leh
a lemonade	**une limonade** oon leemonad
a lemon squash	**une citronnade** oon seetronad
a mineral water	**un Perrier** an pair-yeh
an orangeade	**une orangeade** oon orahn-shad
an orange juice	**un jus d'orange** an shoo dorahnsh
a grape juice	**un jus de raisin** an shoo der rehzan
a pineapple juice	**un jus d'ananas** an shoo dahnahnah
a beer	**une bière** oon be-air
a draught beer	**une bière pression** oon be-air pressee-on
a half	**un demi** an der-me
I'd like . . . please	**Je voudrais . . . s'il vous plaît** sher voodreh . . . sil voo pleh
a cheese sandwich	**un sandwich au fromage** an sandwich o fromash
a ham sandwich	**un sandwich au jambon** an sandwich o shahmbon
a pancake	**une crêpe** oon crep

These are some other snacks you may like to try:

une choucroûte garnie	sauerkraut usually served with
oon shoo-croot gahrnee	ham, smoked bacon and sausage
un croque-monsieur	toasted ham and cheese sandwich
an crok-mer-see-er	
des frites	chips
deh freet	
un hot-dog	a hot dog
an ot-dog	
un sandwich au saucisson	a salami sandwich
an sandwich o so-see-son	
un sandwich au pâté	a pâté sandwich
an sandwich o pah-teh	

In a restaurant

ESSENTIAL INFORMATION

- The place to ask for: **UN RESTAURANT**
- You can eat at these places:
  RESTAURANT
  CAFÉ
  BUFFET (at stations)
  ROUTIERS (roadside cafés)
  BRASSERIE (limited choice here)
  RELAIS
  AUBERGE
  RÔTISSERIE
  DRUGSTORE
  BISTRO
  LIBRE-SERVICE (self-service cafeterias)
- By law, the menus must be displayed outside or in the window
  – and that is the *only* way to judge if a place is right for your
  needs.
- Self-service restaurants are not unknown (see above), but all
  other places have waiter service.

- Leave a tip unless you see **SERVICE COMPRIS** on the bill or on the menu.
- Children's portions are not usually available.
- Eating times: usually from 11.30–2, and from 7–10, but these vary a great deal according to the type of establishment.

WHAT TO SAY

May I book a table?	**Puis-je réserver une table?**
	pweesh reh-zairveh oon tab
I've booked a table	**J'ai réservé une table**
	sheh reh-zairveh oon tab
A table . . .	**Une table . . .**
	oon tab . . .
for one	**pour une personne**
	poor oon pair-son
for three	**pour trois personnes**
	poor trwah pair-son
The à la carte menu, please	**La carte, s'il vous plaît**
	la cart sil voo pleh
The fixed price menu	**Le menu à prix fixe**
	ler mer-noo ah pree fix
The 25 franc menu	**Le menu à vingt-cinq francs**
	ler mer-noo ah vant-san frahn
The tourist menu	**Le menu touristique**
	ler mer-noo touristeek
Today's special menu	**Le menu du jour**
	ler mer-noo doo shoor
The wine list	**La carte des vins**
	lah cart deh van
What's this, please? [*point to menu*]	**Qu'est ce que c'est ça, s'il vous plaît?**
	kesk seh sah sil voo pleh
A carafe of wine, please	**Une carafe de vin, s'il vous plaît**
	oon car-af der van sil voo pleh
A quarter (25 cc)	**Un quart**
	an car
A half (50 cc)	**Une demi-carafe**
	oon der-me car-af
A glass	**Un verre**
	an vair

A bottle/a litre	**Une bouteille/un litre**
	oon bootay/an leet
A half-bottle	**Une demi-bouteille**
	oon der-me bootay
Red/white/rosé/house wine	**Du vin rouge/blanc/rosé/maison**
	doo van roosh/blahn/roseh/mehzon
Some more bread, please	**Encore du pain, s'il vous plaît**
	ahncor doo pan sil voo pleh
Some more wine	**Encore du vin**
	ahncor doo van
Some oil	**De l'huile**
	der lweel
Some vinegar	**Du vinaigre**
	doo veeneg
Some salt	**Du sel**
	doo sel
Some pepper	**Du poivre**
	doo pwahv
Some water	**De l'eau**
	der lo
With/without (garlic)	**Avec de/sans (l'ail)**
	ahvec der/sahn (lie)
How much does that come to?	**Ça fait combien?**
	sah feh combee-an
Is service included?	**Est-ce que le service est compris?**
	esk ler sairvees eh compree
Where is the toilet, please?	**Où sont les WC s'il vous plaît?**
	oon son leh veh-seh sil voo pleh
Miss! [*this does not sound abrupt in French*]	**Mademoiselle!**
	mad-mwahzel
Waiter!	**Garçon!**
	gar-son
The bill, please	**L'addition, s'il vous plaît**
	laddisee-on sil voo pleh

Key words for courses, as seen on some menus: [*Only ask this question if you want the waiter to remind you of the choice.*]

What have you got in the way of . . .	**Qu'est-ce que vous avez comme . . .**
	kesk voozahveh com
starters?	**hors d'œuvre?**
	or derv

soup?	**soupe?**
	soup
egg dishes?	**œufs?**
	er
fish?	**poisson?**
	pwah-son
meat?	**viande?**
	vee-ahnd
game?	**gibier?**
	sheeb-yeh
fowl?	**volaille?**
	vol-eye
vegetables?	**légumes?**
	lehgoom
cheese?	**fromages?**
	fromash
fruit?	**fruits?**
	frwee
ice-cream?	**glaces?**
	glass
dessert?	**dessert?**
	deh-sair

UNDERSTANDING THE MENU

- You will find the names of the principal ingredients of most dishes on these pages:

  Starters p. 83   Fruit p. 85
  Meat p. 87   Cheese p. 84
  Fish p. 89   Ice-cream p. 81
  Vegetables p. 86   Dessert p. 81

  Used together with the following lists of cooking and menu terms, they should help you to decode the menu.

- These cooking and menu terms are for understanding only – not for speaking.

Cooking and menu terms

à l'anglaise	boiled
au beurre	with butter
au beurre noir	fried in sizzling butter
bien cuit	well done

bisque	shellfish soup
blanquette	cooked in a creamy sauce
au bleu	boiled in water, oil and thyme (fish) very rare (meat)
bonne femme	baked with wine and vegetables
bouilli	boiled
braisé	braised
en broche	spit-roasted
en cocotte	stewed
coquilles	cooked in a white sauce and browned under the grill
en croûte	in a pastry case
en daube	braised in a wine stock
à l'étouffée	stewed
farci	stuffed
au four	baked
à la française	cooked with lettuce and onion
frit	fried
froid	cold
fumé	smoked
garni	served with vegetables or chips
au gratin	sprinkled with breadcrumbs and browned under the grill
grillé	grilled
haché	minced
maître d'hôtel	served with butter mixed with parsley and lemon juice
Marengo	cooked in oil, tomatoes and white wine
mousseline	mousse
Parmentier	containing potatoes
poché	poached
à point	medium
à la provençale	cooked with garlic, tomatoes, olive oil, olives, onions and herbs
rôti	roasted
saignant	rare
salade	served with oil and vinegar dressing
sauce béarnaise	vinegar, egg yolks, white wine, butter, shallots and tarragon
sauce béchamel	flour, butter and milk

sauce bourguignonne	red wine sauce with herbs, onions and spices
sauce madère	cooked in Madeira wine
sauce Mornay	cheese sauce
sauce piquante	sharp vinegar sauce with chopped gherkins and herbs
sauté	fried slowly in butter
en terrine	preparation of meat, game or fowl baked in a terrine (casserole) and served cold
à la vapeur	steamed
Vichy	garnished with carrots
vinaigrette	with oil and vinegar dressing

Further words to help you understand the menu

assiette anglaise	cold meat and salad
boudin	black pudding
bouillabaisse	rich fish soup in which a variety of fish and shell fish have been cooked. Soup and fish are served in separate dishes
champignons	mushrooms
chantilly	cream whipped with icing sugar
choucroûte	sauerkraut
compote	stewed fruit
consommé	clear broth
crudités	raw vegetables and salads served as starters
cuisses de grenouilles	frogs' legs
escalopes panées	veal escalopes fried in egg and breadcrumbs
escargots	snails
flan	egg custard
moules	mussels
potage	vegetable soup
quenelles	fish or meat fingers cooked in a white sauce
ragoût	stew
ratatouille	a vegetable stew
ris de veau	veal sweetbreads
sorbet	water ice
tournedos	fillet steak

Health

ESSENTIAL INFORMATION

- Be sure to have medical insurance.
- For minor disorders and treatment at a drugstore, see p. 73.
- For finding your way to a doctor, dentist, drugstore or Health and Social Security Office, see p. 66.
- To find a doctor in an emergency, look for:
  Médecins (in the Yellow Pages of the telephone directory)
  Les Urgences (emergency ward)

What's the matter?

I have a pain here [*point*]	**J'ai mal ici** sheh mal ee-see
I have a toothache	**J'ai mal aux dents** sheh mal o dahn
I have broken . . .	**J'ai cassé . . .** sheh casseh . . .
my dentures	**mon dentier** moon dahnt-yeh
my glasses	**mes lunettes** meh loonet
I have lost . . .	**J'ai perdu . . .** sheh pairdoo . . .
my contact lenses	**mes verres de contact** meh vair der contact
a filling	**un plombage** an plombash
My child is ill	**Mon enfant est malade** mon ahnfahn eh mal-ad

Already under treatment for something else?

I take . . . regularly [*show*]	**Je prends . . . régulièrement**
	sher prahn . . . rehgool-yair-mahn
this medicine	**ce médicament**
	ser meh-deecah-mahn
these pills	**ces pilules**
	seh peelool
I have . . .	**J'ai . . .**
	sheh . . .
a heart condition	**le cœur malade**
	ler ker mal-ad
haemorrhoids	**des hémorroïdes**
	deh zeh-moro-eed
rheumatism	**des rhumatismes**
	deh rheumateesm
I am . . .	**Je suis . . .**
	sher swee . . .
diabetic	**diabétique**
	dee-ah-beh-teek
asthmatic	**asthmatique**
	asthmateek
pregnant	**enceinte**
	ahn-sant
allergic to (penicillin)	**allergique à (la pénicilline)**
	allersheek ah (lah penicillin)

Problems: loss, theft

ESSENTIAL INFORMATION

- If worse comes to worst, find the police station. To ask the way, see p. 64.
- Look for:
  GENDARMERIE (police)
  COMMISSARIAT DE POLICE (police station)

- If you lose your passport report the loss to the police and go to the nearest U.S. consulate.
- In an emergency, dial 17 for police/ambulance and 18 for the fire brigade.

LOSS
[See also 'Theft' below: the lists are interchangeable]

I have lost . . .	J'ai perdu . . .
	sheh pairdoo . . .
my camera	**mon appareil photo**
	mon appah-ray photo
my car keys	**les clés de ma voiture**
	leh cleh der mah vwahtoor
my car registration	**ma carte grise**
	mah cart greez
my driver's license	**mon permis de conduire**
	mon pairmee der condweer
my insurance certificate	**mon assurance**
	mon assoorahns

THEFT

Someone has stolen . . .	On m'a volé . . .
	on mah voleh . . .
my car	**ma voiture**
	mah vwahtoor
my money	**mon argent**
	mon arshahn
my tickets	**mes billets**
	meh bee-yeh
my travellers' cheques	**mes traveller chèques**
	meh traveller shek
my wallet	**mon portefeuille**
	mon port-fey
my luggage	**mes bagages**
	meh baggash

The post office and phoning home

ESSENTIAL INFORMATION

POSTES TELECOMMUNICATIONS

- To find a post office, see p. 65.
- Key words to look for:
  POSTES
  POSTE, TÉLÉGRAPHE, TÉLÉPHONE (PTT)
  POSTES ET TÉLÉCOMMUNICATIONS (PT)
- It is best to buy stamps at a tobacco shop.
- Unless you read and speak French well, it's best not to make phone calls by yourself. Go to the main post office and write the town and number you want on a piece of paper.
- For international calls, dial 19. Wait for the second buzzing noise and then dial 44 for Great Britain or 1 for the United States. Then dial the area code and number.

WHAT TO SAY

To England, please
Pour l'Angleterre, s'il vous plaît
poor lahng-tair sil voo pleh

[*Hand letters, cards or parcels over the counter*]

To Australia
Pour l'Australie
poor lostrah-lee

To the United States
Pour les États-Unis
poor leh zehtah-zoonee

I'd like to send a telegram
Je voudrais envoyer un télégramme
sher voodreh ahn-vwah-yeh an telegram

I'd like this number . . .
Je voudrais ce numéro . . .
sher voodreh ser noomehro . . .

[*show number*]

in England
en Angleterre
ahn ahng-tair

in Canada
au Canada
o canada

Can you dial it for me, please?
Pouvez-vous me l'appeler, s'il vous plaît?
pooveh-voo mer lap-leh sil voo pleh

Cashing checks and changing money

ESSENTIAL INFORMATION

- Finding your way to a bank or exchange bureau, see p. 65.
- Look for these words on buildings:
  BANQUE
  CRÉDIT
  SOCIÉTÉ GÉNÉRALE
  BUREAU DE CHANGE
  CHANGE
- To cash checks, use your bank card where you see the Eurocheque sign. Write in English.
- Have your passport handy.

WHAT TO SAY

I'd like to cash . . .	**Je voudrais encaisser . . .** sher voodreh ahn-kesseh . . .
these travellers' cheques	**ces traveller chèques** seh traveller shek
this cheque	**ce chèque** ser shek
I'd like to change this . . .	**Je voudrais changer ceci . . .** sher voodreh shan-sheh ser-see . . .
into French francs	**en francs français** ahn frahn frahn-seh
into schillings	**en schillings autrichiens** ahn shilling otreesh-yan
into Belgian francs	**en francs belges** ahn frahn belsh
into marks	**en marks** ahn mark
into lire	**en lires** ahn leer
into pesetas	**en pesetas** ahn pesetas
into Swiss francs	**en francs suisses** ahn frahn sweess

Car travel

ESSENTIAL INFORMATION

- Finding a filling station or garage, see p. 66.
- Is it a self-service station? Look out for **LIBRE SERVICE** or **SERVEZ-VOUS**.
- Grades of gasoline:
  NORMALE
  ORDINAIRE (regular)
  SUPER (CARBURANT) (premium)
  GAS-OIL (diesel)
- 1 gallon is about 3¾ liters.
- For car repairs, look for:
  DÉPANNAGE (repairs)
  GARAGE (garage)
  MÉCANICIEN (mechanic)
  CARROSSERIE (for body work)
- Gas stations outside towns will sometimes close from 12–3.
- In case of a breakdown or an emergency look for the **TCF** (French Touring Club) sign, or dial 6969 **(Touring Secours)** from any public telephone.

WHAT TO SAY

[*For numbers, see p. 106*]

(Nine) litres	**(Neuf) litres** (nerf) leet
(Two hundred) francs . . .	**(Deux cents) francs . . .** (der sahn) frahn . . .
of standard	**d'ordinaire** dordeenair
of premium	**de super** der soopair
of diesel	**de gas-oil** der gazwahl
Fill it up, please	**Faites le plein, s'il vous plaît** fet ler plan sil voo pleh
Can you check . . .	**Pouvez-vous vérifier . . .** pooveh voo vehrif-yeh . . .
the oil?	**l'huile?** lweel

Can you check . . .	**Pouvez-vous vérifier . . .** pooveh voo vehrif-yeh . . .
the battery?	**la batterie?** lah battree
the radiator?	**le radiateur?** ler raddee-atter
the tyres?	**les pneus?** leh pner
I've run out of petrol	**Je suis en panne d'essence** sher swee ahn pan dessahns
Can you help me, please?	**Pouvez-vous m'aider, s'il vous plaît?** pooveh voo med-eh sil voo pleh
Do you do repairs?	**Est-ce que vous faites les réparations?** esk voo fet leh rehpahrah-see-on
I have a puncture	**J'ai une crevaison** sheh oon crer-veh-zon
I have a broken windscreen	**Mon pare-brise est cassé** mon par-breez eh casseh
I think the problem is here . . . [*point*]	**Je crois que c'est ça qui ne va pas . . .** sher crwah ker seh sah kee ner vah pah . . .

LIKELY REACTIONS

I don't do repairs	**Je ne fais pas les réparations** sher ner feh-pah leh rehpahrah- see-on
Where's your car?	**Où est votre voiture?** oo eh vot vwahtoor
What make is it?	**C'est quelle marque?** seh kel mark
Come back tomorrow/on Monday	**Revenez demain/lundi** rer-venneh der-man/lerndee
[*For days of the week, see p. 109*]	
We don't hire cars	**On ne fait pas la location** on ner feh pah lah locah-see-on
Your driving licence, please	**Votre permis, s'il vous plaît** vot pairmee sil voo pleh
The mileage is unlimited	**Le kilométrage n'est pas limité** ler keelomeh-trash neh pah limiteh

Public transport

ESSENTIAL INFORMATION

- Key words on signs:
  ACCÈS AUX QUAIS (to the trains)
  ARRÊT D'AUTOBUS (bus stop)
  BILLETS (tickets, ticket office)
  CONSIGNE (left luggage)
  ENTRÉE (entrance)
  HORAIRE (timetable)
  INTERDIT(E) (forbidden)
  LOCATIONS (bookings)
  MONTÉE (entrance for buses)
  N'OUBLIEZ PAS DE COMPOSTER (don't forget to validate)
  RENSEIGNEMENTS (information)
  QUAI (platform)
  SORTIE (exit)
  VOIE (platform)
- As French Railways have abolished ticket control at platform barriers, *you* must validate your ticket by using one of the orange-coloured date stamping machines provided at platform entrances *before* departure. If you fail to do so, you will be liable to a fine of up to 20% of your fare. However, these regulations do not apply to international tickets purchased outside France.
- There is a flat rate for subway tickets and it is cheaper to buy a **carnet** (a book of ten tickets). In Paris, bus and subway tickets are interchangeable.

WHAT TO SAY

Where does the train for (Paris) leave from?	**De quelle voie part le train de (Paris)?**
	der kel vwah par ler tran der (pahree)
Is this the train for (Paris)?	**Est-ce le train de (Paris)?**
	ess ler tran der (pahree)
Where does the bus for (Toulouse) leave from?	**D'où part l'autobus de (Toulouse)?**
	doo par lotoboos der (too-looz)

Is this the bus for (Toulouse)?	**Est-ce l'autobus de (Toulouse)?** ess lotoboos der (too-looz)
Do I have to change?	**Faut-il changer?** fo-til shahn-sheh
Where can I get a taxi?	**Où puis-je trouver un taxi?** oo pweesh trooveh an taxee
Can you put me off at the right stop, please?	**Pouvez-vous me dire où je dois descendre?** pooveh-voo mer deer oo sher dwah dessahnd
Can I book a seat?	**Puis-je réserver une place?** pweesh reh-zairveh oon plass
A single	**Un aller** an alleh
A return	**Un aller-retour** an alleh rer-toor
First class	**Première classe** prem-yair class
Second class	**Deuxième classe** der-zee-em class
One adult	**Un adulte** an ahdoolt
Two adults	**Deux adultes** der zahdoolt
and one child	**et un enfant** eh an ahnfahn
and two children	**et deux enfants** eh der zahnfahn
How much is it?	**C'est combien?** seh combee-an

Reference

NUMBERS

0	**zéro**	zehro
1	**un**	an
2	**deux**	der
3	**trois**	trwah

4	**quatre**	kat
5	**cinq**	sank
6	**six**	seess
7	**sept**	set
8	**huit**	weet
9	**neuf**	nerf
10	**dix**	deess
11	**onze**	onz
12	**douze**	dooz
13	**treize**	trez
14	**quatorze**	kattorz
15	**quinze**	kanz
16	**seize**	sez
17	**dix-sept**	dee-set
18	**dix-huit**	deezweet
19	**dix-neuf**	deez-nerf
20	**vingt**	van
21	**vingt et un**	vanteh an
22	**vingt-deux**	vant-der
23	**vingt-trois**	vant-trwah
24	**vingt-quatre**	vant-kat
25	**vingt-cinq**	vant-sank
26	**vingt-six**	vant-seess
27	**vingt-sept**	vant-set
28	**vingt-huit**	vant-weet
29	**vingt-neuf**	vant-nerf
30	**trente**	trahnt
31	**trente et un**	trahnteh an
35	**trente-cinq**	trahnt sank
38	**trente-huit**	trahnt weet
40	**quarante**	kah-rahnt
41	**quarante et un**	kahrahnteh an
45	**quarante-cinq**	kah-rahnt sank
48	**quarante-huit**	kah-rahnt weet
50	**cinquante**	sankahnt
55	**cinquante-cinq**	sankahnt sank
60	**soixante**	swah-sahnt
65	**soixante-cinq**	swah-sahnt sank
70	**soixante-dix**	swah-sahnt deess
75	**soixante-quinze**	swah-sahnt kanz
80	**quatre-vingts**	kat van
85	**quatre-vingt-cinq**	kat van sank

90	**quatre-vingt-dix**	kat van deess
95	**quatre-vingt-quinze**	kat van kanz
100	**cent**	sahn
101	**cent un**	sahn an
102	**cent deux**	sahn der
125	**cent vingt-cinq**	sahn vant sank
150	**cent cinquante**	sahn sankahnt
175	**cent soixante-quinze**	sahn swah-sahnt kanz
200	**deux cents**	der sahn
300	**trois cents**	trwah sahn
400	**quatre cents**	kat sahn
500	**cinq cents**	san sahn
1,000	**mille**	meel
1,500	**mille cinq cents**	meel san sahn
2,000	**deux mille**	der meel
5,000	**cinq mille**	san meel
10,000	**dix mille**	dee meel
100,000	**cent mille**	sahn meel
1,000,000	**un million**	an meel-yon

TIME

What time is it?	**Quelle heure est-il?**
	keller eh-til
It's one o'clock	**Il est une heure**
	il eh ooner
It's . . .	**Il est . . .**
	il eh . . .
two o'clock	**deux heures**
	der-zer
three o'clock	**trois heures**
	trwah-zer
noon	**midi**
	meedee
midnight	**minuit**
	meenwee
a quarter past five	**cinq heures et quart**
	sanker eh kar
half past five	**cinq heures et demie**
	sanker eh der-me
a quarter to six	**six heures moins le quart**
	seezer mwen ler kar

DAYS AND MONTHS

Monday	**lundi**
	lerndee
Tuesday	**mardi**
	mardee
Wednesday	**mercredi**
	mairk-dee
Thursday	**jeudi**
	sher-dee
Friday	**vendredi**
	vahnd-dee
Saturday	**samedi**
	samdee
Sunday	**dimanche**
	deemahnsh
January	**janvier**
	shahnv-yeh
February	**février**
	fehvree-eh
March	**mars**
	marss
April	**avril**
	avreel
May	**mai**
	meh
June	**juin**
	shoo-an
July	**juillet**
	shwee-yeh
August	**août**
	oot
September	**septembre**
	septahmb
October	**octobre**
	octob
November	**novembre**
	novahmb
December	**décembre**
	dessahmb

Index

German

D. L. Ellis, A. Cheyne

Pronunciation **Dr J. Baldwin**

Useful addresses

Austrian National Tourist Office
545 5th Ave.
New York, NY 10017

German National Tourist Office
630 5th Ave.
New York, NY 10020

Swiss National Tourist Office
608 5th Ave.
New York, NY 10020

Contents

Pronunciation hints

In German it is important to stress or emphasize the syllables in italics, just as you would if we were to take as an English example: *li*ttle Jack *Hor*ner *sat* in the *cor*ner. Here we have ten syllables, but only four stresses. German will pose no problems as there is an obvious and consistent relationship between pronunciation and spelling.
Viel Spass!

Everyday expressions

[*See also 'Shop talk', p. 128*]

Hello	**Guten Tag** g*oo*-ten t*ah*k
Hello (Austria)	**Grüss Gott** gr*oo*ss g*o*t
Good morning	**Guten Morgen** g*oo*-ten m*o*rgen
Good day ⎤ Good afternoon ⎦	**Guten Tag** g*oo*-ten t*ah*k
Good evening	**Guten Abend** g*oo*-ten *a*h-bent
Good night	**Gute Nacht** g*oo*-teh n*a*kt
Good-bye	**Auf Wiedersehn** owf v*ee*der-zain
Yes	**Ja** yah
Please	**Bitte** b*i*tteh
Yes, please	**Ja, bitte** yah b*i*tteh
Thank you	**Danke** d*a*nkeh
That's right	**Das stimmt** das sht*i*mmt
No	**Nein** nine
I disagree	**Das stimmt nicht** das sht*i*mmt n*i*sht
Excuse me ⎤ Sorry ⎦	**Entschuldigen Sie** ent-sh*oo*l-dig-en zee
It doesn't matter	**Es macht nichts** es m*a*kt n*i*shts
Where's the toilet, please?	**Wo sind die Toiletten?** v*o* zint dee twa-l*e*tten
Do you speak English?	**Sprechen Sie Englisch?** shpr*e*shen zee *e*ng-lish
What's your name?	**Wie ist Ihr Name?** vee ist eer n*a*hmeh
My name is . . .	**Mein Name ist . . .** mine n*a*hmeh ist . . .

Asking the way

ESSENTIAL INFORMATION

- Keep a look out for all these place names as you will find them on shops, maps and notices.

WHAT TO SAY

Excuse me, please
Entschuldigen Sie, bitte
ent-shool-dig-en zee bitteh

How do I get . . .
Wie komme ich . . .
vee kommeh ish . . .

to Hamburg?
nach Hamburg?
nahk hum-boork

to (Station) Road?
zur (Bahnhof) strasse?
tsoor (bahn-hof-)shtrahsseh

to the hotel (Krone)?
zum Hotel (Krone)?
tsoom hotel (krone-eh)

to the airport?
zum Flughafen?
tsoom flook-hahfen

to the beach?
zum Strand?
tsoom shtrant

to the bus station?
zum Busbahnhof?
tsoom boos-bahn-hof

to the market?
zum Markt?
tsoom markt

to the police station?
zur Polizeiwache
tsoor poli-tsy-vakkeh

to the port?
zum Hafen?
tsoom hahfen

to the post office?
zum Postamt?
tsoom post-amt

to the railway station?
zum Bahnhof?
tsoom bahn-hof

to the sports stadium?
zum Stadion?
tsoom shtah-dee-on

to the tourist information office?
zum Fremdenverkehrsbüro?
tsoom fremden-ferkairs-buro

to the town centre?
zum Stadtzentrum?
tsoom shtatt-tsent-room

to the town hall?	**zum Rathaus?**
	tsoom r*a*ht-house
Is there . . . near by?	**Gibt es . . . in der Nähe?**
	geept es . . . in der n*ay*-eh
a baker's	**eine Bäckerei**
	*i*neh becker-ry
a bank	**eine Bank**
	*i*neh b*a*nk
a bar	**eine Bar**
	*i*neh b*a*r
a bus stop	**eine Bushaltestelle**
	*i*neh b*oo*s-halteh-shtelleh
a butcher's	**eine Metzgerei**
	*i*neh mets-ga-ry
a café	**ein Café**
	ine caff*ay*
a cake shop	**eine Konditorei**
	*i*neh con-dee-to-ry
a campsite	**eine Campingplatz**
	*i*nen c*a*mping-plats
a car park	**einen Parkplatz**
	*i*nen p*a*rk-plats
a change bureau	**eine Wechselstube**
	*i*neh v*e*ksel-shtoobeh
a chemist's	**eine Apotheke**
	*i*neh ah-pot*a*ke-eh
a delicatessen	**ein Feinkostgeschäft**
	ine f*i*ne-kost-gash*e*ft
a dentist's	**einen Zahnarzt**
	*i*nen ts*a*hn-artst
a department store	**ein Kaufhaus**
	ine k*o*wf-house
a disco	**eine Diskothek**
	*i*neh disco-t*a*ke
a doctor's surgery	**eine Arztpraxis**
	*i*neh artst-prak-sis
a dry cleaner's	**eine Reinigung**
	*i*neh ry-nee-goong
a fishmonger's	**ein Fischgeschäft**
	ine f*i*sh-gash*e*ft
a garage (for repairs)	**eine Autowerkstatt**
	*i*neh *o*wto-vairk-shtatt

Is there . . . near by?	Gibt es . . . in der Nähe?
	geept es . . . in der nay-eh
a hairdresser's	einen Frisör
	inen free-zer
a greengrocer's	eine Gemüsehandlung
	ineh ga-moozeh-hant-loong
a grocer's	ein Lebensmittelgeschäft
	ine labens-mittel-gasheft
a hospital	ein Krankenhaus
	ine kranken-house
a hotel	ein Hotel
	ine hotel
an ice-cream parlour	eine Eisdiele
	ineh ice-deeleh
a local sickness insurance office	eine Krankenkasse
	ineh kranken-kasseh
a laundry	eine Wäscherei
	ineh vesheh-ry
a newsagent's	einen Zeitungshändler
	inen tsy-toongs-hentler
a night club	einen Nachtklub
	inen nakt-kloop
a park	einen Park
	inen park
a petrol station	eine Tankstelle
	ineh tank-shtelleh
a post box	einen Briefkasten
	inen breef-kasten
a public telephone	eine Telefonzelle
	ineh telefone-tselleh
a public toilet	öffentliche Toiletten
	erffent-lish-eh twa-letten
a restaurant	ein Restaurant
	ine rest-o-rung
a supermarket	einen Supermarkt
	inen zooper-markt
a taxi stand	einen Taxistand
	inen taxi-shtant
a tobacconist's	einen Zigarettenladen
	inen tsee-garetten-lahden
a travel agent's	ein Reisebüro
	ine ryzeh-buro

a youth hostel	**eine Jugendherberge** ineh yoogent-hair-bairgeh

DIRECTIONS

Left	**Links** links
Right	**Rechts** reshts
Straight ahead	**Geradeaus** grahdeh-ows
There	**Dort** dort
First left/right	**Erste Strasse links/rechts** airsteh shtrahsseh links/reshts
Second left/right	**Zweite Strasse links/rechts** twvy-teh shtrahsseh links/reshts

---

Accommodation

ESSENTIAL INFORMATION
Hotel

- If you want hotel-type accommodation, all the following words in capital letters are worth looking for on signs:
  HOTEL
  HOTEL GARNI (room and breakfast, no other meals provided)
  MOTEL
  PENSION (boarding house)
  GASTHOF (inexpensive type of inn with a limited number of rooms)
  ZIMMER FREI (rooms to rent in private houses, bed and breakfast)
- A list of hotels in the town or district can usually be obtained at the local tourist information office.
- Not all hotels and boarding-houses provide meals apart from breakfast; inquire about this, on arrival, at the reception desk.

- The cost is displayed in the room itself, so you can check it when having a look round before agreeing to stay.
- The displayed cost is for the room itself, per night and not per person. It usually includes service charges and taxes, but quite often does not include breakfast.
- Breakfast is continental style, with rolls, butter and jam; boiled eggs, cheese and cold meats are usually available on request. Some larger hotels also offer a **FRÜHSTÜCKS-BUFFET** where you can help yourself to cereals, yoghurt, fresh fruit etc.
- It is customary to tip the porter and leave a tip for the chambermaid in the hotel room.

WHAT TO SAY

I have a booking	**Ich habe reserviert** ish hahbeh reserveert
Have you any vacancies, please?	**Haben Sie noch Zimmer frei?** hahben zee nok tsimmer fry
Can I book a room?	**Kann ich ein Zimmer reservieren lassen?** kan ish ine tsimmer reser-veeren lassen
It's for . . .	**Es ist für . . .** es ist foor . . .
one adult/one person	**einen Erwachsenen/eine Person** inen er-vaksen-en/ineh per-zone
two adults/two people	**zwei Erwachsene/zwei Personen** tsvy er-vaksen-eh/tsvy per-zonen
and one child	**und ein Kind** oont ine kint
and two children	**und zwei Kinder** oont tsvy kin-der
It's for . . .	**Es ist für . . .** es ist foor . . .
one night	**eine Nacht** ineh nakt
two nights	**zwei Nächte** tsvy nesh-teh
one week	**eine Woche** ineh vok-eh
two weeks	**zwei Wochen** tsvy vokken

I would like . . .	**Ich möchte . . .**
	ish mershteh . . .
a room	**ein Zimmer**
	ine tsimmer
two rooms	**zwei Zimmer**
	tsvy tsimmer
a room with a single bed	**ein Einzelzimmer**
	ine ine-tsel-tsimmer
a room with two single beds	**ein Zweibettzimmer**
	ine tsvy-bett-tsimmer
a room with a double bed	**ein Doppelzimmer**
	ine doppel-tsimmer
I would like a room . . .	**Ich möchte ein Zimmer . . .**
	ish mershteh ine tsimmer . . .
with a toilet	**mit Toilette**
	mit twa-letteh
with a bathroom	**mit Bad**
	mit baht
with a shower	**mit Dusche**
	mit doo-sheh
with a cot	**mit einem Kinderbett**
	mit inem kin-der-bett
with a balcony	**mit Balkon**
	mit bal-kone
I would like . . .	**Ich möchte . . .**
	ish mershteh . . .
full board	**Vollpension**
	foll-penzee-on
half board	**Halbpension**
	hal-penzee-on
bed and breakfast [see essential information]	**Übernachtung mit Frühstück**
	oober-naktoong mit froo-shtok
Do you serve meals?	**Kann man bei Ihnen essen?**
	kan man by eenen essen
Can I look at the room?	**Kann ich mir das Zimmer ansehen?**
	kan ish meer das tsimmer un-zay-en
OK, I'll take it	**Gut, ich nehme es**
	goot ish nay-meh es
No thanks, I won't take it	**Nein, danke, ich nehme es nicht**
	nine dankeh ish nay-meh es nisht

The bill, please	**Die Rechnung, bitte**
	dee resh-noong bitteh
Is service included?	**Ist Bedienung inbegriffen?**
	ist bed*ee*-noong *i*n-begriffen
I think this is wrong	**Ich glaube, hier ist ein Fehler**
	ish gla-oobeh here ist ine failer
May I have a receipt?	**Kann ich eine Quittung haben?**
	kan ish *i*neh kv*i*t-oong hahben

Camping

- Look for: **CAMPINGPLATZ** or **ZELTPLATZ**
- Be prepared for the following charges:
  per person
  for the car (if applicable)
  for the tent or for trailer space
  for electricity
  for hot showers
- You must provide proof of identity, such as your passport.
- If you cannot find an official camping site and want to camp elsewhere, get the permission of the farmer/landowner or the local police first.
- It is usually not possible to make advance reservations on camping sites. Try and secure a site in mid-afternoon if you are travelling during the high season.
- Owners of camping sites in Germany are not liable for losses. You should make your own insurance arrangements in advance.

Youth hostels

- Look for the word **JUGENDHERBERGE**.
- You must have a YHA card with a photograph.
- There is no upper age limit at German youth hostels, except in Bavaria where the age limit is twenty-seven.
- Accommodation is usually in small dormitories.
- Many German youth hostels do *not* provide a kitchen in which visitors can prepare their own meals; but usually meals at a reasonable price are provided by the house-parents.
- You may have to help with domestic chores in some hostels.

WHAT TO SAY

Have you any vacancies?	**Haben Sie noch etwas frei?**
	h*a*hben zee nok *e*tvas fry
How much is it . . .	**Wie hoch ist die Gebühr . . .**
	vee hoke ist dee gab*oo*r . . .
for the tent?	**für das Zelt?**
	foor das tselt
for the trailer?	**für den Wohnwagen?**
	foor den v*o*ne-vahgen
for the car?	**für das Auto?**
	foor das *o*wto
for the electricity?	**für Elektrizität**
	foor elektri-tsee-t*a*te
per person?	**pro Person?**
	pro per-z*o*ne
per day/night?	**pro Tag/Nacht?**
	pro t*a*hk/naht
May I look round?	**Kann ich mich etwas umsehen?**
	kan ish mish *e*tvas *oo*m-zay-en
Do you provide anything . . .	**Kann man bei Ihnen etwas . . . bekommen?**
	kan man by *ee*nen *e*tvas . . . bek*o*mmen
to eat?	**zu essen**
	tsoo *e*ssen
to drink?	**zu trinken**
	tsoo tr*i*nken
Do you have . . .	**Haben Sie . . .**
	h*a*hben zee . . .
a bar?	**eine Bar?**
	*i*neh b*a*r
hot showers?	**heisse Duschen?**
	hysseh d*oo*-shen
a kitchen?	**eine Küche?**
	*i*neh k*oo*-sheh
a launderette?	**einen Waschsalon?**
	*i*nen v*a*sh-zal*o*ng
a restaurant?	**ein Restaurant?**
	ine resto-r*u*ng
a shop?	**ein Geschäft?**
	ine gash*e*ft

Do you have . . .   **Haben Sie . . .**
                              hahben zee . . .

    a swimming pool?   **ein Schwimmbad?**
                              ine shvimm-baht

    a snack-bar?   **eine Imbisstube?**
                              ineh im-bis-shtoobeh

[*For food shopping, see p. 131, and for eating and drinking out, see p. 141*]

Problems

The toilet   **Die Toilette**
                    dee twa-letteh

The shower   **Die Dusche**
                    dee doosheh

The tap   **Der Wasserhahn**
                 der vasser-hahn

The razor point   **Die Steckdose für den**
                              Rasierapparat
                          dee shteck-doze-eh foor den
                              razeer-apparaht

The light   **Das Licht**
                   das lisht

. . . is not working   **. . . funktioniert nicht**
                               . . . foonk-tsee-o-neert nisht

My camping gas has run out   **Ich habe kein Camping-Gas mehr**
                                     ish hahbeh kine camping-gahs mair

LIKELY REACTIONS

Have you an identity
document?   **Haben Sie einen Pass oder**
                       Personalausweis?
                   hahben zee inen pass oder
                       per-zonahl-ows-vice

Your membership card, please   **Ihre Mitgliedskarte, bitte**
                                       eereh mit-gleets-karteh bitteh

What's your name [*see p. 115*]   **Wie ist Ihr Name?**
                                          vee ist eer nahmeh

Sorry, we're full   **Est tut mir leid, wir sind voll**
                               besetzt
                           es toot meer lite veer zint foll
                               bezetst

How many people is it for?   **Für wieviele Personen?**
                                     foor vee-feeleh per-zonen

How many nights is it for?	**Für wieviele Nächte?**
	foor vee-feeleh nesh-teh
It's (4) marks . . .	**Es kostet (vier) Mark . . .**
	es kostet (feer) mark . . .
per day/per night	**pro Tag/pro Nacht**
	pro tahk/pro nakt
I haven't any rooms left	**Ich habe keine Zimmer mehr frei**
	ish hahbeh kineh tsimmer mair fry
Do you want to have a look?	**Wollen Sie es sich ansehen?**
	vollen zee es zish un-zay-en

General shopping

The drugstore/The chemist's

ESSENTIAL INFORMATION

- Look for the word **APOTHEKE** (drugstore) or this sign:
- There are two kinds of drugstores in Germany. The **APOTHEKE** (dispensing pharmacy) is the place to go for prescriptions, medicines etc.; toilet and household articles, as well as patent medicines, are sold at the **DROGERIE.**
- Try a pharmacist *before* going to a doctor: they are usually qualified to treat minor injuries.
- Drugstores are open during normal business hours, i.e. from 8.30 a.m. to 12.30 p.m., and from 2.30 to 6.30 p.m. on weekdays. On Saturdays they close at 2.00 p.m.
- Drugstores take turns staying open all night and on Sunday. If a drugstore is shut, a notice on the door will give the address of the nearest night **(NACHDIENST)** and Sunday service **(SONNTAGSDIENST).**
- Some toiletries can be bought at a **PARFÜMERIE** but they will be more expensive.

WHAT TO SAY

I'd like . . .	**Ich möchte . . .** ish mershteh . . .
some Alka Seltzer	**Alka Seltzer** alka zeltser
some antiseptic	**ein antiseptisches Mittel** ine anti-zeptishes mittel
some aspirin	**Aspirin** ahs-pee-reen
some baby food	**Babynahrung** baby-nah-roong
some contraceptives	**ein Verhütungsmittel** ine fer-hootoongs-mittel
some cotton	**Watte** vatteh
some disposable diapers	**Papierwindeln** papeer-vin-deln
some eye drops	**Augentropfen** owghen-tropfen
some inhalant	**ein Inhaliermittel** ine in-hahleer-mittel
some insect repellent	**ein Insektenschutzmittel** ine in-zekten-shoots-mittel
some paper tissues	**Papiertücher** papeer-toosher
some sanitary napkins	**Monatsbinden** monahts-bin-den
some sticking plaster	**Heftpflaster** heft-pflaster
some suntan lotion/oil	**Sonnenmilch/öl** zonnen-milsh/erl
some Tampax	**eine Packung Tampax** ineh pack-oong tampax
some throat lozenges	**Halspastillen** hals-past-ill-en
some toilet paper	**Toilettenpapier** twa-letten-papeer
I'd like something for . . .	**Ich möchte etwas gegen . . .** ish mershteh etvas gay-ghen . . .
bites (snakes, dogs)	**Bisswunden** bis-voon-den

burns	**Verbrennungen**
	fer-bren-oong-en
a cold	**Erkältung**
	er-kelt-oong
constipation	**Verstopfung**
	fer-shtopf-oong
a cough	**Husten**
	hoosten
diarrhoea	**Durchfall**
	doorsh-fahl
ear-ache	**Ohrenschmerzen**
	or-en-shmairts-en
flu	**Grippe**
	grippeh
scalds	**Verbrühung**
	fer-broo-oong
sore gums	**wundes Zahnfleisch**
	voondes tsahn-flysh
stings (mosquitos, bees)	**Insektenstiche**
	in-zekten-shtee-sheh
sunburn	**Sonnenbrand**
	zonnen-brant
car (air)/sea sickness	**Reisekrankheit/Seekrankheit**
	ryzeh-krank-hite/zeh-krank-hite

[*For other essential expressions, see 'Shop talk', p. 128*]

Holiday items

ESSENTIAL INFORMATION

- Places to shop at and signs to look for:
  SCHREIBWARENGESCHÄFT (stationery)
  PHOTOGESCHÄFT (films)
  KUNSTGEWERBE (arts and crafts)
  GESCHENKARTIKEL (gifts)
- and the main department stores:
KARSTADT	HERTIE
HORTEN	KAUHOF

WHAT TO SAY

I'd like . . .	**Ich möchte . . .**
	ish mershteh . . .
a bag	**eine Tasche**
	*i*neh t*a*sheh
a beach ball	**einen Strandball**
	*i*nen shtr*a*nt-bal
a bucket	**einen Eimer**
	*i*nen *i*mer
an English newspaper	**eine englische Zeitung**
	*i*neh *e*ng-lisheh tsy-toong
some envelopes	**Breifumschläge**
	br*ee*f-oom-shlaig-eh
a guide book	**einen Reiseführer**
	*i*nen ryzeh-foorer
some postcards	**Ansichtskarten**
	*u*n-zishts-karten
a spade	**eine Schaufel**
	*i*neh sh*a*-oofel
a straw hat	**einen Strohhut**
	*i*nen shtr*o*-hoot
some sunglasses	**eine Sonnenbrille**
	*i*neh z*o*nnen-brilleh
some writing paper	**Schreibpapier**
	shr*i*pe-papeer
a colour film	**einen Farbfilm**
[*show the camera*]	*i*nen farp-film
a black and white film	**einen Schwarzweiss-Film**
	*i*nen shvarts-v*i*ce film

Shop talk

ESSENTIAL INFORMATION

- Know how to say the important weights and measures: note that though Germany is metric, people still use the word **Pfund** (pound).

50 grams	**fünfzig Gramm**
	foonf-tsik gramm
100 grams	**einhundert Gramm**
	ine-hoondert gramm
200 grams	**zweihundert Gramm**
	tsvy-hoondert gramm
½ lb (250 grams)	**ein halbes Pfund**
	ine halbes pfoont
1 lb	**ein Pfund**
	ine pfoont
1 kilo	**ein Kilo**
	ine kilo
2 kilos	**zwei Kilo**
	tsvy kilo
½ litre	**einen halben Liter**
	inen halben litre
1 litre	**einen Liter**
	inen litre
2 litres	**zwei Liter**
	tsvy litre

[*For numbers, see p. 159*]

CUSTOMER

I'm just looking	**Ich sehe mich nur um**
	ish zay-eh mish noor oom
How much is this/that?	**Wieviel kostet dies/das?**
	vee-feel kostet dees/das
What is that?/What are those?	**Was ist das?**
	vas ist das
Is there a discount?	**Gibt es einen Rabatt?**
	geept es inen rah-batt
I'd like that, please	**Ich möchte das da, bitte**
	ish mershteh das dah bitteh
Not that	**Nicht das**
	nisht das
Like that	**Wie das da**
	vee das dah
That's enough, thank you	**Das ist genug, danke**
	das ist ganook dankeh
More, please	**Mehr, bitte**
	mair bitteh

Less than that	**Etwas weniger** *etvas vay-neeg-er*
That's fine	**Das ist gut so** das ist goot zo
I won't take it, thank you	**Ich nehme es nicht, danke** ish nay-meh es nisht dankeh
It's not right	**Es ist nicht das Richtige** es ist nisht das rish-teeg-eh
Have you got something . . .	**Haben Sie etwas . . .** hahben zee etvas . . .
better?	**Besseres?** besser-es
cheaper?	**Billigeres?** billig-er-es
different?	**anderes?** ander-es
larger?/smaller?	**Grösseres?/Kleineres?** gresser-es/kliner-es
Can I have a bag, please?	**Kann ich bitte eine Tragetasche haben?** kan ish bitteh ineh trahg-eh-tasheh hahben
Can I have a receipt?	**Kann ich eine Quittung haben?** kan ish ineh kvitt-oong hahben
Do you take . . .	**Nehmen Sie . . .** nay-men zee . . .
English/American money?	**englisches/amerikanisches Geld?** eng-lishes/ameri-kah-nishes ghelt
travellers' cheques?	**Reiseschecks?** ryzeh-shecks
credit cards?	**Kreditkarten?** kredeet-karten

SHOP ASSISTANT

Can I help you?	**Kann ich Ihnen behilflich sein?** kan ish eenen behilf-lish zine
What would you like?	**Was darf es sein** vas darf es zine
Will that be all?	**Kommt noch etwas dazu?** komt nok etvas dah-tsoo

Is that all?	**Ist das alles?**
	ist das *a*lles
Anything else?	**Sonst noch etwas?**
	*zo*nst nok *e*tvas
Would you like it wrapped?	**Soll ich es einwickeln?**
	zoll ish es *ine*-vickeln
Sorry, none left	**Leider ausverkauft**
	l*i*der *o*ws-fer-kowft
I haven't got any	**Wir haben keine**
	veer h*a*hben k*i*neh
I haven't got any more	**Wir haben keine mehr**
	veer h*a*hben k*i*neh mair
How many do you want?	**Wieviele möchten Sie?**
	vee-feeleh m*e*rshten zee
How much do you want?	**Wieviel möchten Sie?**
	vee-feel m*e*rshten zee
Is that enough?	**Ist das genug?**
	ist das gan*oo*k

Shopping for food

Bread

ESSENTIAL INFORMATION

- Key words to look for:
  BÄCKEREI (bakery)
  BÄCKER (baker)
  BROT (bread)
- Bakeries are open from 7:30 a.m. to 12:30 p.m. and from 2:30 to 6:30 p.m. on weekdays. On Saturdays they close at lunchtime. Many bakeries will open on Sunday mornings from 10 a.m. to noon and close one afternoon during the week, usually on Wednesdays.

WHAT TO SAY

A loaf (like that)	**Ein Brot (wie das da)**
	ine brote (vee das dah)
A bread roll	**Ein Brötchen**
	ine brert-shen
A bread roll (Bavaria, Austria)	**Eine Semmel**
	ineh zemmel
A crescent roll	**Ein Hörnchen**
	ine hern-shen
Sliced bread	**Geschnittenes Brot**
	ga-shnitten-es brote
White bread	**Weissbrot**
	vice-brote
Rye bread	**Graubrot**
	gra-oo-brote
(Black) rye bread	**Schwarzbrot**
	shvarts-brote
Wholemeal bread	**Vollkornbrot**
	foll-korn-brote

[*For other essential expressions, see 'Shop talk', p. 128*]

Cakes and ice cream

ESSENTIAL INFORMATION

- Key words to look for:
  BÄCKEREI (bread and cake shop)
  KONDITOREI (cake shop, often with a tea-room in the back)
  EIS (ice cream)
  EISDIELE (ice cream parlor)
  EISCAFÉ (ice cream parlor/tea room)
  SÜSSWARENLADEN (candy shop)
- **CAFÉ or KAFFEEHAUS** in Austria: a place to buy cakes and have a drink at a table, usually in the afternoon. See also p. 141, 'Ordering a drink and a snack'.

WHAT TO SAY

The type of cakes you find in the shops varies slightly from region to region but the following are some of the most common.

der Berliner	jam filled doughnut
der ber-leener	
der Florentiner	almond flakes on a thin cake and
der flor-en-teener	chocolate base
die Schwarzwälder	Black Forest gâteau
Kirschtorte	
dee shvarts-velder keersh-torteh	
die Obsttorte	fruit on a sponge base with glazing
dee obst-torteh	over
der Apfelstrudel	flaky pastry filled with apple, nuts,
der apfel-shtroodel	and raisins
der Mohrenkopf	ball-shaped pastry filled with
der moren-kopf	pudding, covered with chocolate
der Käsekuchen	cheesecake
der kaizeh-kooken	
die Sachertorte	rich Viennese chocolate cake with
dee zahker-torteh	jam
der Sandkuchen	Madeira cake
der zant-kooken	
die Sahnetorte	cream cake
dee zah-neh-torteh	
der Bienenstich	cream cake sprinkled with flaky
der beenen-shtish	almonds and honey
A . . . ice cream, please	**Ein . . . Eis, bitte**
	ine . . . ice bitteh
strawberry	**Erdbeer**
	airt-bear
chocolate	**Schokoladen**
	shoko-lahden
vanilla	**Vanille**
	vanilyeh
lemon	**Zitronen**
	tsee-tronen
caramel	**Karamel**
	kara-mel
raspberry	**Himbeer**
	him-bear

A cone . . .	**Ein Hörnchen . . .** ine hern-shen . . .
a tub . . .	**Einen Becher . . .** inen besher . . .
(60 Pfennig's) worth of ice-cream	**Ein Eis zu (sechzig)** ine ice tsoo (zek-tsig)

Picnic food

ESSENTIAL INFORMATION

- Key words to look for:
  DELIKATESSENGESCHÄFT
  FEINKOSTGESCHÄFT ⎤ (delicatessen)
  METZGEREI
  SCHLACHTEREI ⎤ (butcher shop)

WHAT TO SAY

Two slices of . . .	**Zwei Scheiben . . .** tsvy shy-ben . . .
roast beef	**Rostbraten** rost-brahten
tongue sausage	**Zungenwurst** tsoongen-voorst
Saveloy sausage	**Zervelatwurst** zervelaht-voorst
raw cured ham	**rohen Schinken** ro-en shinken
cooked ham	**gekochten Schinken** gakokten shinken
garlic sausage	**Knoblauchwurst** knop-lowk-voorst
salami	**Salami** zalah-mi

You might also like to try some of these:
eine Pizza   a pizza
ineh pizza

ein Stück Gänseleberpastete ine shtook gh*e*n-zeh-laber-past*ai*teh	some goose liver pâté
ein Stück Fleischwurst ine shtook fl*y*sh-voorst	some luncheon sausage
einen Matjeshering *i*nen m*a*t-yes-hering	white salted herring
eine Frikadelle *i*neh frikah-d*e*lleh	a spicy thick hamburger (often eaten cold)
einen Räucheraal *i*nen roy-sher-*a*hl	a smoked eel
ein paar Frankfurter ine par fr*a*nk-foorter	two Frankfurter sausages
eine Weisswurst *i*neh v*i*ce-voorst	a Bavarian sausage
eine Thüringer Bratwurst *i*neh t*oo*ring-er br*a*ht-voorst	a spicy sausage from Thuringia
einen Elsässer Wurstsalat *i*nen *e*l-zesser v*oo*rst-zalaht	shredded meat and cheese salad
ein Stück Leberkäse ine shtook l*a*ber-kay-zeh	some meatloaf
eine Wurstpastete *i*neh v*oo*rst-past*ai*teh	a sausage roll
eine Königin-Pastete *i*neh k*e*rneeg-in past*ai*teh	a vol-au-vent
eine Geflügelpastete *i*neh gafl*oo*g-el-past*ai*teh	a chicken vol-au-vent
einen Kräuterquark *i*nen kr*o*yter-kwark	soft cream cheese with herbs
Tilsiter t*i*l-zit-er	mild cheese
Kümmelkäse k*oo*mmel-kaizeh	cheese with caraway seeds
einen Harzer Roller *i*nen h*a*rtser r*o*ller	sharp roll-shaped cheese
Emmentaler emmen-tahler	Swiss cheese
Gouda g*o*wdah	Dutch cheese
Camembert/Brie c*a*men-bair/br*e*e	Camembert/Brie

[*For other essential expressions, see 'Shop talk', p. 128*]

Fruit and vegetables

ESSENTIAL INFORMATION

- Key words to look for:
  OBST (fruit)
  GEMÜSE (vegetables)
  OBST-UND GEMÜSEHÄNDLER (greengrocer)

WHAT TO SAY

1 kilo of . . .	**Ein Kilo . . .**
	*in*e k*i*lo . . .
apples	**Äpfel**
	*e*pfel
bananas	**Bananen**
	ban*a*h-nen
cherries	**Kirschen**
	k*ee*r-shen
grapes	**Weintrauben**
	vine-tra-ooben
oranges	**Apfelsinen**
	apfel-z*ee*nen
pears	**Birnen**
	b*ee*r-nen
peaches	**Pfirsiche**
	pf*ee*r-zisheh
plums	**Pflaumen**
	pfl*a-oo*men
strawberries	**Erdbeeren**
	*ai*rd-bairen
A pineapple, please	**Eine Ananas, bitte**
	*i*neh *a*h-nanas b*i*tteh
A grapefruit	**Eine Pampelmuse**
	*i*neh pampel-m*oo*zeh
A melon	**Eine Melone**
	*i*neh mel*o*ne-eh
A water melon	**Eine Wassermelone**
	*i*neh v*a*sser-mel*o*ne-eh

1lb of . . .	**Ein Pfund . . .**
	*i*ne pfoont . . .
artichokes	**Artischocken**
	arti-sh*o*ken
eggplant	**Auberginen**
	ober-g*ee*nen
avocado pears	**Avokados**
	ahvo-k*a*hdos
carrots	**Karotten**
	kar*o*tten
courgettes	**Zucchini**
	tsoo-k*i*ni
green beans	**grüne Bohnen**
	gr*oo*neh b*o*ne-en
leeks	**Lauch/Porree**
	lowk/p*o*r-ray
mushrooms	**Pilze**
	p*i*l-tseh
onions	**Zwiebeln**
	tsv*ee*-beln
peas	**Erbsen**
	*ai*rpsen
potatoes	**Kartoffeln**
	kar-t*o*ffeln
red cabbage	**Rotkohl**
	r*o*te-kole
spinach	**Spinat**
	shpee-n*a*ht
tomatoes	**Tomaten**
	tom*a*hten
A bunch of . . .	**Ein Bund . . .**
	*i*ne boont . . .
parsley	**Petersilie**
	pater-z*ee*l-yeh
radishes	**Radieschen**
	rah-d*ee*s-shen
shallots	**Schalotten**
	shah-l*o*tten
A head of garlic	**Knoblauch**
	kn*o*pe-la-ook
A lettuce	**Einen Kopfsalat**
	*i*nen k*o*pf-zalaht

A cucumber

Eine Salatgurke
*i*neh zal*a*ht-goorkeh

Like that, please

So eine, bitte
zo *i*neh b*i*tteh

Meat and fish

ESSENTIAL INFORMATION

- Key words to look for:
  METZGEREI
  FLEISCHEREI ⎤ (butcher
  SCHLACHTEREI ⎦ shop)

  METZGER
  FLEISCHER ⎤ (butcher)
  SCHLACHTER ⎦

- When buying fish look for:
  FISCHGESCHÄFT (fish store)
  FISCHABTEILUNG (fish section in store)
  NORDSEE (fish-shop chain selling fresh fish as well as smoked and marinated specialties)

WHAT TO SAY

For roasts, choose the type of meat and then say how many people it is for:

Some beef, please

Rindfleisch, bitte
r*i*nt-flysh b*i*tteh

Some lamb

Lamm
l*a*mm

Some mutton

Hammelfleisch
h*a*mmel-flysh

Some pork

Schweinefleisch
shv*i*ne-eh-flysh

Some veal	**Kalbfleisch** kalp-flysh
A roast . . .	**Einen Braten . . .** inen brahten . . .
for two people	**für zwei Personen** foor tsvy per-zonen
for four people	**für vier Personen** foor feer per-zonen
Some steak, please	**Steak, bitte** steak bitteh
Some liver	**Leber** laber
Some kidneys	**Nieren** neeren
Some sausages	**Würstchen** voorst-shen
Some minced meat	**Hackfleisch** hack-flysh
Two veal scallops, please	**Zwei Kalbsschnitzel, bitte** tsvy kalps-shnitsel bitteh
Three pork chops	**Drei Schweinekotelletts** dry shvine-eh-kotlets
Five lamb chops	**Fünf Lammkoteletts** foonf lamm-kotlets

You may also want:

A chicken	**Ein Huhn** ine hoon
A tongue	**Eine Zunge** ineh tsoong-eh

Purchase large fish and small shellfish by weight:

1lb (½ kilo) of . . .	**Ein Pfund . . .** ine pfoont . . .
cod	**Kabeljau** kahbel-yow
haddock	**Schellfisch** shell-fish
turbot	**Steinbutt** shtine-boott
carp	**Karpfen** karp-fen

1 lb (½ kilo) of . . .	**Ein Pfund . . .**
	*in*e pfoont . . .
red sea-bass	**Rotbarsch**
	r*o*te-barsh
halibut	**Heilbutt**
	h*i*le-boott
pike	**Hecht**
	hesht
shrimps	**Garnelen**
	gar-n*ay*-len
shrimps (N. Germany)	**Granat**
	grah-n*a*ht
prawns	**Krabben**
	kr*a*bben
mussels	**Muscheln**
	m*oo*sheln
salmon	**Lachs**
	laks

For some shellfish and 'frying pan' fish, specify the number you want:

A crab, please	**Einen Krebs, bitte**
	*i*nen kr*e*ps b*i*tteh
A lobster	**Einen Hummer**
	*i*nen h*oo*mmer
A spiny lobster	**Eine Languste**
	*i*neh lang*oo*st-eh
A plaice	**Eine Scholle**
	*i*neh sh*o*ll-eh
A trout	**Eine Forelle**
	*i*neh for*e*ll-eh
A sole	**Eine Seezunge**
	*i*neh z*ay*-tsoong-eh
A mackerel	**Eine Makrele**
	*i*neh mak-r*ai*leh
A herring	**Einen Hering**
	*i*nen h*ai*r-ing

Eating and drinking out

Ordering a drink and a snack

ESSENTIAL INFORMATION

- The places to ask for: **EIN CAFÉ.**
  EINE WIRTSCHAFT (a type of tavern)
  EINE WEINSTUBE (a wine bar)
- By law, the price list of drinks (**GETRÄNKEKARTE**) must be displayed outside or in the window.
- There is always waiter service in cafés, taverns and wine bars. In a tavern you can also drink at the bar if you wish (cheaper).
- A service charge of 10–15% is almost always included in the bill (**BEDIENUNG INBEGRIFFEN**), but it is customary to leave some additional small change.
- Cafés serve non-alcoholic and alcoholic drinks, and are normally open all day.

WHAT TO SAY

I'll have . . . please	**Ich hätte gern . . . bitte**
	ish hetteh gairn . . . bitteh
a black coffee	**einen schwarzen Kaffee**
	inen shvar-tsen kaffeh
a coffee with cream	**einen Kaffee mit Sahne**
	inen kaffeh mit zahneh
a tea	**einen Tee**
	inen tay
with milk/lemon	**mit Milch/Zitrone**
	mit milsh/tsee-trone-eh
a glass of milk	**ein Glas Milch**
	ine glass milsh
a hot chocolate	**eine heisse Schokolade**
	ineh hysseh shoko-lahdeh
a mineral water	**ein Mineralwasser**
	ine minerahl-vasser
a lemonade	**eine Limonade**
	ineh lim-o-nahdeh

I'll have . . . please	**Ich hätte gern . . . bitte**
	ish hetteh gairn . . . bitteh
an orangeade	**einen Orangensprudel**
	inen o-rung-shen-shproodel
a fresh orange juice	**einen frischen Orangensaft**
	inen frishen o-rung-shen-zaft
a grape juice	**einen Traubensaft**
	inen tra-ooben-zaft
an apple juice	**einen Apfelsaft**
	inen apfel-zaft
a beer	**ein Bier**
	ine beer
a draught beer	**ein Bier vom Fass**
	ine beer fom fass
a bitter	**ein Altbier**
	ine alt-beer
a brown ale	**ein dunkles Bier**
	ine doonk-les beer
a half	**ein Kleines**
	ine kly-nes
I'll have . . . please	**Ich hätte gern . . . bitte**
	ish hetteh gairn . . . bitteh
a cheese sandwich/roll	**ein Käsebrot/Käsebrötchen**
	ine kaizeh-brote/kaizeh-brertshen
a ham sandwich/roll	**ein Schinkenbrot/**
	Schinkenbrötchen
	ine shinken-brote/shinken-
	brertshen
a roll with fish	**ein Fischbrötchen**
	ine fish-brertshen
an omelet	**ein Omelett**
	ine omelet
with mushrooms	**mit Pilzen**
	mit pil-tsen
with diced ham	**mit Schinken**
	mit shinken

These are some other snacks you may like to try:

eine Bratwurst   a fried spicy pork sausage
ineh braht-voorst
eine Bockwurst   a large Frankfurter
ineh bock-voorst

eine Currywurst	a grilled sausage topped with curry
*i*neh c*u*rry-voorst	and ketchup
ein halbes Hähnchen	half a (roast) chicken
*i*ne h*a*lbes h*ai*n-shen	
ein Deutsches Beefsteak	a hamburger steak
*i*ne d*o*yt-shes b*ee*fsteak	
ein paar Spiegeleier	two fried eggs
*i*ne par shp*ee*g-el-eye-er	
eine Gulaschsuppe	spicy beef soup
*i*neh g*oo*lash-z*oo*ppeh	

In a restaurant

ESSENTIAL INFORMATION

- You can eat at these places:
  RESTAURANT
  HOTEL-RESTAURANT
  GASTSTÄTTE/GASTHOF
  RASTHOF (highway restaurant)
  GASTWIRTSCHAFT
  BAHNHOFSBÜFETT (at stations)
  GRILLSTUBE
  CAFÉ (limited choice here)
- By law, the menus must be displayed outside or in the window
  – and that is the *only* way to judge if a place is right for you.
- Self-service restaurants are not unknown, but most places have
  waiter service.
- A service charge of 10–15% is usually included in restaurant
  bills, but if satisfied with the service you should always leave
  some small change.
- Most restaurants offer small portions for children. Look for
  KINDER-TELLER (children's portions) on the menu.
- Hot meals are served from 12.00 to 2.00 p.m. at lunchtime and
  from 6.00 to 9.00–10.00 p.m. at night. After that many res-
  taurants offer snacks for latecomers (soups, sausages, salads etc.)
  Ask for the 'small menu': **die kleine Karte** (dee kly-neh k*a*rteh).

WHAT TO SAY

May I book a table?	**Kann ich einen Tisch reservieren lassen?**
	kan ish _i_nen t_i_sh reser-v_ee_ren l_a_ssen
I've booked a table	**Ich habe einen Tisch reservieren lassen**
	ish h_a_hbeh _i_nen t_i_sh reser-v_ee_ren l_a_ssen
A table . . .	**Einen Tisch . . .**
	_i_nen t_i_sh . . .
for one	**für eine Person**
	foor _i_neh per-z_o_ne
for three	**für drei Personen**
	foor dry per-z_o_nen
The à la carte menu, please	**Die Speisekarte, bitte**
	dee shp_y_zeh-karteh b_i_tteh
The fixed-price menu	**Die Gedeck-Karte**
	dee gad_e_ck-karteh
The tourist menu	**Das Touristen-Menü**
	das tour_i_sten-men_oo_
Today's special menu	**Die Karte mit Tagesgedecken**
	dee k_a_rteh mit t_a_hg-es-gad_e_cken
What's this, please [_point to menu_]	**Was ist dies, bitte?**
	v_a_s ist d_ee_s b_i_tteh
The wine list	**Die Weinkarte**
	dee v_i_ne-karteh
A carafe of wine, please	**Eine Karaffe Wein, bitte**
	_i_neh ka-r_a_ffeh v_i_ne b_i_tteh
A quarter (250cc)	**Einen Viertelliter**
	_i_nen f_ee_r-tel-litre
A half (500cc)	**Einen halben Liter**
	_i_nen h_a_lben l_i_tre
A glass	**Ein Glas**
	ine glass
A (half) bottle	**Eine (halbe) Flasche**
	_i_neh (h_a_lbeh) fl_a_sheh
A litre	**Einen Liter**
	_i_nen l_i_tre
Red/white/rosé/house wine	**Rotwein/Weisswein/Rosé/Hauswein**
	r_o_te-vine/v_i_ce-vine/roz_ay_/h_o_use-vine

Some more bread, please	**Noch etwas Brot, bitte**
	nok etvas brote bitteh
Some more wine	**Noch etwas Wein**
	nok etvas vine
Some oil	**Etwas Öl**
	etvas erl
Some vinegar	**Etwas Essig**
	etvas essick
Some salt/pepper	**Etwas Salz/Pfeffer**
	etvas zalts/pfeffer
Some water	**Etwas Wasser**
	etvas vasser
With/without garlic	**Mit/ohne Knoblauch**
	mit/o-neh knope-la-ook
How much does that come to?	**Wieviel macht das insgesamt?**
	vee-feel makt das ins-gazamt
Is service included?	**Ist Bedienung inbegriffen?**
	ist be-deen-ong in-begriffen
Where is the toilet, please?	**Wo sind die Toiletten?**
	vo zint dee twa-letten
Miss!/Waiter!	**Fräulein!/Herr Ober!**
	froy-line/hair o-ber
The bill, please	**Die Rechnung, bitte**
	dee resh-noong bitteh

Key words for courses, as seen on some menus

[*Only ask this question if you want the waiter to remind you of the choice.*]

What have you got in the way of . . .	**Was für . . . haben Sie?**
	vas foor . . . hahben zee
STARTERS?	**VORSPEISEN**
	for-shpyzen
SOUP?	**SUPPEN**
	zooppen
EGG DISHES?	**EIERSPEISEN**
	eye-er-shpyzen
FISH?	**FISCHGERICHTE**
	fish-garisht-eh
MEAT?	**FLEISCHGERICHTE**
	flysh-garisht-eh

What have you got in the way of . . .	**Was für . . . haben Sie?** vas foor . . . hahben zee
GAME?	**WILDGERICHTE** vilt-garisht-eh
FOWL?	**GEFLÜGELGERICHTE** ga-floogel-garisht-eh
VEGETABLES?	**GEMÜSE** ga-moozeh
CHEESE?	**KÄSE** kay-zeh
FRUIT?	**OBST** opst
ICE-CREAM?	**EIS** ice
DESSERT?	**NACHSPEISEN** nahk-shpyzen

UNDERSTANDING THE MENU

You will find the names of the principal ingredients of most dishes on these pages:

Starters, see p. 134
Meat, see p. 138
Fish, see p. 139
Vegetables, see p. 137

Fruit, see p. 136
Dessert, see p. 133
Cheese, see p. 135
Ice-cream, see p. 133

Used together with the following lists of cooking and menu terms, they should help you to decode the menu.

Cooking and menu terms

angemacht	in a special dressing
Auflauf	soufflé
blau	steamed and served with butter
blutig	rare
Bouillon	broth, clear soup
Brat-	fried
-braten	roast, joint
-brühe	broth
-brust	breast
Butter-	buttered
durchgebraten	well done
gebacken	baked

gedämpft	steamed
gedünstet (Austria)	steamed, stewed
gefüllt	stuffed
gegrillt	grilled
gekocht	boiled
in Gelee	jellied
gemischt	mixed
gepökelt	salted, pickled
geräuchert	smoked
gerieben	grated
geschmort	braised, stewed
gespickt	larded, smoked
halbdurch	medium
Hausfrauenart	with apple, sour cream and onions
hausgemacht	homemade
Holländisch	with mayonnaise
Holstein	topped with fried egg, garnished with anchovies and vegetables
Jägerart	served in red wine sauce with mushrooms
-Kaltschale	chilled fruit soup
-Kompott	stewed fruit
Kraftbrühe	broth, beef consommé
Kräuter-	with herbs
mariniert	marinated
Meerrettich-	with horse radish
Müllerin	baked in butter, dressed with breadcrumbs and egg
paniert	dressed with egg and breadcrumbs
Pell-	boiled in the jacket
Petersilien-	parsleyed
-püree	mashed
Rahm-	with cream
roh	raw
Röst-	fried
Sahne-	creamed
sauer	sour
Schlemmer-	for the gourmet
Schnitzel	escalope (of veal)
Senf-	with mustard
Sosse	sauce
Sülz-	in aspic

süss	sweet
überbacken	au gratin
Zwiebel-	with onions

Further words to help you understand the menu

Aalsuppe	eel soup, a speciality of Hamburg
Aufschnitt	sliced cold meat and sausages
Austern	oysters
Bauernomelett	bacon and onion omelette
Bierwurst	beer sausage
Birne Helene	vanilla ice-cream with pear and hot chocolate sauce
Bismarckhering	soused herring with onions
Blutwurst	black pudding
Bockwurst	large Frankfurter sausage
Bratkartoffeln	fried potatoes
Bratwurst	fried sausage (with herbs)
Deutsches Beefsteak	Hamburger steak
Eisbein	pig's knuckle
Ente	duck
Erbsensuppe	thick pea soup
Fasan	pheasant
Fleischkäse	type of meatloaf, sliced and fried
Forelle	trout
Frühlingssuppe	fresh vegetable soup
Gänseleberpastete	goose liver pâté
Gefrorenes	ice-cream specialities
Grünkohl	kale
Hackbraten	hamburger steak
Kaiserschmarren	shredded pancake with raisins and almonds
Kartoffelpuffer	small potato and onion pancakes
Kasseler Rippenspeer	cured pork chops with mustard sauce
Klösse ⎤ Knödel ⎦	dumplings
Königsberger Klopse	meat balls in a white caper sauce
Kohlrouladen	cabbage stuffed with minced meat
Labskaus	pork and potato stew served with fried eggs and gherkins
Lachs	salmon

Leberknödelsuppe	soup with liver dumplings
Leberwurst	liver pâté
Linsensuppe	lentil soup
Matjeshering	young salted herring
Ochsenschwanzsuppe	oxtail soup
Ölsardinen	tinned sardines
Paprikaschoten	green peppers
Pfannkuchen	pancake
Pfirsich Melba	peach with vanilla ice-cream, whipped cream, raspberry syrup
Räucheraal	smoked eel
Rauchwurst	smoked sausage
Rehrücken	saddle of deer
Rollmops	pickled herring fillet, rolled around onion slices
Rosenkohl	Brussels sprouts
Rösti	hashed brown potatoes
Röstkartoffeln	roast potatoes
Rote Beete	beetroot
Rotkraut	red cabbage
Rouladen	thin slices of meat, rolled up and braised in rich brown sauce
Russische Eier	hard-boiled eggs, with caper and mayonnaise dressing
Sardellen	anchovies
Sauerkraut	pickled white cabbage
Sauerbraten	beef marinated in vinegar, sugar and spices, and then braised
Schildkrötensuppe	turtle soup
Schinkenwurst	ham sausage
Schlachtplatte	assorted cold meat and sausages
Schweinshaxe	pig's knuckle
Serbische Bohnensuppe	spicy Serbian bean soup
Spargel	asparagus
Spätzle	South German variety of pasta
Speck	bacon
Strammer Max	raw ham and fried eggs, served on rye-bread
Truthahn	turkey
Weinbergschnecken	snails with garlic, herbs and butter
Wienerschnitzel	veal escalope in breadcrumbs

Health

ESSENTIAL INFORMATION

- Be sure to have medical insurance.
- For minor disorders, and treatment at a drugstore, see p. 125.
- For finding your way to a doctor, dentist, drugstore or Health and Social Security Office, see p. 118.
- In an emergency dial 110 for ambulance service.

  ÄRZTE (in the telephone directory) or these signs:

  PRAXIS (doctor's office)

  ERSTE HILFE (first aid)

  KRANKENHAUS
  HOSPITAL ⎤ (hospital)

  UNFALLSTATION (emergency ward of a hospital)

What's the matter?

I have a pain here [*point*]	**Ich habe hier Schmerzen** ish hahbeh here shmairts-en
I have a toothache	**Ich habe Zahnschmerzen** ish hahbeh tsahn-shmairts-en
I have broken my dentures	**Mein Gebiss ist zerbrochen** mine gabis ist tsair-brocken
I have broken my glasses	**Meine Brille ist zerbrochen** mineh brilleh ist tsair-brocken
I have lost . . .	**Ich habe . . . verloren** ish hahbeh . . . fer-loren
my contact lenses	**meine Kontaktlinsen** mineh kontakt-lin-zen
a filling	**eine Füllung** ineh foolloong
My child is ill	**Mein Kind ist krank** mine kint ist krank

Already under treatment for something else?

I take . . . regularly [*show*]	**Ich nehme regelmässig . . .** ish n*ay*-meh r*ai*g-el-masik . . .
this medicine	**dieses Medikament** d*ee*zes medikament
these tablets	**diese Tabletten** d*ee*zeh tabletten
I have . . .	**Ich habe . . .** ish h*ah*beh . . .
a heart condition	**ein Herzleiden** ine h*ai*rts-ly-den
haemorrhoids	**Hämorrhoiden** hemorro-*ee*-den
rheumatism	**Rheuma** r*oy*mah
I'm . . .	**Ich bin . . .** ish bin . . .
diabetic	**Diabetiker** dee-ah-b*e*ticker
asthmatic	**Asthmatiker** ast-m*ah*-ticker
pregnant	**schwanger** shv*a*nger
allergic to (penicillin)	**allergisch gegen (Penicillin)** all*ai*r-gish g*ay*-ghen (peni-tsee-l*ee*n)

Problems: loss, theft

ESSENTIAL INFORMATION

- If worse comes to worst, find the police station. To ask the way, see p. 116.
- Look for:
  POLIZEI (police)
  POLIZEIWACHE (police station)

- Ask for:
  FUNDBÜRO (lost property)
- If you lose your passport go to the nearest U.S. consulate.
- In an emergency dial 110 (for police) or 112 (if there's a fire).

LOSS
[See also 'Theft' below: the lists are interchangeable]

I have lost . . .	**Ich habe . . . verloren**
	ish hahbeh . . . fer-loren
my camera	**meine Kamera**
	mineh kamerah
my car keys	**meine Autoschlüssel**
	mineh owto-shloossel
my car registration	**meinen Kraftfahrzeugschein**
	minen kraft-far-tsoyk-shine
my driver's license	**meinen Führerschein**
	minen foorer-shine
my insurance certificate	**meine Versicherungskarte**
	mineh fer-zisheroongs-karteh

THEFT

Someone has stolen . . .	**Man hat . . . gestohlen**
	man hat . . . ga-shtolen
my car	**mein Auto**
	mine owto
my money	**mein Geld**
	mine ghelt
my tickets	**meine Fahrkarten**
	mineh far-karten
my travellers' cheques	**meine Reiseschecks**
	mineh ryzeh-shecks
my wallet	**meine Brieftasche**
	mineh breef-tasheh
my luggage	**mein Gepäck**
	mine gapeck

The post office and phoning home

ESSENTIAL INFORMATION

- Key words to look for:
  POST
  POSTAMT
  BUNDESPOST or this sign
- For stamps look for the words **BRIEFMARKEN** or **POSTWERTZEICHEN** on a post office counter.
- Some stationery shops and newsstands which sell postcards, also sell stamps.
- Unless you read and write German well, it's best not to make phone calls by yourself. Go to the main post office and write the town and number you want on a piece of paper and then hand it to the operator.

WHAT TO SAY

To England, please	**Nach England, bitte** nahk eng-lant bitteh

[*Hand letters, cards or parcels over the counter*]

To Australia	**Nach Australien** nahk owstrah-lee-en
To the United States	**In die Vereinigten Staaten** in dee ferine-nik-ten shtahten
I'd like this number . . . [*show number*]	**Ich möchte diese Nummer . . .** ish mershteh deezeh noommer . . .
in England	**in England** in eng-lant
in Canada	**in Kanada** in kanadah
Can you dial it for me, please?	**Können Sie für mich wählen?** kernnen zee foor mish vay-len

Cashing checks and changing money

ESSENTIAL INFORMATION

- Look for these words on buildings:
  BANK (bank)
  SPARKASSE (bank, savings bank)
  WECHSELSTUBE
  GELDWECHSEL] (exchange bureau)
- Changing money or traveller's checks is usually a two-stage process. The formalities are completed at a desk called **DEVISEN**; you will then be sent to the cashier (**KASSE**) to get your money.
- To cash checks, exactly as at home, use your bank card where you see the Eurocheque sign. Write in English.
- Have your passport handy.

WHAT TO SAY

I'd like to cash . . .	**Ich möchte . . . einlösen** ish mershteh . . . ine-lerzen
these travellers' cheques	**diese Reiseschecks** deezeh ryzeh-shecks
this cheque	**diesen Scheck** deezen sheck
I'd like to change this . . .	**Ich möchte dies . . . wechseln** ish mershteh dees . . . vexeln
into German marks	**in deutsche Mark** in doytsheh mark
into Austrian schillings	**in österreichische Schillinge** in erster-ry-kisheh shilling-eh
into Belgian francs	**in belgische Franken** in bel-ghish-eh franken
into Danish kroner	**in dänische Kronen** in da-nisheh kro-nen
into Dutch guilders	**in holländische Gulden** in hollendisheh gool-den

into French francs

in französische Franken
in fran-tser-zisheh franken

into Swiss francs

in Schweizer Franken
in shvyster franken

Car travel

ESSENTIAL INFORMATION

- Is it a self-service station? Look out for:
  SELBSTBEDIENUNG or **SB**.
- Grades of gasoline:
  BENZIN
  NORMAL ⎤ (regular)
  SUPER (premium)
  DIESEL
- 1 gallon is about 3¾ liters.
- The minimum sale is often 5 liters (often less at self-service pumps).
- Filling stations are usually able to deal with minor mechanical problems. For major repairs you have to find a garage (**REPARATURWERKSTATT**).

WHAT TO SAY

(9) litres of . . .	**(Neun) Liter . . .**
	(noyn) litre . . .
(20) marks of . . .	**Für (zwanzig) Mark . . .**
	foor (tsvan-tsik) mark . . .
standard/premium/diesel	**Normal/Super/Diesel**
	nor-mahl/zooper/deezel
Fill it up, please	**Volltanken, bitte**
	folltanken bitteh

Will you check . . .	**Bitte prüfen Sie . . .** b*i*tteh pr*oo*fen zee . . .
the oil	**das Öl** das *e*rl
the battery	**die Batterie** dee batter*ee*
the radiator	**das Kühlwasser** das k*oo*l-vasser
the tyres	**die Reifen** dee ryfen
I've run out of petrol	**Ich habe kein Benzin mehr** ish h*a*hbeh kine ben-ts*ee*n mair
Can you help me, please?	**Können Sie mir bitte helfen?** k*e*rnnen zee meer b*i*tteh helf-en
Do you do repairs?	**Machen Sie Reparaturen?** m*a*k-en zee repara-t*oo*ren
I have a puncture	**Ich habe eine Reifenpanne** ish h*a*hbeh *i*neh ryfen-panneh
I have a broken windscreen	**Die Windschutzscheibe ist zerbrochen** dee v*i*nt-shoots-shybeh ist tsair-br*o*cken
I don't know what's wrong	**Ich weiss nicht, woran es liegt** ish v*i*ce nisht vor*a*n es leekt
I think the problem is here . . . [*point*]	**Ich glaube, es liegt hieran . . .** ish gl*a*-oobeh es leekt here-un . . .

LIKELY REACTIONS

I don't do repairs	**Wir machen keine Reparaturen** veer m*a*k-en k*i*neh repara-t*oo*ren
Where's your car?	**Wo steht Ihr Wagen?** vo sht*ai*t eer v*a*hg-en
What make is it?	**Was für ein Wagen ist es?** v*a*s foor ine v*a*hg-en ist es
Come back tomorrow/on Monday	**Kommen Sie morgen/Montag wieder** kommen zee m*o*rgen/m*o*ne-tahk veeder

[*For days of the week, see p. 161*]

Public transport

ESSENTIAL INFORMATION

- Finding the way to the bus station, a bus stop, a tram stop, the railway station and a taxi stand, see p. 116.
- Remember that lining up for buses is unheard of!
- To get a taxi you usually have to telephone the local **TAXI-ZENTRALE** (taxi center) or go to a taxi stand. Hailing a taxi is less common and doesn't always work.
- Types of trains:
  Tee (Trans-Europe-Express; luxury high-speed train with first class only)
  INTER CITY
  EXPRESS ⎤ (long distance trains, often
  SCHNELLZUG ⎟ between countries, stopping only
  D-ZUG ⎦ at principal stations)
  EILZUG (medium-distance, domestic train, stopping only at bigger towns)
  PERSONENZUG (slow local train, stopping at all stations)
  NAHVERKEHRSZUG (short distance train, often to suburbs)
- Key words on signs:
  FAHRKARTEN (tickets, ticket office)
  EINGANG (entrance)
  AUSGANG (exit)
  VERBOTEN (forbidden)
  GLEIS (platform, literally: track)
  BAHNSTEIG (platform)
  BAHNHOFSMISSION (Travellers' Aid Office)
  AUSKUNFT (information, information office)
  DB (initials for German railways)
  GEPÄCKAUFBEWAHRUNG (left-luggage)
  BUSHALTESTELLE (bus stop)
  ABFAHRT (timetable, departures)
  ANKUNFT (timetable, arrivals)
  GEPÄCKABFERTIGUNG ⎤ (luggage office/forwarding office)
  GEPÄCKANNAHME ⎦

- Buying a ticket:
  Buy your train ticket at the ticket office inside the station.
  When travelling by bus or tram you usually pay as you enter.
  When travelling by subway (**U-BAHN**) you buy your
  ticket from an automatic machine at the station. This also
  applies to trams in the larger cities where there is a ticket
  machine at each tram stop.

  In most German cities you can purchase a ticket which
  allows you to transfer between trams, subway and
  buses, in the one direction. (These can often be bought at
  tobacco shops.) You can also buy a 'Rover' ticket for a specified
  number of days; ask for a **TOURISTEN-FAHRKARTE**
  (tooristen-far-karteh) at a main station ticket office.

WHAT TO SAY

Where does the train for (Bonn) leave from?	**Auf welchem Gleis fährt der Zug nach (Bonn) ab?** owf velshem glyss fairt der tsook nahk (bonn) up
Is this the train for (Bonn)?	**Ist dies der Zug nach (Bonn)?** ist dees der tsook nahk (bonn)
Where does the bus for (Köln) leave from?	**Wo fährt des Bus nach (Köln) ab?** vo fairt der boos nahk (kerln) up
Is this the bus for (Köln)?	**Ist dies der Bus nach (Köln)?** ist dees der boos nahk (kerln)
Do I have to change?	**Muss ich umsteigen?** moos ish oom-shtyg-en
Can you put me off at the right stop, please?	**Können Sie mir bitte sagen, wann ich aussteigen muss?** kernnen zee meer bitteh zahg-en vann ish ows-shtyg-en-moos
Where can I get a taxi?	**Wo Kann ich ein Taxi bekommen?** vo kan ish ine taxi bekommen
Can I book a seat?	**Kann ich einen Sitzplatz reservieren?** kann ish inen zits-plats reserveeren
A single	**Eine einfache Fahrt** ineh ine-fak-eh fart
A return	**Eine Rückfahrkarte** ineh rook-far-karteh

First class	**Erster Klasse**
	*ai*rster kl*a*sseh
Second class	**Zweiter Klasse**
	tsvy-ter kl*a*sseh
One adult	**Ein Erwachsener**
	ine er-v*a*ksen-er
Two adults	**Zwei Erwachsene**
	tsvy er-v*a*ksen-eh
and one child	**und ein Kind**
	oont ine k*i*nt
and two children	**und zwei Kinder**
	oont tsvy k*i*n-der
How much is it?	**Wieviel kostet das?**
	v*ee*-feel k*o*stet das

Reference

NUMBERS

0	**null**	nool
1	**eins**	ines
2	**zwei**	tsvy
3	**drei**	dry
4	**vier**	feer
5	**fünf**	foonf
6	**sechs**	zex
7	**sieben**	z*ee*ben
8	**acht**	ahkt
9	**neun**	noyn
10	**zehn**	tsain
11	**elf**	elf
12	**zwölf**	tsverlf
13	**dreizehn**	dry-tsain
14	**vierzehn**	f*ee*r-tsain
15	**fünfzehn**	foonf-tsain
16	**sechzehn**	zek-tsain
17	**siebzehn**	z*ee*p-tsain
18	**achtzehn**	*a*hk-tsain

19	**neunzehn**	n*o*yn-tsain
20	**zwanzig**	tsv*a*n-tsik
21	**einundzwanzig**	*i*ne-oont-tsvan-tsik
22	**zweiundzwanzig**	tsv*y*-oont-tsvan-tsik
23	**dreiundzwanzig**	dr*y*-oont-tsvan-tsik
24	**vierundzwanzig**	f*ee*r-oont-tsvan-tsik
25	**fünfundzwanzig**	f*oo*nf-oont-tsvan-tsik
30	**dreissig**	dry-sik
35	**fünfunddreissig**	f*oo*nf-oont-dry-sik
36	**sechsunddreissig**	z*e*x-oont-dry-sik
37	**siebenunddreissig**	z*ee*ben-oont-dry-sik
38	**achtunddreissig**	*a*kt-oont-dry-sik
39	**neununddreissig**	n*o*yn-oont-dry-sik
40	**vierzig**	f*ee*r-tsik
41	**einundvierzig**	*i*ne-oont-feer-tsik
50	**fünfzig**	f*oo*nf-tsik
51	**einundfünfzig**	*i*ne-oont-foonf-tsik
60	**sechzig**	z*e*k-tsik
61	**einundsechzig**	*i*ne-oont-zek-tsik
70	**siebzig**	z*ee*p-tsik
71	**einundsiebzig**	*i*ne-oont-zeep-tsik
80	**achtzig**	*a*hk-tsik
81	**einundachtzig**	*i*ne-oont-ahk-tsik
90	**neunzig**	n*o*yn-tsik
91	**einundneunzig**	*i*ne-oont-noyn-tsik
100	**hundert**	h*oo*ndert
101	**hunderteins**	hoondert-*i*nes
102	**hundertzwei**	hoondert-tsv*y*
125	**hundertfünfundzwanzig**	hoondert-f*oo*nf-oont-tsvan-tsik
150	**hundertfünfzig**	hoondert-f*oo*nf-tsik
175	**hundertfünfundsiebzig**	hoondert-f*oo*nf-oont-zeep-tsik
200	**zweihundert**	tsv*y*-hoondert
250	**zweihundertfünfzig**	tsv*y*-hoondert-f*oo*nf-tsik
300	**dreihundert**	dry-hoondert
400	**vierhundert**	f*ee*r-hoondert
500	**fünfhundert**	f*oo*nf-hoondert
700	**siebenhundert**	z*ee*ben-hoondert
1,000	**tausend**	t*o*wzent
1,100	**tausendeinhundert**	towzent-*i*ne-hoondert
2,000	**zweitausend**	tsv*y*-towzent
5,000	**fünftausend**	f*oo*nf-towzent
10,000	**zehntausend**	fs*ai*n-towzent

| 100,000 | **hunderttausend** | hoondert-towzent |
| 1,000,000 | **eine Million** | ineh mill-yon |

TIME

What time is it?	**Wie spät ist es?**
	vee shpait ist es
It's . . .	**Es ist . . .**
	es ist . . .
one o'clock	**ein Uhr**
	ine oor
two o'clock	**zwei Uhr**
	tsvy oor
noon	**zwölf Uhr mittags**
	tsverlf oor mittahks
midnight	**Mitternacht**
	mitter-nakt
a quarter past five	**viertel nach fünf**
	feertel nahk foonf
half past five	**halb sechs**
	halp zex
a quarter to six	**viertel vor sechs**
	feertel for zex

DAYS AND MONTHS

Monday	**Montag**
	mone-tahk
Tuesday	**Dienstag**
	deens-tahk
Wednesday	**Mittwoch**
	mitt-vok
Thursday	**Donnerstag**
	donners-tahk
Friday	**Freitag**
	fry-tahk
Saturday	**Samstag/Sonnabend**
	zams-tahk/zonn-ahbent
Sunday	**Sonntag**
	zonn-tahk

January	**Januar**	
	yah-noo-ahr	
February	**Februar**	
	fay-broo-ahr	
March	**März**	
	mairts	
April	**April**	
	ah-pril	
May	**Mai**	
	my	
June	**Juni**	
	yoo-nee	
July	**Juli**	
	yoo-lee	
August	**August**	
	ow-goost	
September	**September**	
	zeptember	
October	**Oktober**	
	oktober	
November	**November**	
	november	
December	**Dezember**	
	detsember	

Public holidays

Unless otherwise specified, offices, shops and schools are closed on these days in Austria, Germany and Switzerland.

1 January	**Neujahrstag**	New Year's Day
. . .	**Himmelfahrt**	Ascension
. . .	**Pfingstmontag**	Whit Monday
24 December	**Heiligabend**	Christmas Eve (half day)
25 December	**erster Weihnachtstag**	Christmas Day
26 December	**zweiter Weihnachtstag**	Boxing Day
26 December	**Stephanstag**	St Stephen's Day (Austria and Switzerland)

Index

Greek

D. L. Ellis, H. Rapi

Pronunciation **Dr J. Baldwin**

Useful address

Greek National Tourist Office
Olympic Tower
645 5th Ave.
New York, NY 10022

Contents

Pronunciation hints

In Greek it is important to stress or emphasize the syllables in *italics*, just as you would if we were to take as an English example: Little Jack *Hor*ner *sat* in the *cor*ner. Here we have ten syllables, but only four stresses. This is particularly important in Greek, as meaning can be dependent on stress and many words will be completely unintelligible to a Greek unless the stress is put in the correct place.

καλή επιτυχί!

Everyday expressions

[*See also 'Shop talk', p. 181*]

Hello	Γειά σας yassas
Good morning ⎤ Good day ⎦	Καλημέρα kal-eemehra
Good afternoon (after siesta) ⎤ Good evening ⎦	Καλησπέρα kaleespera
Good night	Καληνύχτα kal-eeneehta
Goodbye	Γειά σας yassas
Yes	Ναί neh
Please	Παρακαλῶ parakalo
Yes, please	Ναί, παρακαλῶ neh, parakalo
Thank you	Εὐχαριστῶ ef-har-eesto
Thank you very much	Ευ'χαριστῶ πάρα πολύ ef-har-eesto para pol-ee
That's right	Σωςτά sosta
No	'Οχι o-hee
No, thank you	'Οχι, ευ'χαριστῶ o-hee ef-har-eesto
I disagree	Διαφωνῶ thee-af-on-o
Excuse me ⎤ Sorry ⎦	Συγγνώμη seeg-nom-ee
Where's the toilet, please?	Ποῦ ειναι ἡ τουαλέτα, παρακαλῶ; poo een-eh ee too-aleh-ta parakalo
Do you speak English?	Μιλᾶπε'Αγγλικά; meelat-eh angleeka
What's your name?	Πῶς λεγεσται; poss leg-es-teh
My name is . . .	Μέ λένε . . . meh len-eh . . .

Asking the way

ESSENTIAL INFORMATION

- Keep a look out for all these place names as you will find them on shops, maps and notices.

WHAT TO SAY

Excuse me, please	Μέ συγχωρεῖτε, παρακαλῶ
	meh seenhor-*eet*-eh parakal*o*
How do I get . . .	Πῶς μπορῶ νά πάω . . .
	p*o*ss bor*o* na p*a*-o . . .
to Athens?	στήν 'Αθήνα;
	steen ath*ee*na
To Ermou Street?	στήν ὁδό Έρμοῦ;
	steen oth*o* ehrm*oo*
to the Hotel Caravel?	στό ξενοδοχεῖο Κάραβελ;
	sto ksen-otho-h*ee*-o karavel
to the airport?	στό ἀεροδρόμιο;
	sto ehr-othrom-yo
to the beach?	στή παραλία;
	stee paral*ee*a
to the bus station?	στή στάση λεωφορείου;
	stee st*a*ssee leh-oforee-oo
to the market?	στήν ἀγορά;
	steen agor*a*
to the police station?	στήν ἀστυνομία;
	steen asteen-om*ee*-a
to the port?	στό Λιμάνι;
	sto leeman-ee
to the post office?	στό ταχυδρομεῖο;
	sto ta-hee-throm*ee*-o
to the railway station?	στό σιδηροδρομικό σταθμό;
	sto see-theerothrom-eek*o* stathm*o*
to the sports stadium?	στό στάδιο;
	sto st*a*thio
to the tourist information office?	στό γραφεῖο πληροφοριῶν γιά τουρίστες;
	sto graf*ee*-o pleerof-oree-on ya toor*ee*st-ess

How do I get . . .

Πῶς μπορῶ νά πάω . . .
poss boro na pa-o . . .

to the town centre?

στό κέντρο τῆς πόλης;
sto kendro teess pol-eess

to the town hall?

στό δημαρχεῖο;
sto theem-ar-hee-o

Is there . . . near by?

Ὑπάρχει ἐδῶ κοντά . . .
eepar-hee eth-o konda . . .

a baker's

ἀρτοποιεῖο;
artop-ee-ee-o

a bank

τράπεζα;
trap-ez-a

a bar

μπάρ;
bar

a bus stop

στάση λεωφορείου;
stassee leh-oforee-oo

a butcher's

κρεοπωλεῖο;
kreh-opolee-o

a café

καφενεῖο
kafen-eeo

a cake and coffee shop

ζαχαροπλαστεῖο;
za-har-oplastee-o

a campsite

κατασκήνωση;
kata-skeenossee

a car park

πάρκιγκ;
parking

a change bureau

γραφεῖο συναλλάγματος;
grafee-o seenal-agmat-oss

a chemist's

φαρμακεῖο;
farma-kee-o

a concert hall

αἴθουσα συναυλιῶν;
eh-thoossa seen-avli-on

a delicatessen

ἐδωδιμοπωλεῖο;
eth-oth-eemopolee-o

a dentist's

ὀδοντιατρεῖο;
othondi-atree-o

a department store

μεγάλο ἐμπορικό κατάστημα;
meh-gal-o emboreeko katasteema

a disco

ντισκοτέκ;
discotek

a doctor's surgery

ἰατρεῖο;
ee-atree-o

a dry-cleaner's	στεγνοκαθαριστήριο; stegno-kathar-eest*ee*rio
a fishmonger's	ψαράδικο; psar*a*th-eeko
a garage (for repairs)	συνεργείο; seenehr-g*ee*o
a hairdresser's	κομμωτήριο; kommot-*ee*rio
a greengrocer's	μανάβικο; man*a*v-eeko
a grocer's	μπακάλικο; bak*a*l-eeko
a hospital	νοσοκομείο; nosokom*ee*-o
a hotel	ξενοδοχείο; ksen-otho-h*ee*-o
a laundry	καθαριστήριο; kathar-eest*ee*rio
a newsagent's	περίπτερο; peh-r*ee*ptero
a nightclub	νάιτ κλάμπ; night club
a petrol station	βενζινάδικο; venzeen-*a*theeko
a postbox	γραμματοκιβώτιο; grammatok-eevot-yo
a toilet	τουαλέτα; too-al-*e*h-ta
a restaurant	ἑστιατόριο; estee-at*o*rio
a supermarket	σούπερ μαρκέτ; supermarket
a sweet shop (kiosk)	περίπτερο; peh-r*ee*ptero
a taxi stand	πιάτσα γιά ταξί; pee-*a*tsa ya taks*ee*
a public telephone	τηλέφωνο· teel*e*f-ono
a tobacconist's kiosk	περίπτερο; peh-r*ee*ptero
a travel agent's	πρακτορείο ταξιδιῶν; praktor*ee*-o takseethee-*o*n

Is there . . . near by?	Ὑπάρχει ἐδῶ κοντά . . .
	eepar-hee eth-*o* kond*a* . . .
a youth hostel	ξενῶν νεότητος;
	ksen-*on* neh-*ot*-eetoss

DIRECTIONS

Left	᾿Αριστερά
	areesteh-r*a*
Right	Δεξιά
	theksy*a*
Straight ahead	᾿Ισια
	*ee*sia
There	᾿Εκεῖ
	ek-*ee*
First left/right	῾Ο πρῶτος δρόμος ἀριστερά/δεξιά
	o pr*ot*-oss thr*om*-oss areesteh-r*a*/ theksy*a*
Second left/right	῾Ο δεύτερος δρόμος ἀριστερά/δεξιά
	o th*ef*teross thr*om*-oss areesteh-r*a*/ theksy*a*

Accommodation

ESSENTIAL INFORMATION
Hotel

- If you want hotel-type accommodation, all the following words in capital letters are worth looking for on signs:
  ΞΕΝΟΔΟΧΕΙΟ (hotel)
  ΜΟΤΕΛ (motel)
  ΕΝΟΙΚΙΑΖΟΝΤΑΙ ΔΩΜΑΤΙΑ (rooms to rent)
  ΞΕΝΙΑ (luxurious hotels and usually more expensive than ordinary hotels)
- A list of hotels in the town or district can usually be obtained at the local tourist office or at the local Tourist Police or police station. These lists are also available from the Greek National Tourist Office in New York.

- Recommended hotels are classified into six categories: De luxe or AA and 1st to 5th class or A to E.
- The cost is displayed in the room itself; so you can check it when having a look around before agreeing to stay.
- The displayed cost is for the room itself, per night and not per person. Breakfast is extra and therefore optional.
- In small hotels and village rooms breakfast is paid for separately, if available.
- A Greek breakfast will usually consist of a cup of coffee or tea with bread, butter and jam or honey.
- A service charge of 15% is usually included in the bill but tipping is optional.
- Your passport is requested when registering at a hotel and will normally be kept overnight.

WHAT TO SAY

I have a booking	Ἔχω κλείσει ἕνα δωμάτιο
	eh-ho kleessee enna thomat-yo
Have you any vacancies, please?	Ἔχετε δωμάτια, παρακαλῶ;
	eh-het-eh thomat-ya parakalo
Can I book a room?	Μπορῶ νά κλείσω ἕνα δωμάτιο;
	boro na kleeso enna thomat-yo
It's for . . .	Εἶναι γιά . . .
	eeneh ya . . .
one adult/one person	ἕναν ἐνήλικο/ἕνα ἄτομο
	ennan en-eeleeko/enna atomo
two adults/two people	δύο ἐνήλικες/δύο ἄτομα
	thee-o en-eeleekess/thee-o atoma
and one child	καὶ ἕνα παιδί
	keh enna peth-ee
and two children	καί δύο παιδιά
	keh theeo peth-ya
It's for . . .	Εἶναι γιά . . .
	eeneh ya . . .
one night	μία βραδιά
	mee-a vrath-ya
two nights	δύο βραδιές
	thee-o vrath-yes
one week	μία βδομάδα
	mee-a vthoma-tha
two weeks	δύο βδομάδες
	thee-o vthomath-ess

I would like . . .	Θά ἤθελα . . . tha *ee*thella . . .
a (quiet) room	ἕνα (ἤσυχο) δωμάτιο *e*nna (*ee*-seeho) thom*a*t-yo
two rooms	δύο δωμάτια th*ee*-o thom*a*t-ya
with a single bed	μέ ἕνα μονό κρεββάτι meh *e*nna mon*o* krevv*a*t-ee
with two single beds	μέ δύο μονά κρεββάτια meh th*ee*-o mon*a* krevv*a*t-ya
with a double bed	μέ ἕνα διπλό κρεββάτι meh *e*nna theepl*o* krevv*a*t-ee
with a toilet	μέ τουαλέτα meh too-al-*e*h-ta
with a bathroom	μέ μπάνιο meh ban-yo
with a shower	μέ ντούς meh d*oo*ss
with a cot	μέ παιδικό κρεββάτι meh peh-theek*o* krevv*a*t-ee
with a balcony	μέ μπαλκόνι meh balk*o*n-ee
Do you serve meals?	Σερβίρετε γεύματα; sehrv*ee*r-et-eh gevmata
Can I look at the room?	Μπορῶ νά δῶ τό δωμάτιο; bor*o* na th*o* toh thom*a*t-yo
OK, I'll take it	Ἐντάξει, θά τό πάρω end*a*ksee tha toh p*a*r-o
No thanks, I won't take it	Οχι εὐχαριστῶ, δέν θά τό πάρω o-hee ef-har-eest*o* then tha toh p*a*r-o.
The bill, please	Τό λογαριασμό, παρακαλῶ toh logaree-*a*zmo parakal*o*
Is service included?	Εἶναι μέ τό σερβίς; *ee*neh meh toh serv*ee*ss
I think this is wrong	Νομίζω πώς αυ'τό εἶναι λάθος nom-*ee*zo poss aft*o* *ee*neh lath-oss
May I have a receipt?	Μπορῶ νά ἔχω μία ἀπόδειξη; bor*o* na *e*hho m*ee*-a apoth-*ee*ksee

Camping

- Look for the word: ΚΑΜΠΙΝΓΚ (camping) or this sign.
  Note μ = metres.

- Be prepared for the following charges:
  per person
  for the car (if applicable)
  for the tent or for trailer space
  for electricity
  for hot showers
- A reduction of 10% is made to the holders of AIT or FIA membership cards.
- You must provide proof of identity, such as your passport.
- Passports or identity cards can be returned to their holders only on settlement of the account.
- For the NTOG camping sites, which are better organized, advance booking is strongly recommended.
- Camping is tolerated almost anywhere outside built-up areas but it is always best to get the landowner's permission beforehand. The police have the right to forbid you camping off-site in case of overcrowding, poor hygiene etc.

Youth hostels

- Look for the word: ΞΕΝΩΝ ΝΕΟΤΗΤΟΣ (youth hostel).
- The charge per night is the same everywhere.
- You must have a YHA card.
- Accommodation is in dormitories.
- In most youth hostels there are cafeterias where light meals and drinks can be bought at reasonable prices.

WHAT TO SAY

Have you any vacancies?	Ἔχετε θέσεις; eh-het-eh thesseess
How much is it . . .	Πόσο κάνει . . . posso kan-ee . . .
for the tent?	ή σκηνή; ee skeenee
for the caravan?	τό κάραβαν; toh karavan
for the car?	τό αὐτοκίνητο; toh aftokeen-eeto
for the electricity?	τό ἠλεκτρικό; toh eelek-treeko
per person?	τό ἄτομο; toh atomo
per day/night?	τή μέρα/βραδιά; tee-meh-ra/vrath-ya
May I look round?	Μπορῶ νά ρίξω μία ματιά; boro na reekso mee-a mat-ya
Do you provide anything . . .	Σερβίρετε . . . sehr-veer-et-eh . . .
to eat?	φαγητό; fag-eeto
to drink?	ποτά; pota
Is there/are there . . .	Ἔχετε . . . eh-het-eh . . .
a bar?	μπάρ; bar
hot showers?	ζεστά ντούς; zesta dooss
a kitchen?	κουζίνα; koozeena
a laundry?	πλυντήριο; pleendeerio
a restaurant?	ἐστιατόριο; estee-atorio
a shop?	μαγαζί; magaz-ee
a swimming pool?	πισίνα; peeseena

[*For food shopping, see p. 184, and for eating and drinking out, see p. 192*]

Problems

The toilet	Ἡ τουαλέτα
	ee too-al-*et*-a
The shower	Τό ντούς
	toh d*oo*ss
The tap	Ἡ βρύση
	ee vr*ee*ssee
The razor point	Ἡ πρίζα γιά τή ξυριστική μηχανή
	ee pr*ee*za ya tee kseer-eesteek-*ee*
	mee-han-*ee*
The light	Τό φῶς
	toh f*o*ss
. . . is not working	. . . χάλασε
	. . . h*a*l-ass-eh
My camping gas has run out	Ἡ φιάλη υ᾽γραερίου τελείωσε
	ee fee-*a*l-ee eegra-ehr-*ee*-oo tel*ee*-osseh
The bill, please	Τό λογαριασμό, παρακαλῶ
	toh logaree-azm*o* parakal*o*

LIKELY REACTIONS

Have you an identity document?	Ἔχετε ταυτότητα;
	*e*h-het-eh taftot-eeta
Your membership card, please	Τήν κάρτα σας, παρακαλῶ
	t*ee*n k*a*rta sas parakal*o*
What's your name?	Πῶς ὀνομάζεστε;
	p*o*ss on-omaz-es-teh
Sorry, we're full	Λυπᾶμαι, ἀλλά δέν ἔχουμε θέση
	leepam-eh all*a* then *e*hoomeh thessee
How many people is it for?	Γιά πόσα ἄτομα εἶναι;
	ya p*o*ssa *a*toma *ee*neh
How many nights is it for?	Γιά πόσες βραδιές εἶναι;
	ya p*o*ssess vrath-yes *ee*neh
It's (80) drachmas . . .	(Ὀγδόντα) δραχμές . . .
	(ogth*o*nda) thra-hmess . . .
per day/per night	τή μέρα/τή βραδιά
	tee m*e*h-ra/tee vrath-ya

I haven't any rooms left

Δέν ἔχουμε δωμάτια
then eh-hoomeh thomat-ya

Do you want to have a look?

Θέλετε νά ρίξετε μία ματιά;
thel-et-eh na reekset-eh mee-a mat-ya

General shopping

The drugstore/The chemist's

ESSENTIAL INFORMATION

ΦΑΡΜΑΚΕΙΟΝ

PHARMACIE

- Look for the word ΦΑΡΜΑΚΕΙΟΝ (drugstore) or this sign.
- Medicines (drugs) are only available at a drugstore. Some non-drugs can be bought at a supermarket or department store.
- Try a pharmacist before going to a doctor: they are usually qualified to treat minor injuries.
- Drugstores take turns staying open all night and on Sundays. A drugstore will display an illuminated list of all-night drugstores (ΔΙΑΝΥΚΤΕΡΥΟΝΤΑ ΦΑΡΜΑΚΕΙΑ).
- Normal opening times are: 8.00 a.m. to 1.00 p.m. and 5.30 p.m. to 8.30 p.m. Drugstores are closed on Monday, Wednesday afternoon and all day Saturday.

WHAT TO SAY

I'd like . . .

Θά ἤθελα . . .
tha eethella . . .

some Alka Seltzer

αλκασέλτζερ
alka seltzer

some antiseptic

ἕνα ἀντισηπτικό
enna antee-seepteeko

some aspirin

ἕνα κουτί ἀσπιρίνες
enna kootee aspeer-eeness

some baby food

βρεφική τροφή
vrefeekee trof-ee

some contraceptives	προφυλακτικά
	prof-eelak-tee*ka*
some cotton	ἕνα βαμβάκι
	enna vamvak-ee
some disposable diapers	πᾶνες μίας χρήσεως
	pan-ess *mee*-ass hreess-eh-oss
some eye drops	σταγόνες γιά τά μάτια
	stagon-ess ya ta mat-ya
some gauze dressing	μερικές γάζες
	mehr-eekess gaz-ess
some inhalant	κάτι γιά εἰσπνοές
	kat-ee ya eess-pno-ess
some insect repellent	ἕνα ἐντομοκτόνο
	enna endomokton-o
some paper tissues	χαρτομάνδηλα
	hart-oman-theela
some sanitary napkins	σερβιέτες ὑγείας
	sehr-vee-et-ess eeg-*ee*-ass
some sticking plaster	ἕνα λευκοπλάστη
	enna lefkoplastee
some suntan lotion/oil	μία ἀντιηλιακή κρέμα/λάδι
	mee-a antee-eelee-ak-*ee* krem-a/ lathee
some Tampax	ἕνα ταμπάξ
	enna tampax
some throat lozenges	παστίλλιες γιά τό λαιμό
	pasteel-ee-ess ya toh lem-*o*
some toilet paper	ἕνα χαρτί ὑγείας
	enna hartee ee-y*ee*-ass
I'd like something for . . .	Θά ἤθελα κάτι γιά . . .
	tha *ee*thella kat-ee ya . . .
bites	τσίμπημα
	tse*em*-beema
burns	ἔγκαυμα
	engavma
a cold	ἕνα κρύωμα
	enna kr*ee*oma
constipation	δυσκοιλιότητα
	theeskeelee-ot-eeta
a cough	τόν βῆχα
	ton v*ee*-ha

I'd like something for . . .	Θά ἤθελα κάτι γιά . . .
	tha *ee*thella k*a*t-ee ya . . .
diarrhoea	διάρροια
	thee-*a*rria
earache	πόνο στό αὐτί
	p*o*n-o sto aft*ee*
flu	γρίππη
	gr*ee*pee
scalds	κάψιμο
	k*a*pseemo
sore gums	σπυράκια
	speer*a*k-ya
stings	κεντρίσματα
	ken-dr*ee*zmata
sunburn	ἔγκαυμα η'λίου
	*e*ngavma eel*ee*-oo
sea/travel sickness	ναυτία
	naft*ee*-a

[*For other essential expressions, see 'Shop talk', opposite*]

Holiday items

ESSENTIAL INFORMATION

- Places to shop at and signs to look for:
  ΒΙΒΛΙΟΠΩΛΕΙΟ (bookshop)
  ΧΑΡΤΟΠΩΛΕΙΟ (stationery store)
  ΦΩΤΟΓΡΑΦΙΚΑ ΕΙΔΗ (photographic items)
- and the main department stores:
  MARINOPOULOS – PRISUNIC
  MINION, ATHENÈE, TSITSOPOULOS, LAMBROPOULOS
- Newsstands (ΠΕΡΙΠΤΕΡΑ) are particularly useful as they are
  open late at night and sell a variety of goods such as aspirin, razor
  blades, playing cards, pens, soft drinks etc.

WHAT TO SAY

I'd like . . .	Θά ἤθελα . . .
	tha *ee*thella . . .

a bag	μία τσάντα
	m*ee*-a ts*a*nda
a beach ball	μία μπάλλα
	m*ee*-a b*a*lla
a bucket	ἔνα κουβᾶ
	*e*nna koov*a*
an English newspaper	μία ἀγγλική ἐφημερίδα
	m*ee*-a ang-leek*ee* ef-eemehr-*ee*tha
some envelopes	μερικούς φακέλους
	mehr-eek-*oo*s fak-el-*oo*ss
some postcards	μερικές κάρτες
	mehr-eek-*e*ss k*a*rtess
a spade	ἔνα φτυάρι
	*e*nna ftee-*a*r-ee
a straw hat	ἔνα ψάθινο καπέλλο
	*e*nna ps*a*thee-no kap*e*llo
some sunglasses	γυαλιά ἡλίου
	yal-y*a* eelee-*oo*
some writing paper	χαρτί ἀλληλογραφίας
	hart*ee* alleel-ograf-*ee*-ass
a colour film [*show the camera*]	ἔνα ἔγχρωμο φίλμ
	*e*nna en-hrom-o film
a black and white film	ἔνα ἀσπρόμαυρο φίλμ
	*e*nna assprom-avro film

[*For other essential expressions, see 'Shop talk', below*]

Shop talk

ESSENTIAL INFORMATION

- Know how to say the important weights and measures:

50 grams	πενῆντα γραμμάρια
	pen-*ee*nda gramm*a*-ria
100 grams	ἐκατό γραμμάρια
	ek-at-*o* gramm*a*-ria
200 grams	διακόσια γραμμάρια
	thee-ak*o*ss-ya gramm*a*-ria

½ kilo	μισό κιλό
	meesso keelo
1 kilo	ἕνα κιλό
	enna keelo
2 kilos	δύο κιλά
	thee-o keela
½ litre	μισό λίτρο
	meesso leetro
1 litre	ἕνα λίτρο
	enna leetro
2 litres	δύο λίτρα
	thee-o leetra

[*For numbers, see p. 209*]

CUSTOMER

I'm just looking	Ρίχνω μία ματιά
	reehno mee-a mat-ya
How much is this/that?	Πόσο κάνει αὐτό/ἐκεῖνο;
	posso kan-ee afto/ek-eeno
What is that?	Τί εἶναι ἐκεῖνο;
	tee eeneh ek-eeno
What are those?	Τί εἶναι ἐκεῖνα;
	tee eeneh ek-eena
Is there a discount?	Κάνετε ἔκπτωση;
	kan-et-eh ekptoss-ee
I'd like that, please	Θά ἤθελα ἐκεῖνο, παρακαλῶ
	tha eethella ek-eeno parakalo
Not that	Οχι ἐκεῖνο
	o-hee ek-eeno
Like that	Σάν ἐκεῖνο
	san ek-eeno
That's enough, thank you	Φτάνει, εὐχαριστῶ
	ftan-ee ef-har-eesto
More, please	Περισσότερο, παρακαλῶ
	perissot-ehro parakalo
Less than that, please	Λιγότερο ἀπό αὐτό, παρακαλῶ
	leegot-ehro apo afto parakalo
I won't take it, thank you	Δέν θά τό πάρω, εὐχαριστῶ
	then tha toh par-o ef-har-eesto
It's not right	Δέν εἶ᾿ναι σωστό
	then eeneh sosto

Thank you very much	Εὐχαριστῶ πάρα πολύ
	ef-har-eesto para pol-ee
Have you got something . . .	Ἔχετε κάτι . . .
	eh-het-eh kat-ee . . .
better?	καλύτερο;
	kal-eet-ehro
cheaper?	φθηνότερο;
	ftheenot-ehro
different?	διαφορετικό;
	thee-afor-et-eeko
larger?/smaller?	μεγαλύτερο;/μικρότερο;
	meg-aleet-ehro/meekrot-ehro
Can I have a bag, please?	Μπορῶ νά ἔχω μία τσάντα, παρακαλῶ;
	boro na eh-ho mee-a tsanda parakalo
Can I have a receipt?	Μπορῶ νά ἔχω μία ἀπόδειξη;
	boro na eh-ho mee-a apoth-eeksee
Do you take . . .	Παίρνετε . . .
	pehr-net-eh . . .
English/American money?	ἐγγλέζικα/ἀμερικάνικα λεφτά;
	englez-eeka/amerikan-eeka lefta
travellers cheques?	τράβελερς τσέκς;
	travelers tseks
credit cards?	πιστωτικές κάρτες;
	peestohteekess kartess

SHOP ASSISTANT

Can I help you?	Μπορῶ νά σᾶς βοηθήσω;
	boro na sas vo-eeth-eeso
What would you like?	Τί θά θέλατε;
	tee tha thellat-eh
Will that be all?	Τίποτα ἄλλο;
Is that all?	teepota allo
Anything else?	
Would you like it wrapped?	Θέλετε νά σᾶς τό τυλίξω;
	thellet-eh na sas toh teeleek-so
Sorry, none left	Λυπᾶμαι, δέν ἔχει μείνεl τίποτα
	leepam-eh then eh-hee meenee teepota

I haven't got any	Δέν ἔχω
	then eh-ho
I haven't got any more	Δέν μοῦ ἔχει μείνει τίποτα
	then moo eh-hee meenee teepota
How many do you want? ⎤	Πόσα θέλετε;
How much do you want? ⎦	possa thellet-eh
Is that enough?	Φτάνει αυτό;
	ftan-ee afto

Shopping for food

Bread

ESSENTIAL INFORMATION

- Key words to look for:
  ΑΡΤΟΠΟΙΕΙΟΝ (bakery)
  ΨΩΜΙ (bread)
- Some supermarkets sell bread.
- All loaves are sold by weight, rolls by number.

WHAT TO SAY

A loaf (like that)	Ἕνα ψωμί (σάν ἐκεῖνο)
	enna psom-ee (san ek-een-o)
A large one	Ἕνα μεγάλο ψωμί
	enna megalo psom-ee
A small one	Ἕνα μικρό ψωμί
	enna meekro psom-ee
A bread roll	Ἕνα ψωμάκι
	enna psomak-ee
Two French-type loaves	Δύο φραντζόλες
	thee-o frant-zol-ess
½ kilo of white bread	Μισό κιλό ασπρο ψωμί
	meesso keelo aspro psom-ee
1 kilo of brown bread	Ἕνα κιλό ψωμί μαῦρο
	enna keelo psom-ee mavr-o

Cakes and ice cream

ESSENTIAL INFORMATION

- Key words to look for:
  ΖΑΧΑΡΟΠΛΑΣΤΕΙΟΝ (a place to buy cakes and have a drink)
  ΓΑΛΑΚΤΟΠΩΛΕΙΟΝ (milk bars specializing in dairy produce,
  e.g. rice puddings, yoghurt, ice creams etc., but which also serve
  cakes.
  ΠΑΓΩΤΑ (ice cream)

[See p. 192 for 'Ordering a drink and a snack'.]

WHAT TO SAY

The types of cake you find in the shops vary from region to region
but the following are some of the most common.

μπακλαβᾶ	mille feuilles pastry with nuts and
baklava	honey
καταΐφι	fine shredded pastry with walnuts
kata-eefee	and honey
γαλακτομπούρεκο	custard pudding with mille feuilles
galakto-boorek-o	pastry
λουκουμάδες	small doughnuts fried in oil and
lookoomath-ess	served with honey
σοκολατίνα	chocolate cake
sokolateena	
πάστα ἀμυγδάλου	almond cake
pasta ameegthal-oo	
μπουγάρσα	flaky pastry filled with custard
boogatsa	
ριζόγαλο	rice pudding
reezogalo	
γιαούρτι	yoghurt
ya-oortee	
A . . . ice cream, please	Ἔνα παγωτό . . . παρακαλῶ
	enna pagoto . . . parakalo
vanilla	βανίλα
	vanilla
chocolate	σοκολάτα
	sokola-ta

A . . . ice, please	Ἔνα παγωτό . . . παρακαλῶ
	enna pagoto . . . parakalo
cream	κρέμα
	krem-a
cassata	κασσάτα
	kassat-a
lemon	λεμόνι
	lemon-ee
strawberry	φράουλα
	fra-oola
cherry	βύσσινο
	veessino

Picnic food

ESSENTIAL INFORMATION

- Key words to look for:
  ΠΑΝΤΟΠΩΛΕΙΟΝ (grocer's)
  ΣΟΥΠΕΡΜΑΡΚΕΤ (supermarket)
  ΣΕ ΠΑΚΕΤΟ (takeout)
- Hot food to take out can be bought in restaurants and pizza houses.

WHAT TO SAY

Two slices of . . .	Δύο φέτες . . .
	thee-o fet-ess . . .
ham	ζαμπόν
	zambon
garlic sausage	λονκάνικο μέ σκόρδο
	lookan-eeko meh skortho
salami	σαλάμι
	salam-ee
mortadella	μορταδέλλα
	mortathella

You may also like to try some of these:

ταραμοσαλάτα	cod's roe mixed with oil and lemon
taramo-sala-ta	
φέτα	white cheese made of goat's milk
fet-a	
κασέρι	yellow cheese, rich in cream
kassehr-ee	
κεφαλοτύρι	very salty yellow cheese
kef-aloteer-ee	
μανούρι	very creamy white cheese
manooree	
μυτζήθρα	white soft cheese made from ewe's
meetzeethra	milk
χαλβάς	sweet made from sesame seeds or
halv-ass	semolina, and honey

[*For other essential expressions see 'Shop talk', p. 181*]

Fruit and vegetables

ESSENTIAL INFORMATION

- Key words to look for:
  ΦΡΟΥΤΑ (fruit)
  ΛΑΧΑΝΙΚΑ (vegetables)
  ΟΠΟΡΟΠΩΛΕΙΟΝ (greengrocer)
- It is customary for you to choose your own fruit and vegetables at the market and for the vendor to weigh and price them. You must take your own shopping bag – paper and plastic bags are not normally provided.

WHAT TO SAY

1 kilo of . . .	Ἕνα κιλό . . .
	enna keelo . . .
apples	μῆλα
	meela
apricots	βερύκοκκα
	vehr-eekoka

1 kilo of . . .	Ἕνα κιλό
	enna keel*o* . . .
bananas	μπανάνες
	ban*an*-ess
cherries	κεράσια
	kehr-*a*ss-ya
figs	σῦκα
	s*ee*ka
grapes (white/black)	σταφύλια (ἄσπρα/μαῦρα)
	staf-*ee*l-ya (*a*spra/m*a*vra)
oranges	πορτοκάλια
	portok*a*l-ya
peaches	ροδάκινα
	roth*a*k-eena
pears	ἀχλάδια
	a-hl*a*th-ya
plums	δαμάσκηνα
	tham*a*sk-eena
strawberries	φράουλες
	fra-*oo*l-ess
A pineapple, please	Ἕναν α'νανᾶ, παρακαλῶ
	*e*nnan anan*a* parakal*o*
A grapefruit	Μία φράπα
	m*ee*-a fr*a*p-a
A melon/water melon	Ἕνα πεπόνι/καρπούζι
	*e*nna pep-*o*n-ee/karp*oo*zee
½ kilo of . . .	Μισό κιλό . . .
	meess*o* keel*o* . . .
aubergines	μελιτζάνες
	mel-eetz*a*n-ess
beetroot	παντζάρια
	pannz*a*r-ya
carrots	καρότα
	kar*o*ta
courgettes	κολοκυθάκια
	kolokee-th*a*k-ya
green beans	φασολάκια
	fassol*a*k-ya
leeks	πράσσα
	pr*a*ssa
mushrooms	μανιτάρια
	maneet*a*-ria

onions	κρεμμύδια
	kremm*ee*th-ya
2 kilos of . . .	Δύο κιλά . . .
	th*ee*-o keel*a* . . .
peas	μπιζέλια
	beez*e*l-ya
peppers (green/red)	πιπεριές (πράσινες/κόκκινες)
	pee-peh-ree-*e*ss (pr*a*sseen-ess/ k*o*keen-ess)
potatoes	πατάτες
	pat*a*t-ess
spinach	σπανάκι
	span*a*k-ee
tomatoes	ντομάτες
	dom*a*t-ess
A bunch of . . .	Ἕνα ματσάκι . . .
	*e*nna mats*a*k-ee . . .
parsley	μαϊντανό
	ma-ee-dan-*o*
radishes	ραπανάκια
	rapan*a*k-ya
A head of garlic	Ἕνα σκόρδο
	*e*nna sk*o*rtho
A lettuce	Ἕνα μαρούλι
	*e*nna mar*oo*lee
A cucumber	Ἕνα ἀγγούρι
	*e*nna ang*oo*ree
Like that, please	Ὅπως ἐκεῖνο, παρακαλῶ
	*o*p-oss ek-*ee*no parakal*o*

Meat and fish

ESSENTIAL INFORMATION

- Key words to look for:
  ΚΡΕΟΠΩΛΕΙΟΝ (butcher shop)
  ΚΡΕΟΠΩΛΗΣ (butcher)
  ΨΑΡΑΔΙΚΟ (fish store)
  ΘΑΛΑΣΣΙΝΑ (seafood)

- There are no labels on counters and supermarket displays in Greece which could help you decide what cut or roast to have, so you will have to ask or simply point. Do not expect, however, to find the same cuts of meat you would find at home.
- Pork in Greece is of a very high quality.
- Markets usually have fresh-fish stands.
- You will find that cod and herring are sold dried and salted: they simply require soaking in water overnight.

WHAT TO SAY

For roasts, choose the type of meat and then say how many people it is for:

Some beef, please	Βοδινό, παρακαλῶ
	vothee-no parakalo
Some lamb	Ἀρνάκι
	arnak-ee
Some pork	Χοιρινό
	heereeno
Some veal	Μοσχαρίσιο
	moss-har-ees-yo
A roast . . .	Ἕνα κομμάτι . . .
	enna kommat-ee . . .
for two people	γιά δύο ἄτομα
	ya thee-o atoma
for four people	γιά τέσσερα ἄτομα
	ya tessera atoma
Some steak, please	Μπόν φιλέ, παρακαλῶ
	bon feeleh parakalo
Some liver	Συκωτάκια
	seekotak-ya
Some kidneys	Νεφρά
	nefra
Some sausages	Λουκάνικα
	lookan-eeka
Some mince	Κιμᾶ
	keema
Two veal scallops, please	Δύο μοσχαρίσιες μπριζόλες, παρακαλῶ
	thee-o moss-ha-rees-yess breezol-ess parakalo
Three pork chops	Τρεῖς χοιρινές μπριζολες
	treess heereen-ess breezol-ess

Five lamb chops	Πέντε ἀρνίσιες μπριζόλες
	pendeh arneess-yess breezol-ess

You may also want:

A chicken	Ένα κοτόπουλο
	enna kotop-oolo
A rabbit	Ἕνα κουνέλι
	enna koonel-ee
A tongue	Μία γλῶσσα
	mee-a glossa

Purchase most fish by weight:

½ kilo of . . .	Μισό κιλό . . .
	meesso keelo . . .
anchovies	ἀντσούγες
	ants-oog-ess
grey mullet	λυθρίνια
	lee-threen-eea
mussels	μύδια
	meeth-ya
octopus	χταπόδια
	htapoth-ya
oysters	στρείδια
	streeth-ya
prawns	γαρίδες
	ga-reethess
red mullet	μπαρμπούνια
	barboon-ya
sardines	σαρδέλες
	sar-thel-ess
smelt (fried)	μαρίδες (τιγανιτές)
	ma-reethess (teeganeetess)
squid	καλαμάρια
	kalama-ria
shrimps	γαρίδες
	ga-reethess
sea bream	συναγρίδες
	seen-agreeth-ess
trout	πέστροφες
	pestrof-ess
cod	μπακαλιάρο
	bakal-ya-ro

For some shellfish and 'frying pan' fish; specify the number:

A crab, please	Ἕνα καβούρι, παρακαλῶ
	enna kavoo-ree parakalo
A lobster	Ἕναν ἀστακό
	ennan astako
A sole	Μία γλῶσσα
	mee-a glossa
A mackerel	Ἕνα σκουμπρί
	enna skoombree
A herring	Μία ρέγγα
	mee-a renga

Eating and drinking out

Ordering a drink and a snack

ESSENTIAL INFORMATION

- The places to ask for: ΜΠΑΡ (bar), ΣΝΑΚ-ΜΠΑΡ (snack bar),
  ΟΥΖΕΡΙ (bar which serves hors d'oeuvres)
  ΖΑΧΑΡΟΠΛΑΣΤΕΙΟ (pastry shop which serves drinks as well)
  ΚΑΦΕΝΕΙΟ (coffee house, where Greek women are rarely seen)
- By law the price list (ΤΙΜΟΛΟΓΙΟΝ) must be on display. Service
  is usually included.
- Bars open late in the afternoon and close at 2.00 a.m. All other
  establishments are normally open all day.
- Bars and cafés serve both non-alcoholic and alcoholic drinks.
  Children are allowed in.
- Greek beer comes in small bottles of 350 g (about ½ pint) and
  500 g (about 1 pint).
- Greek coffee is made by heating water, mixing in the ground
  coffee and sugar, and bringing it to the boil – it is very strong.

WHAT TO SAY

I'll have . . . please	Θέλω . . . παρακαλῶ
	thello . . . parakalo
a black coffee	ἕνα νέσκαφε σκέτο
	enna nescafe sket-o

a coffee with milk	ἕνα καφέ μέ γάλα
	enna kaf-eh meh ga-la
a Greek coffee	ἕνα Ἑλληνικό καφέ
	enna elleen-eeko kaf-eh
without sugar	σκέτο
	sket-o
medium sweet	μέτριο
	metrio
sweet	γλυκό
	gleeko
a tea	ἕνα τσάϊ
	enna tsa-ee
with milk	μέ γάλα
	meh ga-la
with lemon	μέ λεμόνι
	meh lem-on-ee
a glass of milk	ἕνα ποτήρι γάλα
	enna poteeree ga-la
a hot chocolate	μία ζεστή σοκολάτα
	mee-a zestee sokola-ta
an iced coffee	ἕνα νέσκαφε φραπέ
	enna nescafe frap-eh
a mineral water	ἐμφιαλωμένο νερό
	emfee-alomen-o nehro
a lemonade	μία λεμονάδα
	mee-a lem-on-atha
a lemon squash	μία λεμονάδα χυμό
	mee-a lem-on-atha heemo
a Coca-Cola	μία κόκα κόλα
	mee-a koka kola
an orangeade	μία πορτοκαλάδα
	mee-a portokal-atha
an orange juice	μία πορτοκαλάδα χυμό
	mee-a portokal-atha heemo
a pineapple juice	ἕναν ἀνανᾶ χυμό
	ennan anana heemo
a beer	μία μπύρα
	mee-a bee-ra
a large bottle	ἕνα μεγάλο μπουκάλι
	enna megalo bookalee
a small bottle	ἕνα μικρό μπουκάλι
	enna meekro bookal-ee

I'll have . . . please	Θέλω . . . παρακαλῶ
	thello . . . parakalo
a cheese sandwich	ἕνα σάντουϊτς μέ τθρί
	enna sandwits meh teeree
a ham sandwich	ἕνα σάντουϊτς μέ ζαμπόν
	enna sandwits meh zambon
a meat pie	μία κρεατόπιττα
	mee-a kreh-at-op-ita
a spinach pie	μία σπανακόπιττα
	meea-a spanak-op-ita
a cheese pie	μία τυρόπιττα
	mee-a teer-op-ita
a hot dog	ἕνα χότ ντόγκ
	enna hot dog

This is another snack you may like to try:

ἕνα σουβλάκι	pieces of grilled meat wrapped in
enna soovlak-ee	pitta bread; doner kebab

In a restaurant

ESSENTIAL INFORMATION

- You can eat at the following places:
  ΕΣΤΙΑΤΟΡΙΟΝ (restaurant)
  ΤΑΒΕΡΝΑ (typical Greek restaurant)
  ΨΑΡΟΤΑΒΕΡΝΑ (restaurant specialising in seafood)
  ΨΗΣΤΑΡΙΑ (restaurant specialising in charcoal-grilled food)
- In smaller restaurants there may be no printed menu, so you will either have to ask what is available or look at the food displayed and point. The Greeks themselves often go into the kitchen to choose their meal.
- If the menu lists two prices for each item, the second price includes a 10% service charge, but an extra tip is always welcome.
- If there is a wine waiter (he will also serve the water and bread), a small tip should be left for him on the table (not on the plate with the bill).

- Times when restaurants stay open depend on the area and the season. However, they are normally open from midday to 4.00 p.m. and 8.00 p.m. to midnight. Although Greeks tend to eat late in the summer, all restaurants, bars and cafés are obliged by law to close at 2.00 a.m.
- In most tavernas and many restaurants draught wine is available. It is served in small cans and sold by weight. Order 1 kilo (1 litre), ½ kilo (½ litre) or ¼ kilo (a large glass).

WHAT TO SAY

May I book a table?	Μπορῶ νά κλείσω ἕνα τραπέζι; boro na kleeso enna trap-ez-ee
I've booked a table	Ἔχω κλείσει τραπέζι eh-ho kleessee trap-ez-ee
A table . . .	Ἕνα τραπέζι . . . enna trap-ez-ee . . .
for one	γιά ἕναν ya ennan
for three	γιά τρεῖς ya treess
The menu, please	Τόν κατάλογο παρακαλῶ ton katalogo parakalo
What's this please? [point to the menu]	Τί εἶναι αὐτό παρακαλῶ; tee eeneh afto parakalo
1 kilo of wine	Ἕνα κιλό κρασί enna keelo krassee
½ kilo of wine	Μισό κιλό κρασί meeso keelo krassee
¼ kilo of wine	Τέταρτο κρασί tetartoh krassee
A glass	Ἕνα ποτήρι enna poteeree
A bottle	Ἕνα μπουκάλι enna bookal-ee
A half bottle	Ἕνα μικρό μπουκάλι enna meekro bookal-ee
Red/white/rosé	Κόκκινο/ἄσπρο/ροζέ kokino/aspro/roz-eh
Some more bread, please	Καί ἄλλο/ἀκόμα ψωμί, ηαρακαλῶ keh allo/akoma psom-ee parakalo

Some more wine	Καί άλλο/ἀκόμα κραοί
	keh allo/akoma krassee
Some oil	Λίγο λάδι
	leego la-thee
Some vinegar	Λίγο ξύδι
	leego ksee-thee
Some salt/pepper	Λίγο α'λάτι/πιπέρι
	leego alat-ee/peepeh-ree
Some water	Λίγο νερό
	leego nehro
With/without garlic	με/χωρίς σκόρδο
	meh/horeess skortho
How much does that come to?	Πόσο κάνει;
	posso kan-ee
Is service included?	Ειˇναι μέ τό σερβις;
	eeneh meh toh serveess
Where is the toilet, please?	Ποῦ ειˇναι ή τουαλέτα, παρακαλῶ;
	poo eeneh ee too-al-et-a parakalo
Miss!/Waiter!	Δεσποινίς!/Γκαρσόν!
	thespeen-eess/garson
The bill, please	Τό λογαριασμό, παρακαλῶ
	toh logaree-azmo parakalo

Key words for courses, as seen on some menus

[*Only ask if you want the waiter to remind you of the choice.*]

What have you got in the way of . . .	Τί . . . ἔχετε;
	tee . . . eh-het-eh
starters?	ορεκτικα
	orekteeka
soup?	ϛογιιες
	soopess
egg?	αγγα
	avgah
fish?	ψατια
	psareea
meat?	κπεας
	kreass
game?	κωνηγι
	keeneegee

fowl?	πουλερικα
	poolereeka
vegetables?	λαχαρικα
	lahaneeka
cheese?	τυρια
	teereea
fruit?	φρουτα
	froota
ice-cream?	παγωγα
	pagota
dessert?	γλυκα
	gleeka

UNDERSTANDING THE MENU

You will find the names of the principal ingredients of most dishes on these pages:

Starters p. 186	Fruit p. 187
Meat p. 190	Cheese p. 187
Fish p. 191	Ice-cream p. 185
Vegetables p. 188	Dessert p. 185

Cooking and menu terms

Βραστό	boiled, poached, stewed
vrasto	
γεμιστό	stuffed
ghemeesto	
ζεστό	hot
zesto	
καπνιστό	smoked
kapneesto	
στά κάρβουνα	charcoal-grilled
sta karvoona	
τῆς κατσαρόλας	en casserole
teess katsar-olass	
κοκκινιστό	cooked with oil and tomatoes
kokkin-eesto	
σενιάν (κρέας)	rare (meat)
sen-yan (kreh-ass)	
μέτρια ψημένο	medium
metria pseemen-o	

καμοψημένο	well-done
kalops-ee*men*-o	
κρῦο	cold
kr*ee*-o	
μέ μαϊνταυό	with parsley
meh my-dan-*o*	
μαρινάτο	marinated
mareen*a*t-o	
παστό	cured
past*o*	
πουρέ	mashed (potatoes)
poo-r*eh*	
μέ σάλτσα	with sauce
meh s*a*ltsa	
στή σχάρα	grilled
stee sk*a*r-a	
τηγανισμένο σέ πολύ λάδι	deep fried
teegan-ees*men*-o seh pol-*ee* la-thee	
τηγανητό	fried
teegan-ee*to*	
τριμμένο	grated
trimm*en*-o	
στό φοῦρνο	baked
sto f*oo*rno	
ψητό	roasted, baked
psee*to*	
ψητό τῆς κατσαρόλας	pot-roasted
psee*to* teess katsar-olass	
ψηλοκομμένο	finely chopped
psee-lokomm*en*-o	
ὠμό	raw
om-*o*	

Further words to help you understand the menu

ἀγγοῦρι	cucumber
ang*oo*ree	
αὐγολέμονο	rice, egg and lemon soup
avgol-*em*-ono	
γαριδοσαλάτα	shrimps in oil and lemon sauce
gareeth-osal*a*-ta	

γιουβαρλάκια yoo-varlak-ya	minced meat and rice balls
γιουβέτσι yoo-vet-see	meat with noodles baked in the oven
κεφτέδες kefteth-ess	meatballs made with bread and herbs
κοκορέτσι kokoret-see	lamb innards roasted on a spit
κρεμμύδι kremmeethee	onion
μελιτζάνες γεμιστές mel-eetzan-ess ghe-meess-tess	stuffed aubergines
μουσακά moossaka	layers of baked aubergines and minced meat
μπιζέλια beezel-ya	peas
μπιφτέκια beeftekya	grilled meatballs
ντολμάδες dolmath-ess	vine or cabbage leaves stuffed with rice and/or meat
ντοσάτες γεμιστές domat-ess ghemeess-tess	stuffed tomatoes with rice and/or minced meat
παστίτσιο pasteetsio	minced meat and macaroni baked and completed by a sauce
παστρουμάς pastroom-ass	heavily spiced, dried or smoked meat
πατσάς patsass	tripe soup
πιπεριές γεμιστές peepeh-ree-ess ghemeess-tess	stuffed peppers
ρεβύθια reh-veethia	chick-peas
σκορδαλιά skor-thal-ya	garlic sauce
σκόρδο skortho	garlic
σουβλάκι soovlak-ee	cubes of meat grilled on a spit
σουτζουκάκια soot-zookak-ya	spicy meatballs in sauce
ταραμοσαλάτα taramo-sala-ta	dip of fish roe blended with bread, oil and lemon

τζατζίκι tsat-*zee*kee	dip of yoghurt, cucumber, garlic, olive oil and mint
φακιές fak-*yess*	lentils
φασολάδα fassol-*atha*	kidney bean soup with tomatoes
χόρτα σαλάτα *horta sala-ta*	made from greens resembling spinach
χθλόπιττες hee*lop-eet-ess*	noodles
χωριάτικη σαλάτα hor*eeat-eekee* sala-ta	mixed salad, (tomatoes, cucumber, green peppers, cheese, onion)
ψαρόσουπα psar*oss-oopa*	fish soup

Health

ESSENTIAL INFORMATION

- It is *essential* to have proper medical insurance.
- Take your own first aid kit with you.
- See p. 178 for minor disorders and treatment at a drugstore.
- See p. 170 for asking the way to a doctor, dentist, or a pharmacist.
- To find a doctor in an emergency look for: ΝΟΣΟΚΟΜΕΙΟΝ (hospital) or contact the police.
- Because of the limited ambulance service in Greece, taxis are frequently used to take people to the hospital.

What's the matter?

I have a pain here [*point*]	Ἔχω ἕνα πόνο ἐδῶ *e*h-ho *e*nna pon-o eth-*o*
I have toothache	Ἔχω πονόδοντο *e*h-ho pon-*o*thondo

I have broken . . .	Ἔσπασα . . .
	*e*spassa . . .
my dentures	τή μασέλα μου
	tee mas*se*lla moo
my glasses	τά γυαλιά μου
	ta yal-y*a* moo
I have lost . . .	Ἔχασα . . .
	eh-hassa . . .
my contact lenses	τούς φακούς ἐπαφῆς μου
	tooss fak-*oo*ss ep-af*ee*ss moo
a filling	ἔνα σφράγισμα
	*e*nna sfr*a*g-eesma
My child is ill	Τό παιδί μου εἶναι αρρωστο
	toh peth-*ee* moo *ee*neh *a*rrosto

Already under treatment for something else?

I take . . . regularly [*show*]	Παίρνω συνήθως . . .
	p*eh*r-no seen*ee*th-oss . . .
this medicine	αὐτό τό φάρμακο
	aft*o* toh f*a*rmako
these pills	αυ'τά τά χάπια
	aft*a*ta h*a*p-ya
I have . . .	Ἔχω . . .
	eh-ho . . .
haemorrhoids	αἱμορροϊδες
	em-orro-*ee*thess
rheumatism	ρευματισμούς
	revma-teezm*oo*ss
I'm . . .	Εἶμαι . . .
	*ee*meh . . .
diabetic	διαβητικός/διαβητική*
	thee-av-eeteek-*o*ss/thee-av-eeteek-*ee**
asthmatic	ἀσθματικός/ἀσθματικν̆*
	as-thmat-eek-*o*ss/as-thmat-eek-*ee**
pregnant	ἔγκυος
	engee-oss
I have a heart condition	Εἶμαι καρδιακός/καρδιακή*
	*ee*meh karthee-ak*o*ss/karthee-ak*ee**

*For men use the first alternative, for women the second.

I am allergic to (pencillin) Εἶμαι ἀλλεργικός/α'λλεργική*
στή (πενικιλλίνη)
*ee*meh allehr-geek-*oss*/allehr-geek-
ee st*ee* (pen-eekeel-*ee*nee)

Problems: loss, theft

ESSENTIAL INFORMATION

- If worse comes to worst, find the police station; to ask the way, see p. 169.
- Look for:
  ΑΣΤΥΝΟΜΙΑ (police in towns) or ΧΩΡΟΦΥΛΑΚΗ (gendarmerie, i.e. rural police)
- If you lose your passport go to the nearest U.S. consulate.
- In an emergency, dial 100 for the police.

LOSS

[*See also 'Theft' below; the lists are interchangeable*]

I have lost . . .   Ἔχασα . . .
                                       eh-hassa . . .

  my camera   τήν φωτογραφική μηχανή μου
                                       teen fotograffeek*ee* meehan*ee* moo

  my car registration   τήν ἄδεια κθκλοφορίας
                                       teen *ath*-eya keek-lofor*ee*-ass

  my driver's license   τήν αδεια ὀδηωήσεφς
                                       teen *athee*-a othee-g*ee*s-eh-oss

  my insurance certificate   τήν ἀσφαλεια τοῦ αυ'τοκινήτου
                                       μου
                                       teen asf*ah*lee-a too aftokeen-*ee*too
                                       moo

THEFT

Someone has stolen . . .	Κάποιος μοῦ ἔκλεψε . . .
	kap-ee-oss moo eklepseh . . .
my car	τό αὐτοκίνητο μου
	toh aftokeen-eeto moo
my keys	τά κλειδιά μου
	ta kleeth-ya moo
my money	τά χρήματα μου
	ta hreem-ata moo
my tickets	τά εἰσιτήρια μου
	ta eess-eeteeree-a moo
my travellers cheques	τά τράβελερς τσέκς μου
	ta travelers' tseks moo
my wallet	τό πορτοφόλι μου
	toh portofol-ee moo
my luggage	τά πράγματα μου
	ta pragmata moo

The post office and phoning home

ESSENTIAL INFORMATION

- Key words to look for:
  ΤΑΧΥΔΡΟΜΕΙΟΝ (post office)
  ΕΛ.ΤΑ, (abbreviation for Greek post office:
  look out for this symbol)
  OTE (telecommunications)
- For stamps, look for the word ΓΡΑΜΜΑΤΟΣΗΜΑ.
- Telegrams are not sent from post offices, but from the offices of
  the OTE.
- Unless you read and speak Greek well, it's best not to make
  phone calls by yourself. Go to OTE (Telecommunications Organization of Greece, look out for this symbol)
  – and not to the post office – and write the town
  and number you want on a piece of paper.

- To phone the UK from Greece, dial 0044 and then the number you want.
- To phone the USA, the code is 001.

WHAT TO SAY

To England, please	Γιά τήν 'Αγγλία, παρακαλῶ
	ya teen anglee-a parakalo
[Hand letters, cards or parcels over the counter]	
To Australia	Γιά τήν Αὐστραλία
	ya teen af-straleea
To the United States	Γιά τήν 'Αμερική
	ya teen amerik-ee
I'd like this number . . .	Θελω αὐτό τόν ἀριθμό . . .
	thello afto ton a-reethmo . . .
in England	στήν 'Αγγλία
	steen angleea
in Canada	στόν Καναδᾶ
	ston kana-tha
Can you dial it for me, please?	Μπορεῖτε νά μοῦ πάρετε τόν ἀριθμό, σᾶς παρακαλῶ;
	boreeteh na moo par-et-eh ton a-reethmo sas parakalo
I'd like to send a telegram	Θέλω νά στείλω ενα τηλεγράφημα
	thello na steelo enna teelegraf-eema

Cashing checks and changing money

ESSENTIAL INFORMATION

- Look for these signs:
  ΤΡΑΠΕΖΑ (bank)
  BUREAU DE CHANGE (exchange bureau)
- To cash checks, exactly as at home, use your bank card where you see the Eurocheque sign. Write in English.

- Have your passport handy.
- Banks are open between 8.00 a.m. and 2.00 p.m. except on Saturdays, Sundays and public holidays. However, during the high season some banks will remain open during the afternoons.

WHAT TO SAY

I'd like to cash .	Θέλω νά ἐξαργυρώσω . . .
	the*ll*o na ek-sarg-eer*o*sso . . .
these travellers' cheques	αὐτά τά τράβελερς τσέκ
	a*ft*a ta travelers tseks
this cheque	αὐτό τό τσέκ
	a*ft*o toh tsek
I'd like to change this . . .	Θά ἤθελα νά ἀλλάξω αὐτό . . .
	tha *ee*thella na all*a*kso a*ft*o . . .
into Italian lira	σέ Ἰταλικές λιρέττες
	seh eetal-eek*e*ss leer*e*t-ess
into Turkish pounds	σέ τούρκικες λίρες
	seh t*oo*r-keekess l*ee*ress
into Yugoslav dinar	σέ γιουγκοσλαυικά δηνάρια
	seh yoogoslavika deen*a*reeya

Car travel

ESSENTIAL INFORMATION

- Is it a self-service filling station? Look out for:
  ΣΕΛΦ-ΣΕΡΒΙΣ
- Grades of gasoline:
  ΒΕΝΖΙΝΗ (gasoline)   ΣΟΥΠΕΡ (premium)
  ΑΠΛΗ (regular)
  ΝΤΗΖΕΛ (diesel)
- One gallon is about 3¾ liters.
- Most filling stations in Greece (ΓΚΑΡΑΖ) do not do major repairs. The place to go to for repairs is ΣΥΝΕΡΓΕΙΟΝ.

- The Greek Automobile and Touring Club (ELPA) offers assistance to foreign motorists free of charge.
- Dial 104 for assistance in Athens and Thessaloniki (up to a radius of 60 km) and Larissa, Patras, Herakleion, Volos, Lamia, Kalamata and Yannina (up to a radius of 25 km).

WHAT TO SAY

[*For numbers, see p. 209*]

(Nine) litres of . . .	(Ἐννέα) νίτρα . . .
	(enneh-a) leetra . . .
(150) drachmas of . . .	(ἑκατὸ πενῆντα) δραχμές . . .
	(ek-at-o pen-eenda) thra-hmess . . .
standard	ἁπλή
	aplee
premium	σοῦπερ
	soopehr
diesel	ντῆζελ
	diesel
Fill it up, please	Νά τό γεμίσετε, παρακαλω8
	na toh gemeesset-eh parakalo
Will you check . . .	Μπορεῖτε νά κοιτάξετε . . .
	boreeteh na keetak-set-eh . . .
the oil?	τό λάδι;
	toh la-thee
the battery?	τήν μπαταρία;
	teen bataree-a
the radiator?	τό ψηγεῖο;
	toh pseeg-ee-o
the tyres?	τά λάστιχα;
	ta lastee-ha
I've run out of petrol	Ἔμεινα ἀπό πετρέλαιο
	em-eena apo petrel-eh-o
Can you help me, please?	Μπορεῖτε νά μέ βοηθήσετε, σᾶς παρακαλῶ;
	boreeteh na meh vo-eeth-eeset-eh sas parakalo
Do you do repairs?	Κάνετε ἐπισκευές;
	kan-et-eh ep-eeskev-ess
I have a puncture	Τρύπησε τό λάστιχο
	treepees-eh toh lastee-ho

I have a broken windscreen	Ἔσπασε τό μπροστινό τζάμι espas-eh toh brosteeno tzam-ee
I think the problem is here . . . [point]	Νομίζω ὅτι τό πρόβλημα εἶναι εδω . . . nomeezo otee toh prov-leema eeneh eth-o

LIKELY REACTIONS

I don't do repairs	Δέν κάνω ἐπισκευές then kan-o ep-eeskev-ess
Where's your car?	Ποῦ εἰναι τό αὐτοκίνητο σας; poo eeneh toh aftokeen-eeto sas
What make is it?	Τί μάρκα εἶναι; tee marka eeneh
Come back tomorrow/on Monday	Ἐλᾶτε αὔριο/τή Δευτέρα ellat-eh anrio/tee thef-tehra

[*For days of the week, see p. 212*]

Public transport

ESSENTIAL INFORMATION

- For finding the way to the bus station, a bus stop, a trolley stop, the railway station and a taxi stand, see p. 169.
- If you flag down a taxi, there's a flat rate of 15 drs.
- Remember that lining up for buses is not strictly followed.
- The railway network in Greece is not very extensive. The national railways connect Athens with the most important regions of the country. Buses are more frequent (much faster than trains).
- The subway in Athens is called 'Ο ΗΛΕΚΤΡΙΚΟΣ, and joins Piraeus with Athens and Kifissia.
- There are frequent ferry-boats to most islands from Piraeus.
- In Athens there are electric trolleys in addition to bus service. For urban buses and trolleys there is a flat rate which you pay to the conductor. Some of these have no conductors, so no

change is available and you drop the fare into a box. They have a large sign on the front: ΧΩΡΙΣ ΕΙΣΠΡΑΚΤΟΡΑ (without conductor) and you get in and pay at the front and get out at the back.

- Key words on signs:
  ΓΡΑΦΕΙΟΝ ΕΙΣΤΗΡΙΩΝ (ticket office)
  ΕΙΣΟΔΟΣ (entrance)
  ΑΠΑΓΟΡΕΥΕΤΑΙ Η ΕΙΣΟΔΟΣ (no entrance)
  ΑΝΟΔΟΣ (entrance, for buses)
  ΚΑΘΟΔΟΣ (exit, for buses)
  ΠΡΟΣ ΤΑΣ ΑΠΟΒΑΘΡΑΣ (to the platforms)
  ΓΡΑΦΕΙΟΝ ΠΛΗΡΟΦΟΡΙΩΝ (information office)
  ΟΣΕ (initials for Greek railways)
  ΚΤΕΛ (initials for Greek coach services)
  ΕΞΟΔΟΣ (exit)
  ΘΥΡΙΔΕΣ ΑΠΟΣΚΕΥΩΝ (left luggage)
  ΣΤΑΣΙΣ stop: in Athens the stops are yellow for trolleys and blue for buses. The sign shows a bus stop.
  ΔΡΟΜΟΛΟΓΙΟΝ (timetable)

WHAT TO SAY

Where does the ferry-boat for (Piraeus) leave from?	Ἀπό ποῦ φεύγει τό φέρυ μπότ γιά (τόν Πειραιᾶ);
	apo poo fev-ghee toh feh-ree-bot ya (ton peereya)
Is this the ferry-boat for (Piraeus)?	Εἶναι αὐτό τό φέρυ μπότ γιά (τόν Πειραιᾶ);
	eeneh afto toh feh-ree-bot ya (ton peereya)
Where does the bus for (Delphi) leave from?	Ἀπό ποῦ φεύγει τό λεωφορεῖο γιά (τούς Δελφούς);
	apo poo fev-ghee toh leh-oforee-o ya (tooss thelfooss)
Is this the bus for (Delphi)?	Αὐτό εἶναι τό λεωφορεῖο γιά (τούς Δελφούς);
	afto eeneh toh leh-oforee-o ya (tooss thelfooss)
Do I have to change?	Πρέπει νά ἀλλάξω;
	prep-ee na allak-so

Can you put me off at the right stop, please?	Μπορεῖτε νά μέ κατεβάσετε στή σωστή στάση, παρακαλῶ; boreeteh na meh kat-ev-asset-eh stee sostee stassee parakalo
Where can I get a taxi?	Ποῦ μπορῶ νά βρῶ ἕνα ταξί; poo boro na vro enna taksee
Can I book a seat?	Μπορῶ νά κλείσω μιά θέση; boro na kleeso mee-a thessee
A single	Ἕνα ἁπλό εἰσιτήριο enna aplo eess-eeteerio
A return	Ἕνα εἰσιτήριο μετ'ἐπιστροφῆς enna eess-eeteerio met-ep-eestr-of-eess
First class	Πρώτη θέση prot-ee thess-ee
Second class	Δεύτερη θέση thef-tehree thessee
One adult	Ἕνας ἐνήλικας ennas en-eeleek-ass
Two adults	Δύο ἐνήλικες thee-o en-eeleek-ess
and one child	καί ενα παιδί. keh enna peth-ee
and two children	καί δύο παιδιά keh thee-o peth-ya
How much is it?	Πόσο κάνει; posso kan-ee

Reference

NUMBERS

0	μηδέν	meethen
1	ἕνας, μία, ἕνα	ennas mee-a enna
2	δύο	thee-o
3	τρία	tree-a
4	τέσσερα	tessera
5	πέντε	pendeh

6	ἕξη	eksee
7	ἐπτά	epta
8	ὀκιὼ	okto
9	ἐννέα	enneh-a
10	δέκα	theh-ka
11	ἕντεκα	endek-a
12	δώδεκα	thothek-a
13	δεκατρία	thek-atree-a
14	δεκατέσσεπα	thek-atesser-a
15	δεκαπέντε	thek-apendeh
16	δεκαέξη	theh-ka-eksee
17	δεκαεπτά	theh-ka-ept-a
18	δεκαοκτώ	theh-ka-okto
19	δεκαεννέα	theh-ka-enneh-a
20	εἴκοσι	eekossee
21	εἴκοσι ἕνα	eekossee enna
22	εἴκοσι δύο	eekossee thee-o
23	εἴκοσι τρία	eekossee tree-a
24	εἴκοσι τέσσερα	eekossee tessera
25	εἴκοσι πέντε	eekossee pendeh
26	εἴκοσι ἕξη	eekosse eksee
27	εἴκοσι ἐπτά	eekossee epta
28	εἴκοσι ὀκτώ	eekossee okto
29	εἴκοσι ἐννέα	eekossee enneh-a
30	τριάντα	tree-anda
35	τριάντα πέντε	tree-anda pendeh
38	τριάντα ὀκτώ	tree-anda okto
40	σαράντα	saranda
41	σαράντα ἕνα	saranda enna
45	σαράντα πέντε	saranda pendeh
48	σαράντα ὀκτώ	saranda okto
50	πενῆντα	pen-eenda
55	πενῆντα πέντε	pen-eenda pendeh
56	πενῆντα εξη	pen-eenda eksee
60	ἑξῆντα	ekseenda
65	ἑξῆντα πέντε	ekseenda pendeh
70	ἑβδομῆντα	ev-thomeenda
75	ἑβδομῆντα πέντε	ev-thomeenda pendeh
80	ὀγδόντα	ogthonda
85	ὀγδόντα πέντε	ogthonda pendeh
90	ἐνενῆντα	enneh-neenda
95	ἐνενῆντα πέντε	enneh-neenda pendeh

100	ἑκατό	ek-at-*o*
101	ἑκατόν ἕνα	ek-at-*on* enna
102	ἑκατόν δύο	ek-at-*on* thee-o
125	ἑκατόν εἴκοσι πέντε	ek-at-*on* *ee*kossee pendeh
150	ἑκατόν πενήντα	ek-at-*on* pen-*ee*nda
175	ἑκατόν ἑβδομῆντα πέντε	ek-at-*on* ev-thom*ee*nda pendeh
200	διακόσια	thee-ak*oss*-ya
300	τριακόσια	tree-ak*oss*-ya
400	τετρακόσια	tetra-k*oss*-ya
500	πεντακόσια	pend-ak*oss*-ya
1,000	χίλια	heel-ya
1,500	χίλια πεντακόσια	heel-ya pend-ak*oss*-ya
2,000	δύο χιλιάδες	thee-o heel-y*a*thess
5,000	πέντε χιλιάδες	pendeh heel-y*a*thess
10,000	δέκα χιλιάδες	theh-ka heel-y*a*thess
100,000	ἑκατόν χιλιάδες	ek-at-*on* heel-y*a*thess
1,000,000	ἕνα ἑκατομμύριο	enna ekatomeereeo

TIME

What time is it?	Τί ὥνα εἶναι;
	tee ora *ee*neh
It's . . .	Εἶναι . . .
	*ee*neh . . .
one o'clock	μία
	mee-a
two o'clock	δύο
	thee-o
three o'clock	τρεῖς
	treess
noon	μεσημέρι
	mess-eemehree
midnight	μεσάνυχτα
	mess*an*-ee-hta
a quarter past five	πέντε καί τέταρτο
	pendeh keh tet-arto
half past five	πέντε καί μισή
	pendeh keh mees*see*
a quarter to six	ἕξη παρά τέταρτο
	*ek*see par*a* tet-arto

DAYS AND MONTHS

Monday	Δευτέρα thef-t*e*hra
Tuesday	Τρίτη tr*ee*tee
Wednesday	Τετάρτη tet-*a*rtee
Thursday	Πέμπτη p*e*mp-tee
Friday	Παρασκευή paraskev-*ee*
Saturday	Σάββατο s*a*vvato
Sunday	Κυριακή keeree-ak-*ee*
January	Ἰανουάριος yanoo-*a*r-ee-oss
February	Φεβρουάριος fevroo-*a*r-ee-oss
March	Μάρτιος m*a*rtee-oss
April	Ἀπρίλος apr*ee*lee-oss
May	Μάιος ma-ee-oss
June	Ἰούνιος ee-*ou*nee-oss
July	Ἰούλιος ee-*ou*lee-oss
August	Αυγουστος *a*vgoost-oss
September	Σεπτέμβριος septem-vree-oss
October	Ὀκτώβριος okt*o*vree-oss
November	Νοέμβριος no-*e*m-vree-oss
December	Δεκέμβριος thek-*e*m-vree-oss

Index

Italian

D. L. Ellis, C. Mariella

Pronunciation **Dr J. Baldwin**

Useful address

Italian Government Travel Office
630 5th Ave.
New York, NY 10020

Contents

Reference

Pronunciation hints

In Italian it is important to stress, or emphasize the syllables in *italics*, just as you would if we were to take as an English example: *li*ttle Jack *Ho*rner *sa*t in the *co*rner. Here we have ten syllables, but only four stresses. This Italian sentence also has ten syllables but only four stresses: qu*e*sta m*a*cchina è rumor*o*sa (this car is noisy).
Divertitevi!

Everyday expressions

[*See also 'Shop talk', p. 231*]

Hello	**Buon giorno**
	boo-*o*n j*o*rno
Good morning	**Ciao** (friends only)
Good day (before lunch)	chow
Good afternoon (after lunch)	**Buona sera**
Good evening	boo-*o*na s*e*h-ra
Good night	**Buona notte**
	boo-*o*na n*o*t-teh
Good-bye	**A rivederci**
	ah reeveh-d*a*irchee
Yes	**Sí**
	see
Please	**Per favore**
	pair fav-*o*reh
Yes, please	**Sí, grazie**
	s*ee* gr*a*tzee-eh
Thank you	**Grazie**
	gr*a*tzee-eh
Thank you very much	**Molte grazie**
	m*o*lteh gr*a*tzee-eh
That's right	**Esatto**
	ez*a*t-to
No	**No**
	noh
I disagree	**Non sono d'accordo**
	non sonno dak-k*o*rdo
Excuse me	**Scusi**
Sorry	sc*oo*zee
It doesn't matter	**Non importa**
	non imp*o*rta
Where's the toilet, please?	**Dov'è il bagno, per favore?**
	dov-*e*h il b*a*n-yo pair fav-*o*reh
Do you speak English?	**Parla inglese?**
	p*a*rla ingl*ai*zeh
What's your name?	**Come si chiama?**
	c*o*m-eh see kee-*a*m-ah
My name is . . .	**Mi chiamo . . .**
	mee kee-*a*m-o . . .

Asking the way

ESSENTIAL INFORMATION

- Keep a look-out for all these place names as you will find them on shops, maps and notices.

WHAT TO SAY

Excuse me, please	**Scusi, per favore** sc*oo*zee pair fav-*o*reh
How do I get . . .	**Per andare . . .** pair and*a*r-eh . . .
to Rome?	**a Roma?** ah roma
to the Via Nomentana?	**in via Nomentana?** in vee-ah noment*a*n-ah
to the Hotel Torino?	**all'hotel Torino?** al-lot-*e*l tor*ee*no
to the airport?	**all'aeroporto?** al-la-airop*o*rto
to the beach?	**alla spiaggia?** al-la spee-*a*d-ja
to the bus station?	**alla stazione degli autobus?** al-la statzi*o*neh del-yee ah-*oo*tobus
to the market?	**al mercato?** al mairc*a*t-o
to the police station?	**alla stazione di polizia?** al-la statzi*o*neh dee politz*ee*-ah
to the port?	**al porto?** al p*o*rto
to the post office?	**all'ufficio postale?** al-loof-f*ee*cho post*a*l-eh
to the railway station?	**alla stazione ferroviaria?** al-la statzi*o*neh ferrovee-*a*r-ee-ah
to the sports stadium?	**allo stadio?** al-lo st*a*d-eeo
to the tourist information office?	**all'ufficio informazioni turistiche?** al-loof-f*ee*cho informatzi*o*nee toor*ee*stikeh

How do I get . . .

Per andare . . .
pair and*a*r-eh . . .

   to the town centre?

in centro?
in ch*e*ntro

   to the town hall?

al Municipio?
al moonich*ee*-peeo

Excuse me, please

Scusi, per favore
sc*oo*zee pair fav-*o*reh

Is there . . . near by?

C'è . . . qui vicino?
cheh . . . quee veech*ee*no

   a baker's

una panetteria
oona panet-ter*ee*-ah

   a bank

una banca
oona b*a*nca

   a bar

un bar
oon bar

   a bus stop

una fermata d'autobus
oona fairm*a*t-ah d*a-oo*tobus

   a butcher's

una macelleria
oona machel-ler*ee*-ah

   a café

un caffè
oon caf-f*e*h

   a cake shop

una pasticceria?
oona pasteet-chair*ee*-ah

   a campsite

un campeggio
oon camp*e*d-jo

   a car park

un parcheggio
oon park*e*d-jo

   a change bureau

un ufficio del cambio
oon oof-f*ee*cho del c*a*mbeeo

   a chemist's

una farmacia
oona farmach*ee*-ah

   a delicatessen

una salumeria
oona saloomer*ee*-ah

   a dentist's

un dentista
oon dent*ee*sta

   a department store

un grande magazzino
oon gr*a*ndeh magad-dz*ee*no

   a disco

una discoteca
oona discot*e*c-ah

   a doctor's surgery

una sala medica
oona s*a*l-ah m*e*d-eeca

a dry-cleaner's	**una lavanderia a secco**
	oona lavander*ee*-ah ah s*e*c-co
a fishmonger's	**una pescheria**
	oona pesker*ee*-ah
a garage (for repairs)	**un' autoriparazioni**
	oon a-ootoriparatzi-*o*nee
a hairdresser's	**un parrucchiere**
	oon par-rooc-kee-*ai*reh
a greengrocer's	**un verduriere**
	oon vairdoo-ree-*ai*reh
a grocer's	**un alimentari**
	oon alimen-t*a*r-ee
a Health and Social Security Office	**una sezione dell'INAM**
	oona setzi*o*neh del-l*ee*nam
a hospital	**un ospedale**
	oon osped*a*l-eh
a hotel	**un hotel**
	oon ot*e*l
an ice-cream parlour	**una gelateria**
	oona jelat-er*ee*-ah
a laundry	**una lavanderia**
	oona lavander*ee*-ah
a newsagent's	**un'edicola**
	ooned*ee*cola
a night club	**un night**
	oon night
a petrol station	**un distributore**
	oon distribo*o*toreh
a post box	**una buca per lettere**
	oona b*oo*ca pair l*e*t-tereh
a public toilet	**un gabinetto pubblico**
	oon gabin*e*t-to p*oo*b-blico
a restaurant	**un ristorante**
	oon ristor*a*nteh
a supermarket	**un supermercato**
	oon sooper-mairc*a*t-o
a taxi stand	**una stazione taxi**
	oona statzi*o*neh t*a*xi
a telephone	**un telefono**
	oon tel*e*phono
a tobacconist's	**un tabaccaio**
	oon tabac-c*a*h-yo

Is there . . . near by?	**C'è . . . qui vicino?** cheh . . . quee veecheeno
a travel agent's	**un'agenzia di viaggi** oonajentzee-ah dee vee-ad-jee
a youth hostel	**un ostello per la gioventú** oon ostel-lo pair la joventoo

DIRECTIONS

Left	**Sinistra** sineestra
Right	**Destra** destra
Straight on	**Sempre diritto** sempreh deereet-to
There	**Là** la
First left/right	**La prima a sinistra/destra** la preema ah sineestra/destra
Second left/right	**La seconda a sinistra/destra** la seconda ah sineestra/destra

---

Accommodation

ESSENTIAL INFORMATION
Hotel

- If you want hotel-type accommodation, all the following words in capital letters are worth looking for on signs:
  HOTEL   ⎤
  ALBERGO ⎦   (hotel)
  MOTEL (two main chains are run by **ACI** and **Agip**)
  PENSIONE (boarding house)
- Hotels are divided into five classes (from luxury to tourist class) and **pensioni** into three.
- Lists of hotels and **pensioni** can be obtained from local tourist offices or the Italian Government Travel Office in New York.
- The cost is displayed in the room itself, so you can check it when having a look around before agreeing to stay.

- The displayed cost is for the room itself, per night and not per person. Breakfast is extra and therefore optional.
- Service and VAT are always included in the cost of the room, so tipping is voluntary.
- Not all hotels provide meals, apart from breakfast. A **pensione** always provides meals. Breakfast is continental-style: coffee or tea, with rolls and jam.
- An identity document is requested when registering at a hotel and will normally be kept overnight. Passports or driver's licenses are accepted.

WHAT TO SAY

I have a booking	**Ho una prenotazione** o oona prenotatzi-oneh
Have you any vacancies, please?	**Avete delle camere libere, per favore?** avet-eh del-leh camereh leebereh pair fav-oreh
Can I book a room?	**Potrei prenotare una camera?** potray prenot-ar-eh oona camera
It's for . . .	**È per . . .** eh pair . . .
one adult/one person	**un adulto/una persona** oon adoolto/oona pairsona
two adults/two people	**due adulti/due persone** dooeh adooltee/dooeh pairsoneh
and one child	**e un bambino** eh oon bambeeno
and two children	**e due bambini** eh dooeh bambeenee
It's for . . .	**È per . . .** eh pair . . .
one night	**una notte** oona not-teh
two nights	**due notti** dooeh not-tee
one week	**una settimana** oona set-timan-ah
two weeks	**due settimane** dooeh set-timan-eh

I would like . . .
Vorrei . . .
vorr*a*y . . .

a (quiet) room
una camera (tranquilla)
*oo*na c*a*mera (tranqu*ee*l-la)

two rooms
due camere
d*oo*eh c*a*mereh

with a single bed
singola/e*
s*i*ngola/eh

with two single beds
a due letti
ah d*oo*eh l*e*t-tee

with a double bed
con un letto matrimoniale
con oon l*e*t-to matrimon-y*a*l-eh

with a toilet ⎤
with a bathroom ⎦
con bagno
con b*a*n-yo

with a shower
con doccia
con d*o*t-cha

with a cot
con una culla
con *oo*na c*oo*l-la

with a balcony
con terrazza
con terr*a*t-tza

I would like . . .
Vorrei . . .
vorr*a*y

full board
pensione completa
pen-see*o*neh compl*e*t-ah

half board
mezza pensione
m*e*d-dza pen-see*o*neh

bed and breakfast
[*see essential information*]
solo colazione
solo colatz*i*oneh

Do you serve meals?
Servite i pasti?
sairv*ee*teh ee p*a*stee

Can I look at the room?
Potrei vedere la stanza?
potr*a*y ved-*a*ireh la st*a*ntza

OK, I'll take it
Va bene, la prendo
va b*e*n-eh la pr*e*ndo

No thanks, I won't take it
No grazie, non la prendo
n*o*h gr*a*tzee-eh non la pr*e*ndo

The bill, please
Il conto, per favore
il c*o*nto pair fav-*o*reh

Is service included?
Il servizio è compreso?
il sairv*i*tzio eh compr*a*izo

*Use '**a**' for one single bed, '**e**' for two single beds.

I think this is wrong	**Penso che questo sia sbagliato**
	penso keh questo see-ah sbal-y*a*t-o
May I have a receipt?	**Potrei avere una ricevuta?**
	pot*ray* av*ai*reh oona reechev*oo*ta

Camping

- Look for the words: **CAMPING** or **CAMPEGGIO**.
- Be prepared to have to pay:
  per person
  for the car (if applicable)
  for the tent or for trailer space
  for electricity
  for hot showers
- You must provide proof of identity, such as your passport.
- You can obtain lists of campsites from local tourist offices and from the Italian Travel Office in New York.
- To book space in advance (particularly recommended in July and August) write to the **Centro Internazionale Prenotazioni Campeggio, Casella Postale 649, 1-50100 Firenze, Italy.**
- Some campsites offer discounts to campers with the International Camping Carnet.
- Camping off-site is allowed except in state forests and national parks. It is always best to ask permission from the landowner.

Youth hostels

- Look for the words:
  OSTELLO PER LA GIOVENTÙ
- You will be asked for a YHA card and your passport on arrival.
- Food and cooking facilities vary from hostel to hostel and you may have to help with domestic chores.
- You will have to rent sheets on arrival.
- In the high season it is advisable to book beds in advance, and your stay will be limited to a maximum of three consecutive nights per hostel.
- Apply to the Italian Travel Office or local tourist offices in Italy for lists of youth hostels and details of regulations for hostellers.

WHAT TO SAY

Have you any vacancies?	**Avete dei posti liberi?** avet-eh day postee leeberee
How much is it . . .	**Quant'è . . .** quanteh . . .
for the tent?	**per la tenda?** pair la tenda
for the caravan?	**per la roulotte?** pair la roolot
for the car?	**per la macchina?** pair la mac-keena
for the electricity?	**per l'elettricità?** pair lelet-treechita
per person?	**per persona?** pair pairsona
per day/night?	**per giorno/notte?** pair jorno/not-teh
May I look round?	**Potrei dare uno sguardo?** potray dar-eh oono zgoo-ardo
Do you provide anything . . .	**È possibile . . .** eh posseebeeleh . . .
to eat?	**mangiare qui?** manjar-eh quee
to drink?	**bere qui?** baireh quee
Do you have . . .	**Avete . . .** avet-eh . . .
a bar?	**un bar?** oon bar
hot showers?	**docce con acqua calda?** dot-cheh con acqua calda
a kitchen?	**una cucina?** oona coocheena
a laundry?	**una lavanderia?** oona lavanderee-ah
a restaurant?	**un ristorante?** oon ristoranteh
a shop?	**un negozio?** oon negotzi-o
a swimming pool?	**una piscina?** oona pisheena

[*For food shopping see p. 234, and for eating and drinking out see p. 244.*]

Problems

The toilet	**Il gabinetto** il gabin*et*-to
The shower	**La doccia** la d*ot*-cha
The tap	**Il rubinetto** il roobin*et*-to
The razor point	**La spina per il rasoio** la sp*ee*na pair il raz*oy*o
The light	**La luce** la l*oo*cheh
. . . is not working	**. . . non funziona** . . . non foontzi-*o*na
My camping gas has run out	**La bombola del gas è finita** la b*o*mbola del gaz eh feen*ee*ta

LIKELY REACTIONS

Have you an identity document?	**Ha un documento di riconoscimento?** ah oon doc*oo*mento dee riconosh*ee*mento
Your membership card, please	**La sua tessera, per favore** la s*oo*-ah t*e*s-saira pair fav-*o*reh
What's your name? [*see p. 218*]	**Come si chiama?** com-eh see kee-*a*m-ah
Sorry, we're full	**Spiacente, siamo al completo** spee-ach*e*nteh see-*a*m-o al compl*e*t-o
How many people is it for?	**Per quante persone?** pair qu*a*nteh pairs*o*neh
How many nights is it for?	**Per quante notti?** pair qu*a*nteh n*o*t-tee
It's (8,000) lira . . .	**Fa (ottomila) lire . . .** fa (*o*t-tomeela) l*ee*reh . . .
per day/per night	**al giorno/per notte** al j*o*rno/pair n*o*t-teh

I haven't any rooms left	**Non ci sono piú camere**
	non chee sonno pew c*a*mereh
Do you want to have a look?	**Vuole vederla?**
	voo-*o*leh ved-*ai*ria

General shopping

The drugstore/The chemist's

ESSENTIAL INFORMATION

- Look for the word **FARMACIA** (drugstore).
- Medicines (drugs) are only available at a drugstore.
- Some non-drugs can be bought at a supermarket or department store.
- Try a pharmacist *before* going to a doctor: they are usually qualified to treat minor injuries.
- Drugstores take turns staying open all night and on Sundays. A notice on the door headed **FARMACIE DI TURNO** or **SERVIZIO NOTTURNO** gives details of opening times.
- Some toiletries can also be bought at a **PROFUMERIA**, but they will be more expensive.

WHAT TO SAY

I'd like . . .	**Vorrei . . .**
	vorr*ay* . . .
some Alka Seltzer	**dell'Alka Seltzer**
	del-lalka s*e*ltzer
some antiseptic	**dell'antisettico**
	del-lantis*e*t-tico
some aspirin	**dell'aspirina**
	del-laspir*ee*na
some baby food	**cibi per bambini**
	ch*ee*bee pair bamb*ee*nee
some contraceptives	**contraccettivi**
	contrat-chet-t*ee*vee

some cotton	**del cotone**
	del cot*o*neh
some disposable diapers	**pannolini per bambini**
	pan-nol*ee*nee pair bamb*ee*nee
some eye drops	**del collirio**
	del col-*lee*-reeo
some inhalant	**dell'inalante**
	del-linal*a*nteh
some insect repellent	**della crema anti-insetti**
	del-la cr*e*m-ah anti-ins*e*t-tee
some paper tissues	**fazzoletti di carta**
	fat-tzolet-tee dee c*a*rta
some sanitary napkins	**assorbenti igienici**
	as-sorbenti eejen-eechi
some sticking plaster	**del cerotto**
	del chair*o*t-to
some suntan lotion/oil	**crema/olio solare**
	cr*e*m-ah/*o*lyo sol*a*r-eh
some Tampax	**Tampax**
	t*a*mpax
some throat lozenges	**delle pastiglie per la gola**
	del-leh past*ee*l-yeh pair la g*o*la
some toilet paper	**carta igienica**
	c*a*rta eejen-e*e*ca
I'd like something for . . .	**Vorrei qualcosa per . . .**
	vorr*ay* qualc*o*za pair . . .
bites	**morsicature**
	mor-seecat*oo*reh
burns	**bruciature**
	broo-chat*oo*reh
a cold	**il raffreddore**
	il raf-fred-d*o*reh
constipation	**stitichezza**
	stitik*e*t-tza
a cough	**la tosse**
	la t*o*s-seh
diarrhoea	**diarrea**
	dee-arr*e*h-ah
ear-ache	**mal d'orecchie**
	mal dorr*e*k-kee-eh
flu	**influenza**
	*i*nflu*e*ntza

I'd like something for . . .	**Vorrei qualcosa per . . .**
	vorray qualcoza pair . . .
scalds	**scottature**
	scot-tatooreh
sore gums	**mal di gengive**
	mal dee jenjeeveh
stings	**punture**
	poontooreh
sunburn	**scottature da sole**
	scot-tatooreh da sol-eh
car (sea/air) sickness	**mal d'auto (di mare/d'aereo)**
	mal da-ooto (dee mareh/da-eh-reho)

[*For other essential expressions see 'Shop talk' opposite.*]

Holiday items

ESSENTIAL INFORMATION

- Places to shop at and signs to look for:

LIBRERIA-CARTOLERIA	(bookshop/stationery store)
TABACCHERIA	(tobacco shop)
ARTICOLI DA REGALO	(presents)
FOTO-OTTICO	(photographer-optician)
ARTICOLI FOTOGRAFICI	(photography items)

- and the main department stores:
  UPIM, STANDA, RINASCENTE

WHAT TO SAY

I'd like . . .	**Vorrei . . .**
	vorray . . .
a bag	**una borsa**
	oona borsa
a beach ball	**un pallone da spiaggia**
	oon pal-loneh da speead-ja
a bucket	**un secchiello**
	oon sec-kee-ello

an English newspaper	**un giornale inglese**
	oon jornal-eh inglaizeh
some envelopes	**delle buste**
	del-leh boosteh
some postcards	**delle cartoline**
	del-leh cartoleeneh
a spade	**una paletta**
	oona palet-ta
a straw hat	**un cappello di paglia**
	oon cap-pel-lo dee pal-ya
some sunglasses	**degli occhiali da sole**
	del-yee oc-kee-al-ee da soleh
some writing paper	**della carta da lettere**
	del-la carta da let-tereh
a colour film [*show the camera*]	**una pellicola a colori**
	oona pel-leecola ah coloree
a black and white film	**una pellicola in bianco e nero**
	oona pel-leecola in bee-anco eh nairo

Shop talk

ESSENTIAL INFORMATION

- Know how to say the important weights and measures:

50 grams	**cinquanta grammi**	
	chinquanta gram-mee	
100 grams	**cento grammi**	
	chento gram-mee	
200 grams	**duecento grammi**	
	dooeh-chento gram-mee	
½ kilo	**mezzo chilo**	
	med-dzo keelo	
1 kilo	**un chilo**	
	oon keelo	
2 kilos	**due chili**	
	dooeh keelee	
½ litre	**mezzo litro**	
	med-dzo leetro	

1 litre	**un litro**
	oon l*ee*tro
2 litres	**due litri**
	d*oo*eh l*ee*tree

[*For numbers see p. 264*]

- You may see the words **etto** (100 grams) or **all'etto** (per 100 grams) on price tickets. This is a colloquial expression for 100 grams.

CUSTOMER

I'm just looking	**Guardo soltanto**
	gw*a*rdo solt*a*nto
How much is this/that?	**Quanto costa questo/quello?**
	qu*a*nto c*o*sta qu*e*sto/qw*e*l-lo
What's that?	**Che cos' è quello?**
	keh c*o*z-*e*h qu*e*l-lo
What are those?	**Che cosa sono quelli?**
	keh c*o*za s*o*nno qu*e*l-lee
Is there a discount?	**C'è uno sconto?**
	cheh *o*ono sc*o*nto
I'd like that, please	**Vorrei quello, per favore**
	vorr*ay* qu*e*l-lo pair fav-*o*reh
Not that	**Non quello**
	non qu*e*l-lo
Like that	**Come quello**
	com-eh qu*e*l-lo
That's enough, thank you	**Basta così grazie**
	b*a*sta coz*ee* gr*a*tzee-eh
More, please	**Ancora, per favore**
	anc*o*ra pair fav-*o*reh
Less than that	**Meno di così**
	men-o dee coz*ee*
That's fine ⎤	**Va bene**
OK ⎦	va b*e*n-eh
I won't take it, thank you	**Non lo prendo, grazie**
	non lo pr*e*ndo gr*a*tzee-eh
It's not right	**Non va bene**
	non va b*e*n-eh
Have you got something . . .	**Avete qualcosa . . .**
	av*e*teh qualc*o*za . . .

better?	**di meglio?** dee mel-yo
cheaper?	**di meno caro?** dee men-o car-o
different?	**di diverso?** dee deevairso
larger?/smaller?	**di piú grande?/piccolo** dee pew grandeh/pee-colo
Can I have a bag, please?	**Posso avere una borsa, per favore?** pos-so avaireh oona borsa pair fav-oreh
Can I have a receipt?	**Posso avere la ricevuta?** pos-so avaireh la reechevoota
Do you take . . .	**Accettate . . .** at-chet-tat-eh . . .
English/American money?	**soldi inglesi/americani?** soldee inglaizee/american-ee
travellers' cheques?	**travellers' cheques?** travellairs sheck
credit cards?	**carte di credito?** carteh dee cred-eeto

SHOP ASSISTANT

Can I help you?	**È da servire?** eh da sairveereh
What would you like?	**Che cosa desidera?** keh coza dezeedera
Will that be all?	**È tutto?** eh toot-to
Is that all?	**Basta cosí?** basta cozee
Anything else?	**Nient'altro?** nee-entaltro
Would you like it wrapped?	**Glielo incarto?** lee-el-o incarto
Sorry, none left	**Mi dispiace non ne ho piú** mee dispi-ah-cheh non neh o pew
I haven't got any	**Non ne abbiamo** non neh ab-bee-am-o
I haven't got any more	**Non ne abbiamo piú** non neh ab-bee-am-o pew

How many do you want?	**Quanti ne desidera?**
	quantee neh dezeedera
How much do you want?	**Quanto ne vuole?**
	quanto neh vwoleh
Is that enough?	**È abbastanza?**
	eh ab-bastantza

Shopping for food

Bread

ESSENTIAL INFORMATION

- Key words to look for:
PANETTERIA	(bakery)
PANIFICIO	(baker's bread usually baked on premises)
PANETTIERE	(baker)
PANE	(bread)
- Opening times vary slightly from place to place but are generally 9–1 and 3.30–8. Most bakers open earlier than other shops and are closed one day a week – the day varies from town to town.
- Although large and small loaves can be bought, rolls are very popular and it is important to note that bread is usually bought by *weight*.
- Bakers often stock other groceries, particularly milk. There is no milk-delivery service and the dairy (**LATTERIA**) is fast disappearing.

WHAT TO SAY

A loaf (like that)	**Una pagnotta (cosí)**
	oona pan-yot-ta (cozee)
A large one	**Una grande**
	oona grandeh
A small one	**Una piccola**
	oona peec-cola

A bread roll	**Un panino**
	oon pan*ee*no
250 grams of . . .	**Duecentocinquanta grammi di . . .**
	dooeh-chento-chinqu*a*nta gram-mee dee . . .
bread	**pane**
	p*a*n-eh
white bread	**pane bianco**
	p*a*n-eh bee-*a*nco
wholemeal bread	**pane integrale**
	p*a*n-eh integr*a*l-eh
bread rolls	**panini**
	pan*ee*nee
crispy bread sticks	**grissini**
	gris-s*ee*nee

[*For other essential expressions see 'Shop talk', p. 231.*]

Cakes and ice cream

ESSENTIAL INFORMATION

• Key words to look for:

PASTICCERIA	(cake shop)
PASTICCIERE	(pastry maker)
PASTE/DOLCI	(cakes, pastries, candy)
GELATI	(ice cream)
GELATERIA ⎤	(ice-cream parlour)
CREMERIA ⎦	

• **BAR-PASTICCERIA**: a place to buy cakes and have a drink. Italians often go to a bar for a snack at mid-morning as they eat very little for breakfast.
• Most bars only have a few tables and charge more for waiter service. See p. 244, 'Ordering a drink and a snack'.

WHAT TO SAY

The type of cakes in the shops varies from region to region, but it is usual to find a variety of cookies and small cream-filled pastries called **paste fresche**. These are bought by weight and it is best to point to the selection you prefer.

200 grams of . . .	**Duecento grammi di . . .**
	dooeh-chento gram-mee dee . . .
cream pastries	**paste fresche**
	pasteh freskeh
biscuits	**biscotti**
	biscot-tee
A selection, please	**Misto, per favore**
	meesto pair fav-oreh

You may want to buy larger pastries and cakes individually:

A cake (like that), please	**Una torta (cosí), per favore**
	oona tor-ta cozee pair fav-oreh
An (apple) tart	**Una crostata (di mela)**
	oona crostat-a dee mel-a
A doughnut	**Un bombolone**
	oon bomboloneh
A brioche	**Una brioche**
	oona bree-osh
A . . . ice cream, please	**Per favore, un gelato . . .**
	pair fav-oreh oon jelat-o . . .
chocolate	**al cioccolato**
	al choc-colat-o
lemon	**al limone**
	al leemoneh
nougat	**al torroncino**
	al torroncheeno
peach	**alla pesca**
	al-la pesca
pistachio	**al pistacchio**
	al peestac-keeo
strawberry	**alla fragola**
	al-la fragola
vanilla	**alla crema**
	al-la crem-ah
(1,000) lira's worth	**Da (mille) lire**
	da (meeleh) leereh
A single cone [*specify flavour, as above*]	**Un cono**
	oon cono

Picnic food

ESSENTIAL INFORMATION

- Key words to look for:
  SALUMERIA
  SALUMI ⎤
  GASTRONOMIA ⎦   (delicatessen)
- In these shops you can buy a wide variety of food such as ham, salami, cheese, olives, appetizers, sausages, and freshly made take-out dishes. Specialties differ from region to region.

WHAT TO SAY

Two slices of . . .	**Due fette di . . .**
	d*oo*eh fet-teh dee . . .
roast beef	**arrosto**
	ar*ro*sto
roast pork	**arrosto di maiale**
	ar*ro*sto dee mah-y*a*l-eh
tongue	**lingua**
	l*i*n-gwa
veal with mayonnaise	**vitello tonnato**
	veet*e*l-lo ton-n*a*t-o
bacon	**pancetta**
	panch*e*t-ta
salami (raw/cooked)	**salame (crudo/cotto)**
	sal*a*m-eh (cr*oo*do/c*o*t-to)
ham (raw/cooked)	**prosciutto (crudo/cotto)**
	prosh*oo*t-to (cr*oo*do/c*o*t-to)
meat loaf	**polpettone arrosto**
	polpet-t*o*neh ar*ro*sto

You might also like to try some of these:

olive verdi	green olives
ol*ee*veh v*a*irdee	
olive nere	black olives
ol*ee*veh n*a*ireh	
olive nere al forno	baked black olives
ol*ee*veh n*a*ireh al f*o*rno	

olive verdi ripiene	stuffed green olives
ol*ee*veh v*air*dee rip-yen-eh	
funghetti sott'olio	mushrooms preserved in oil
foongh*et*-tee sot-t*ol*-yo	
peperoni sott'olio	peppers preserved in oil
peper*o*nee sot-t*ol*-yo	
peperoni arrosto	roasted peppers
peper*o*nee arr*o*sto	
peperoni ripieni	stuffed peppers
peper*o*nee rip-yen-ee	
pomodori ripieni	stuffed tomatoes
pomod*o*ree rip-yen-ee	
cipolle ripiene	stuffed onions
chip*o*l-leh rip-yen-eh	
melanzane in parmigiana	aubergines cooked in tomato sauce
melandz*a*n-eh in parmij*a*n-ah	and parmesan cheese
zucchini in carpione	courgettes cooked in oil and
zooc-k*ee*nee in carp-y*o*neh	vinegar, sage and garlic
zucchini ripieni	stuffed courgettes
zuc-k*ee*nee rip-yen-ee	
patatine fritte	crisps, freshly made daily
patat*ee*neh fr*ee*t-teh	
lasagne al forno	wide, flat noodles baked in a sauce
laz*an*-yeh al f*o*rno	of meat and bechamel
gnocchi alla romana	small, flat semolina 'dumplings'
n-y*o*c-kee al-la rom*an*-ah	with butter and parmesan cheese
cannelloni ripieni	large tubular pasta stuffed with
can-nel-l*o*nee rip-yen-ee	meat, or spinach and cheese
gnocchi alla fontina	potato 'dumplings' with melted
n-y*o*c-kee al-la font*ee*na	fontina cheese
torta di verdura	vegetable pie
t*o*rta dee vaird*oo*-ra	
torta pasqualina	spinach, eggs and herbs in a puff
t*o*rta pasqwal*ee*na	pastry pie
parmigiano	parmesan, a hard, strong cheese
parmij*a*n-o	used in cooking, usually grated
robiola	a mild fresh white cheese made
rob-y*o*la	from ewe's milk
pecorino	a strong hard cheese, eaten fresh
pecor*ee*no	or grated when mature
ricotta	a soft white, very bland curd
ric*o*t-ta	cheese made from ewe's milk

fontina
font*ee*na
a rich Alpine cheese usually
melted in cooking

provolone
provol*o*neh
a hard yellow cow's milk cheese
displayed hanging up

gorgonzola
gorgon-tz*o*la
a blue-veined cheese with a rich
soft texture

mozzarella
mot-tzar-*e*l-la
a white flavourless curd cheese,
should be eaten very fresh

Fruit and vegetables

ESSENTIAL INFORMATION

- Key words to look for:

FRUTTA	(fruit)
VERDURA	(vegetables)
PRIMIZIE	(an indication of freshness)
ALIMENTARI	(grocery and greengrocery)
MERCATO	(market)

- It is customary for you to choose your own fruit and vegetables at the market (and in some shops) and for the vendor to weigh them and price them. You must take your own shopping bag: paper and plastic bags are not normally provided.

WHAT TO SAY

1 kilo of . . .	**Un chilo di . . .**
	oon k*ee*lo dee . . .
apples	**mele**
	m*e*l-eh
bananas	**banane**
	ban*a*n-eh
cherries	**ciliegie**
	chil-*ye*h-jeh
grapes (white/black)	**uva (bianca/nera)**
	*oo*va (bee-*a*nca/n*ai*ra)

1 kilo of . . .

Un chilo di . . .
oon keelo dee . . .

oranges

arance
arancheh

pears

pere
paireh

peaches

pesche
peskeh

plums

prugne
proon-yeh

strawberries

fragole
fragoleh

A pineapple, please

Un ananas, per favore
oon ananas pair fav-oreh

A grapefruit

Un pompelmo
oon pompelmo

A melon

Un melone
oon meloneh

A water melon

Un'anguria
oon-angoo-ria

½ kilo of . . .

Mezzo chilo di . . .
med-dzo keelo dee . . .

artichokes

carciofi
carchof-ee

aubergines

melanzane
melandzan-eh

carrots

carote
carot-eh

courgettes

zucchini
tzooc-keenee

green beans

fagiolini
fad-joleenee

leeks

porri
porree

mushrooms

funghi
foonghee

onions

cipolle
chipol-leh

peas

piselli
peezel-lee

peppers (green/red)

peperoni (verdi/rossi)
peperonee (vairdee/ros-see)

potatoes	**patate** pat*at*-eh
spinach	**spinaci** speen*a*chee
tomatoes	**pomodori** pomod*o*ree
A bunch of . . .	**Un mazzetto di . . .** oon mat-tz*et*-to dee . . .
parsley	**prezzemolo** pret-tz*em*-olo
radishes	**rapanelli** rapan*e*l-lee
A head of garlic	**Una testa d'aglio** oona t*e*sta d*a*l-yo
Some lettuce	**Dell'insalata** del-linsal*a*t-ah
A stick of celery	**Un sedano** oon s*e*dan-o
A cucumber	**Un cetriolo** oon chetree-*o*lo
Like that, please	**Come quello, per favore** com-eh qu*e*l-lo pair fav-*o*reh

Meat and fish

ESSENTIAL INFORMATION

- Key words to look for:
MACELLAIO	(butcher)
MACELLERIA	(butcher shop)
PESCHERIA	(fish store)
FRUTTI DI MARE	(shellfish)
MERCATO DEL PESCE	(fish market)
- Butchers, especially in small towns and villages, often use a white sheet hung outside the shop as a sign.
- Mutton and lamb are only sold and eaten during the Easter period.
- Large supermarkets usually have a fresh-fish counter.

WHAT TO SAY

For roasts, choose the type of meat and then say how many people it is for:

Some beef, please	**Del manzo, per favore** del man-zo pair fav-oreh
Some lamb	**Dell'agnello** del-lan-yel-lo
Some pork	**Del maiale** del mah-yal-eh
Some veal	**Del vitello** del veetel-lo
A roast . . .	**Un arrosto . . .** oon arrosto . . .
for two people	**per due persone** pair dooeh pairsoneh
for four people	**per quattro persone** pair quat-tro pairsoneh
for six people	**per sei persone** pair say pairsoneh
Some steak, please	**Della bistecca, per favore** del-la beestec-ca pair fav-oreh
Some liver	**Del fegato** del feh-gat-o
Some kidneys	**Dei rognoni** day ron-yonee
Some heart	**Del cuore** del cworeh
Some sausages	**Delle salsiccie** del-leh salseet-cheh
Some mince	**Della carne tritata** del-la carneh treetat-ah
Two veal scallops	**Due fettine di vitello** dooeh fet-teeneh dee-veetel-lo
Three pork chops	**Tre braciole di maiale** treh bracholeh dee mayal-eh
Four lamb chops	**Quattro costolette d'agnello** quat-tro costolet-teh dan-yel-lo
Five beef chops	**Cinque fettine di manzo** chinqueh fet-teeneh dee mandzo

A chicken	**Un pollo**
	oon pol-lo
A rabbit	**Un coniglio**
	oon coneel-yo
A tongue	**Una lingua**
	oona leengwa

Purchase large fish and small shellfish by the weight:

½ kilo of . . .	**Mezzo chilo di . . .**
	med-dzo keelo dee . . .
anchovies	**acciughe**
	at-choogeh
cod	**merluzzo**
	merloot-tzo
dogfish	**palombo**
	palombo
eel	**anguilla**
	angweel-la
fresh tuna	**tonno fresco**
	ton-no fresco
mussels (two names)	**muscoli/cozze**
	moos-colee/cot-tzeh
octopus	**polipo**
	poleepo
oysters	**ostriche**
	ostreekeh
prawns	**gamberi**
	gamberee
red mullet	**triglie**
	treel-yeh
sardines	**sardine**
	sardeeneh
scampi	**scampi**
	scampee
shrimps	**gamberetti**
	gamberet-tee
small squid	**calamaretti**
	calamaret-tee
squid	**calamari**
	calama-ree
swordfish	**pescespada**
	pesheh-spad-ah

For some shellfish and 'frying pan' fish, specify the number you want:

A crab, please	**Un granchio, per favore**
	oon gr*a*nkeeo pair fav-*o*reh
A lobster	**Un'aragosta**
	oonarag*o*sta
A trout	**Una trota**
	oona tr*o*t-a
A sole	**Una sogliola**
	oona s*o*l-yola
A dory [*expensive*]	**Un'orata**
	oonor*a*t-ah
A bass [*expensive*]	**Un branzino**
	oon brandz*ee*no
A mullet	**Un cefalo**
	oon ch*e*falo

Eating and drinking out

Ordering a drink and a snack

ESSENTIAL INFORMATION

- The places to ask for:
  BAR
  BAR-PASTICCERIA   (drinks and cakes)
  CAFFÈ
  BIRRERIA   (beer and snacks)
- By law, the price list of drinks (**LISTINO PREZZI**) must be displayed somewhere in the bar.
- There is waiter service in some cafés, but you can drink at the bar or counter if you wish (cheaper). In this case you should first pay at the cash register (**CASSA**) and then take the receipt (**scontrino**) to the bar and give your order.
- Service is normally included in the bill (**servizio compreso**) but if not should be 10% to 15%.

- Bars and cafés serve both non-alcoholic and alcoholic drinks. There are no licensing hours, and children are allowed in.
- Italians drink a range of aperitifs (**aperitivi**) and digestives (**digestivi**). Their names vary from region to region. Most of the aperitifs are types of vermouth – red or white, sweet or dry – made by different firms such as Campari, Punt e Mes and Martini. The digestives can be made from almonds, fruit, or herbs and are often thick and syrupy.

WHAT TO SAY

I'll have . . . please	**Prendo per favore . . .**
	prendo pair fav-*oreh* . . .
a black coffee (small and strong)	**un caffè**
	oon caf-f*eh*
a black coffee (less strong)	**un caffè lungo**
	oon caf-f*eh* l*oo*ng-go
a coffee with a dash of cream	**un caffè macchiato**
	oon caf-f*eh* mac-kee-*at*-o
a milky coffee (breakfast)	**un caffelatte**
	oon caf-eh-l*at*-teh
a frothy white coffee	**un capuccino**
	oon capooch*ee*no
a tea	**un tè**
	oon teh
with milk	**al latte**
	al l*at*-teh
with lemon	**al limone**
	al leem*o*neh
a glass of milk	**un bicchiere di latte**
	oon beec-kee-*air*eh dee l*at*-teh
a hot chocolate	**una cioccolata calda**
	oona choc-col*at*-ah c*a*lda
a mineral water	**una minerale**
	oona miner*al*-eh
an iced coffee	**una granita di caffè**
	oona gran*ee*ta dee caf-f*eh*
a lemonade	**una limonata**
	oona leemon*at*-a
a fresh lemon juice	**una spremuta di limone**
	oona sprem*oo*ta dee leem*o*neh

I'll have . . . please	**Prendo per favore . . .** prendo pair fav-oreh . . .
an orangeade	**un'aranciata** oonaranchat-a
a fresh orange juice	**una spremuta d'arancia** oona spremoota darancha
a fresh grapefruit juice	**una spremuta di pompelmo** oona spremoota dee pompelmo
a pineapple juice	**un succo di frutta all'ananas** oon sooc-co dee froot-ta al-la pesca
a lager	**una birra** oona beera
a dark beer	**una birra scura** oona beera scoo-ra
I'll have . . . please	**Prendo, per favore . . .** prendo pair fav-oreh . . .
a cheese roll	**un panino al formaggio** oon paneeno al formad-jo
a ham roll	**un panino al prosciutto** oon paneeno al proshoot-to
a salami roll	**un panino al salame** oon paneeno al salam-eh
a sandwich (like that)	**un tramezzino (così)** oon tramed-dzeeno (cozee)
a pizza	**una pizza** oona peet-tza

These are some other snacks you may like to try:

una pizzetta al pomodoro oona pit-tzet-ta al pomodoro	small tomato pizza, usually eaten cold
una focaccia cona focat-cha	a savoury bread, similar to pizza but without tomato spread
una focaccina al prosciutto cona focat-cheena al proshoot-to	a ham sandwich made with **focaccia** bread
un toast (al prosciutto e formaggio) oon tost (al proshoot-to eh formad-djo)	a toasted sandwich, normally made with ham and cheese

In a restaurant

ESSENTIAL INFORMATION

- You can eat at all these places:

  RISTORANTE
  TRATTORIA (cheaper)
  ALBERGO (hotel – often a fixed menu)
  PENSIONE (mainly residents – fixed menu)
  ROSTICCERIA ⎤
  PIZZERIA   ⎥ (hot snacks)
  BIRRERIA   ⎥
  TAVOLA CALDA ⎦

- Menus are always displayed outside the larger restaurants and that is the *only* way to judge if a place is right for your needs.
- Some smaller restaurants do not have a written menu and you must ask the waiter what is available.
- Self-service restaurants are rare.
- Service (of 10% to 15%) is always included on the bill, but an extra tip is usually welcome.
- Restaurants are now obliged, by law, to give receipts, and you should insist on this.
- In the south of Italy the lunch break is longer than in the north, and dinner is eaten later in the evening.

WHAT TO SAY

May I book a table?	**Potrei prenotare un tavolo?**
	potray prenotar-eh oon tavolo
I've booked a table	**Ho prenotato un tavolo**
	o prenotat-o oon tavolo
A table . . .	**Un tavolo . . .**
	oon tavolo . . .
for one	**per una persona**
	pair oona pairsona
for three	**per tre persone**
	pair treh pairsoneh
The à la carte menu, please	**Il menú alla carta, per favore**
	il menoo al-la carta pair fav-oreh

The fixed price menu	**Il menú a prezzo fisso**
	il men*oo* ah pret-tzo f*is*-so
The (8,000) lira menu	**Il menú da (ottomila) lire**
	il men*oo* da (ot-tom*ee*la) l*ee*reh
The tourist menu	**Il menú turistico**
	il men*oo* toor*i*stico
Today's special menu	**I piatti del giorno**
	ee pee-*at*-tee del j*o*rno
What's this, please? [*point to menu*]	**Che cos'è questo, per favore?**
	keh coz-*eh* qu*e*sto pair fav-*o*reh
A carafe of wine, please	**Una caraffa di vino, per favore**
	oona car*a*f-fa dee v*ee*no pair fav-*o*reh
A quarter (25 cc)	**Un quarto**
	oon qu*aa*rto
A half (50 cc)	**Un mezzo litro**
	oon m*e*d-zo l*ee*tro
A glass	**Un bicchiere**
	oon beec-kee-*ai*reh
A (half) bottle	**Una (mezza) bottiglia**
	oona (m*e*d-za) bot-t*ee*l-ya
A litre	**Un litro**
	oon l*ee*tro
Red/white/rosé/house wine	**Vino rosso/bianco/rosé/della casa**
	v*ee*no r*o*s-so/bee-*a*nco/r*o*zeh/d*e*l-la c*a*za
Some more bread, please	**Ancora del pane, per favore**
	anc*o*ra del p*a*n-eh pair fav-*o*reh
Some more wine	**Ancora del vino**
	anc*o*ra del v*ee*no
Some oil	**Dell'olio**
	del-l*o*l-yo
Some vinegar	**Dell'aceto**
	del-lach*e*to
Some salt/pepper	**Del sale/pepe**
	del s*a*l-eh/p*e*h-peh
With/without (garlic)	**Con/senza (aglio)**
	con/s*e*ntza (*a*l-yo)
Some water	**Dell'acqua**
	del-l*a*cqua
How much does that come to?	**Quanto fa?**
	qu*a*nto fa

Is service included?	**Il servizio è compreso?**
	il sairv*i*tzio eh compr*a*iz-o
Where is the toilet, please?	**Dov'è il bagno, per favore?**
	dov-*e*h il b*a*n-yo pair fav-*o*reh
Miss! [*this does not sound abrupt in Italian*]	**Signorina!**
	seen-yor*e*ena
Waiter!	**Cameriere!**
	cameree-*ai*reh
The bill, please	**Il conto, per favore**
	il c*o*nto pair fav-*o*reh
May I have a receipt?	**Potrei avere una ricevuta?**
	potr*ay* av*ai*reh oona reechev*oo*ta

Key words for courses, as seen on some menus

[*Only ask this question if you want the waiter to remind you of the choice.*]

What have you got in the way of . . .	**Che cosa avete come . . .**
	keh c*o*za avet-eh c*o*m-eh . . .
starters?	**antipasti?**
	antip*a*stee
soup?	**minestre?**
	min*e*streh
egg dishes?	**uova?**
	w*o*va
fish?	**pesce?**
	p*e*sheh
meat?	**carne?**
	c*a*rneh
game?	**selvaggina?**
	selvad-j*ee*na
fowl?	**pollame?**
	pol-l*a*m-eh
vegetables?	**contorno?**
	cont*o*rno
cheese?	**formaggi?**
	form*a*d-jee
fruit?	**frutta?**
	fr*oo*t-ta
ice-cream?	**gelati?**
	jel*a*t-ee

dessert?   **dolci?**
                                       dolchee

['*Pasta*', spaghetti, etc., are part of the MINESTRE course, see p. 254]

UNDERSTANDING THE MENU

- You will find the names of the principal ingredients of most
  dishes on these pages:

  Starters p. 237   Fruit p. 239
  Meat p. 242   Cheese p. 238
  Fish p. 243   Ice-cream p. 236
  Vegetables p. 240   Dessert p. 236

  Used together with the following lists of cooking and menu
  terms, they should help you to decode the menu.

- *Remember*, dishes vary considerably from region to region in
  Italy: a dish with the same name, e.g. **gnocchi alla Romana**
  (pasta 'dumplings' Roman style), might be cooked in a
  different way in Rome from Milan – or even from one
  restaurant to another in the same city. Also, the same dish
  might appear on menus all over Italy with a different name in
  each region! If in doubt, always ask the waiter.

- These cooking and menu terms are for understanding only –
  not for speaking.

Cooking and menu terms

affumicato	smoked
all'aglio e olio	with oil and garlic
agrodolce	sweet-sour
arrosto	roast
al basilico	with basil
ben cotto	well cooked
con besciamella	with bechamel sauce
in bianco	boiled, with no sauce
bollito	boiled/stewed
alla bolognese	Bolognese style
brasato	cooked in wine
al burro	cooked in butter
alla cacciatora	cooked in tomato sauce
al cartoccio	baked wrapped in foil
alla casalinga	homely style
al civet	marinated and cooked in wine

cotto	cooked (as opposed to raw)
crudo	raw
al dente	not overcooked, firm texture
dorato	slightly fried (golden)
alle erbe	with herbs
da farsi	to be prepared
ai ferri	grilled without oil
alla fiorentina	Florentine style
alla fonduta	with fondue
al forno	baked
fritto	fried
in gelatina	in savoury jelly
grattuggiato	grated; baked in cheese sauce
alla griglia	grilled on the fire
imbottiti	stuffed
lesso	boiled
in maionese	in/with mayonnaise
alle mandorle	with almonds
alla marinara	with seafood
al marsala	with Marsala wine
alla milanese	fried in egg and breadcrumbs
alla napoletana	Neopolitan style
all'origano	with oregano (herb)
in padella	cooked and served in a frying pan
al pangrattato	with breadcrumbs
alla panna	cooked in cream
al parmigiano	with parmesan cheese
al pecorino	with pecorino cheese
al pesto	with basil and garlic sauce
alla pizzaiola	with tomato sauce and cheese
al prezzemolo	with parsley
ragù	rich tomato and meat sauce for pasta
alla ricotta	with ricotta cheese
ripieno	stuffed
alla romana	Roman style
al rosmarino	with rosemary
salsa	sauce
salsa verde	parsley and garlic sauce
in salmí	cooked in oil, vinegar and herbs
al sangue	rare (steak, etc.)
alla siciliana	Sicilian style

spiedini	skewers
allo spiedo	on the spit
stufato	stew
al sugo	cooked in sauce
trifolato	cooked with tomato and parsley
in umido	steamed; stewed
alla veneziana	Venetian style
alle vongole	with clam (shellfish) sauce
allo zabaglione	with eggs, sugar and Marsala wine
zuppa	soup

Further words to help you to understand the menu:

abbacchio	young, spring lamb
amaretti	macaroons
anguilla	eel
animelle	sweetbreads
anitra	duck
baccalà	dried cod
bagna cauda	raw vegetables dipped in sauce of hot oil, garlic, anchovies and cream
bistecca alla fiorentina	T-bone steak
braciole	chops
brodo	broth
budino	like crème caramel; pudding
cacciagione	game
capperi	capers
capretto	kid
capriolo	deer
cassata	ice-cream cake with dried fruit
cervella	brains
cinghiale	boar
coppa	very lean bacon; cup (of ice-cream)
costate	large chops
costolette	small chops
cotechino	large pork sausage
crema	custard cream; cream soup
crostata	fruit or jam tart
crostini	small pieces of fried bread
fagiano	pheasant

fagioli	fresh or dried beans
fave	broad or butter beans
fegatini	chicken livers
fettine	small tender steaks
filetti	fillets
fragole di bosco	wild strawberries
frittata	omelette
frittelle	fritters
fritto misto	mixed fried meats
fritto di pesce	mixed fried fish
frutti di mare	shellfish
gelati	ice-cream
granita	water ice
grissini	crispy bread sticks
involtini	slices of meat, stuffed and rolled
lepre	hare
limone	lemon
lombata	sirloin
macedonia	fruit salad
mandorle	almonds
minestrone	vegetable soup
mortadella	large mild salami
ossibuchi	dish of shin of veal
pancetta	bacon
panna	cream
pasta asciutta	general name of cooked pasta
pasta frolla	rich shortcrust pastry
pasta sfogliata	puff pastry
peperonata	stew of green and red peppers
peperoncini	chili peppers
pernice	partridge
petti di pollo/tacchino	chicken/turkey breasts
piccata	small veal slices
pignoli	pine nuts
pinzimonio	raw vegetables to dip in oil
polpette	meatballs
prosciutto di Parma	raw ham from Parma
quaglia	quail
riso	rice
risotto	rice cooked in sauce
rolata	meat loaf stuffed with herbs
salame all'aglio	garlic sausage

salsiccia	sausage
saltimbocca alla romana	fried veal with ham and rosemary
scaloppine	small veal slices
semifreddo	ice-cream with biscuits
seppie	cuttle-fish
spezzatino	stew
stracciatella	hot broth with beaten egg
stracotto	beef stew with vegetables
tacchino	turkey
tartuffi	truffles
torta	cake
trippa	tripe
uccelli	small birds (e.g. thrushes)
uova	eggs
vongole	clams, cockles
zampone	pig's trotter stuffed with chopped, seasoned meat
zuppa inglese	chocolate trifle
zuppa pavese	broth, lightly boiled egg and cheese

Types of pasta

agnolini/agnolotti	like ravioli
cannelloni	large tubular pasta, often stuffed
cappelletti	stuffed pasta rings
conchiglie	shell-shaped pasta
ditali	short tubular pasta
farfalle	butterfly-shaped pasta
fettuccine	narrow ribbons of pasta
gnocchi	small potato or semolina 'dumplings'
lasagne	wide flat pasta
maccheroni	large spaghetti with hole in middle
pasta asciutta	general term for cooked pasta
pasta in brodo	small shapes of pasta in broth
pizza	flat 'bread' spread with tomato
polenta	porridge of maize flour
ravioli	stuffed square-shaped pasta
rigatoni	large-grooved tubular pasta
spaghetti	long, thin, round pasta
tagliatelle	narrow ribbon pasta

tortellini	stuffed pasta rings
vermicelli	very thin spaghetti, 'little worms'
ziti	tubular-shaped pasta

Health

ESSENTIAL INFORMATION

- Be sure to have medical insurance.
- The Italian state medical insurance is called **INAM**.
- For minor disorders and treatment at a drugstore, see p. 228.
- For asking the way to a doctor, dentist, drugstore or Health and Social Security Office, see p. 221.
- To find a doctor in an emergency, look for:
  medici (in the Yellow Pages of the telephone directory)
  AMBULATORIO   (doctor's office)
  PRONTO SOCCORSO   (emergency ward, first aid)
  H⎫
  OSPEDALE⎭   (hospital)
- Dial 113 for emergency ambulance service.

What's the matter?

I have a pain here [*point*]	**Ho un dolore qui**
	o oon dol*o*reh quee
I have toothache	**Ho male a un dente**
	o m*a*l-eh ah oon d*e*nteh
I have broken . . .	**Ho rotto . . .**
	o r*o*t-to . . .
my dentures	**la dentiera**
	la dentee-*ai*ra
my glasses	**gli occhiali**
	l-y*ee* oc-kee-*a*l-ee

I have lost . . .	**Ho perso . . .**
	o p*ai*rso . . .
my contact lenses	**le lenti a contatto**
	leh l*e*ntee ah cont*a*t-to
a filling	**un'otturazione**
	oonot-too-ratz*io*neh
My child is ill	**Mio/a figlio/a è ammalato/a***
	mee-o/ah f*ee*l-yo/ah eh am-mal*a*t-o/ah

Already under treatment for something else?

I take . . . regularly [*show*]	**Prendo regolarmente . . .**
	pr*e*ndo regolarment*e*h . . .
this medicine	**questa medicina**
	qu*e*sta medich*ee*na
these pills	**queste pillole**
	qu*e*steh p*ee*l-loleh
I have . . .	**Ho . . .**
	o . . .
a heart condition	**mal di cuore**
	mal dee cw*o*reh
haemorrhoids	**le emorroidi**
	leh em-orr*o*ydee
rheumatism	**i reumatismi**
	ee reh-oomat*i*smee
I'm . . .	**Sono . . .**
	s*o*nno . . .
diabetic	**diabetico/a***
	dee-ab*e*t-eeco/a
asthmatic	**asmatico/a***
	azm*a*t-eeco/a
pregnant	**incinta**
	eench*ee*nta
allergic to (penicillin)	**allergico/a* alla (penicillina)**
	al-l*ai*rjeeco/ah al-la (penich*ee*l-l*ee*na)

*For men and boys use '**o**', for women and girls use '**a**'.

Problems: loss, theft

ESSENTIAL INFORMATION

- If worse comes to worst, find the police station. To ask the way, see p. 219.
- Look for:
  CARABINIERI ⎤   (police)
  POLIZIA   ⎦
  VIGILI URBANI   (traffic wardens)
  QUESTURA   (police station)
- If you lose your passport go to your country's nearest consulate.
- In an emergency, dial 113 for fire and police.

LOSS

[*See also 'Theft' below; the lists are interchangeable*]

I have lost . . .	**Ho perso . . .**
	o p*ai*rso . . .
my camera	**la macchina fotografica**
	la m*ac*-keena fotograf-eeca
my car keys	**le chiavi della macchina**
	leh kee-*ah*v-ee del-la m*ac*-keena
my car registration	**il libretto della macchina**
	il libr*et*-to del-la m*ac*-keena
my driver's license	**la patente**
	la pat*ent*eh
my insurance certificate	**il certificato dell'assicurazione**
	il chairtee-fic*at*-o del-las-sicoo-ratz*i*oneh

THEFT

Someone has stolen . . .	**Qualcuno mi ha rubato . . .**
	qualc*oo*no mee ah roob*at*-o . . .
my car	**la macchina**
	la m*ac*-keena
my money	**i soldi**
	ee s*o*ldee

Someone has stolen . . .   **Qualcuno mi ha rubato . . .**
                                      qualc*oo*no mee ah roob*a*t-o . . .

   my tickets   **i biglietti**
                                      ee beel-y*e*t-tee

   my travellers' cheques   **i travellers cheques**
                                      ee travellairs sh*e*ck

   my wallet   **il portafoglio**
                                      il portafol-yo

   my luggage   **i bagagli**
                                      ee bag*a*l-yee

The post office and phoning home

ESSENTIAL INFORMATION

- Key words to look for:
  POSTA
  POSTE E TELEGRAFI (PT)
  POSTE-TELECOMUNICAZIONI (PTT)
- It is best to buy stamps at the tobacco shop. Only go to the post office for more complicated transactions, like telegrams.
- Unless you read and speak Italian well, it's best not to make telephone calls by yourself. Go to the main post office and write the town and number you want on a piece of paper.
- To call the UK on a direct-dial telephone (**TELESELEZIONE**) dial the code 0044 then the number (less any initial 0).
- For the USA you call the international operator (**ITALCABLE**); dial 170.

WHAT TO SAY

To England, please   **Per l'Inghilterra, per favore**
                                      pair ling-eelt*ai*rra pair fav-*o*reh

[*Hand letters, cards or parcels over the counter*]
To Australia   **Per l'Australia**
                                      pair la-oostr*a*l-ya

To the United States   **Per gli Stati Uniti**
                                      pair l-yee st*a*t-ee oon*ee*tee

I'd like to send a telegram	**Vorrei spedire un telegramma** vorr*ay* sped-*ee*reh oon telegr*a*m-ma
I'd like this number . . . [*show number*]	**Vorrei questo numero . . .** vorr*ay* questo n*oo*mero . . .
in England	**in Inghilterra** in ing-eelt*ai*rra
in Canada	**in Canada** in c*a*nada
Can you dial it for me, please?	**Può farmi il numero, per favore?** poo-*o* f*a*rmee il n*oo*mero pair fav-*o*reh

---

Cashing checks and changing money

ESSENTIAL INFORMATION

- Look for these words on buildings:
BANCA **BANCO** **ISTITUTO BANCARIO** **CASSA DI RISPARMIO**	(bank)
CAMBIO-VALUTE	(exchange bureau)
- To cash checks, exactly as at home use your bank card where you see the Eurocheque sign. Write in English.
- Have your passport handy.

WHAT TO SAY

I'd like to cash . . .	**Vorrei incassare . . .** vorr*ay* incas-s*a*r-eh . . .
these travellers' cheques	**questi travellers cheques** qu*e*stee travell*ai*rs sh*e*ck
this cheque	**questo assegno** qu*e*sto as-s*e*n-yo

I'd like to change this . . .	**Vorrei cambiare questi soldi . . .**
	vorray cambi-ar-eh questee soldee . . .
into Italian lira	**in lire italiane**
	in leereh italian-eh
into Austrian schillings	**in scellini austriaci**
	in shel-leenee ah-oostree-achee
into French francs	**in franchi francesi**
	in frankee franchez-ee
into Swiss francs	**in franchi svizzeri**
	in frankee zveet-tzeree

Car travel

ESSENTIAL INFORMATION

- Is it a self-service station? Look out for **SELF SERVICE.**
- Grades of gasoline:

BENZINA NORMALE	(regular)
BENZINA SUPER	(premium)
GASOLIO	(diesel)

- 1 gallon is about 3¾ liters.
- For car repairs, look for:

AUTORIPARAZIONI	(repairs)
AUTORIMESSA	(garage)
MECCANICO	(mechanic)
ELETTRAUTO	(for electrical repairs)
CARROZZERIA	(for bodywork)

- Gas stations are usually closed from 12 to 3, and very few offer 24-hour service (except on highways).
- In case of a breakdown or an emergency look for the **ACI** (Italian Automobile Club) sign, or dial 116 from any public telephone.

WHAT TO SAY

[*For numbers see p. 264*]

(Nine) litres of . . .	**(Nove) litri di . . .** (nov-eh) leetree dee . . .
(2000) lira of . . .	**(Duemila) lire di . . .** (dooeh meela) leereh dee . . .
standard/premium/diesel	**normale/super/gasolio** normal-eh/sooper/gazol-yo
Full, please	**Pieno, per favore** pee-ehno, pair fav-oreh
Will you check . . .	**Può controllare . . .** poo-o control-lar-eh . . .
the oil?	**l'olio?** lol-yo
the battery?	**la batteria?** la bat-teree-ah
the radiator?	**il radiatore?** il rad-yatoreh
the tyres?	**le gomme?** leh gom-meh
I've run out of petrol	**Sono rimasta senza benzina** sonno reemas-ta sentza bendzeena
Can you help me, please?	**Mi può aiutare, per favore?** mee poo-o ayootar-eh pair fav-oreh
Do you do repairs?	**Ripara le macchine?** reepar-ah leh mac-keeneh
I have a puncture	**Ho una gomma a terra** o oona gom-ma ah terra
I have a broken windscreen	**Ho rotto il parabrezza** o rot-to il parabret-tza
I think the problem is here . . . [*point*]	**Penso che il guasto sia qui . . .** penso keh il goo-asto see-ah quee . . .

LIKELY REACTIONS

I don't do repairs	**Non riparo auto** non reepar-o ah-ooto

Where's your car?	**Dov'è la sua macchina?**
	dov-*eh* la soo-ah m*a*c-keena
What make is it?	**Che tipo di macchina è?**
	keh t*ee*po dee m*a*c-keena eh
Come back tomorrow/on	**Ritorni domani/lunedí**
Monday	reet*o*rnee dom*a*n-ee/loon-ed*ee*

[*For days of the week see p. 266*]

Public transport

ESSENTIAL INFORMATION

- Key words on signs

BIGLIETTI	(tickets)
BINARIO	(platform)
DEPOSITO BAGAGLI	(left luggage)
ENTRATA	(entrance)
FERMATA AUTOBUS	(bus stop)
FS, FERROVIE DELLO STATO	(Italian railways)
INFORMAZIONI	(information)
ORARIO	(timetable)
PROIBITO-VIETATO	(forbidden)
SALITA	(entrance for buses and trams)
USCITA	(exit)

- In the main cities automatic ticket systems are in operation on buses, trams and the underground. Tickets must be bought in advance from bars and tobacco shops. Ask for details at the local tourist information offices.

WHAT TO SAY

Where does the train for (Rome) leave from?	**Da dove parte il treno per (Roma)?**
	da d*o*v-eh p*a*rteh il tr*e*n-o pair (r*o*ma)
Is this the train for (Rome)?	**È questo il treno per (Roma)?**
	eh qu*e*sto il tr*e*n-o pair (r*o*ma)

Where does the bus for (Florence) leave from?	**Da dove parte l'autobus per (Firenze)?**
	da dov-eh parteh la-ootoboos pair (feerentzeh)
Is this the bus for (Florence)?	**È questo l'autobus per (Firenze)?**
	eh questo la-ootoboos pair (feerentzeh)
Do I have to change?	**Devo cambiare?**
	dev-o cambee-ar-eh
Can you put me off at the right stop, please?	**Può farmi scendere alla fermata giusta, per favore?**
	poo-o farmee shendereh al-la fairmat-ah joosta pair fav-oreh
Where can I get a taxi?	**Dove posso trovare un taxi?**
	dov-eh pos-so trovar-eh oon taxi
Can I book a seat?	**Posso prenotare un posto?**
	pos-so prenotar-eh oon posto
A single	**Solo andata**
	solo andat-ah
A return	**Andata e ritorno**
	andat-ah eh reetorno
First class	**Prima classe**
	preema clas-seh
Second class	**Seconda classe**
	seconda clas-seh
One adult	**Un adulto**
	oon adoolto
Two adults	**Due adulti**
	dooeh adooltee
and one child	**e un bambino**
	eh oon bambeeno
and two children	**e due bambini**
	eh dooeh bambeenee
How much is it?	**Quanto costa?**
	quanto costa

Reference

NUMBERS

0	**zero**	dzairo
1	**uno**	oono
2	**due**	dooeh
3	**tre**	treh
4	**quattro**	quaat-tro
5	**cinque**	chinqueh
6	**sei**	say
7	**sette**	set-teh
8	**otto**	ot-to
9	**nove**	noveh
10	**dieci**	dee-echee
11	**undici**	oondeechee
12	**dodici**	dodeechee
13	**tredici**	trehdeechee
14	**quattordici**	quat-tordeechee
15	**quindici**	quindeechee
16	**sedici**	sehdeechee
17	**diciassette**	deechas-set-teh
18	**diciotto**	deechot-to
19	**diciannove**	deechan-noveh
20	**venti**	ventee
21	**ventuno**	ven-toono
22	**ventidue**	ventee-dooeh
23	**ventitré**	ventee-treh
24	**ventiquattro**	ventee-quat-tro
25	**venticinque**	ventee-chinqueh
26	**ventisei**	ventee-say
27	**ventisette**	ventee-set-teh
28	**ventotto**	ventot-to
29	**ventinove**	ventee-noveh
30	**trenta**	trenta

For numbers beyond 20 follow the pattern of **venti**: *keep the final vowel except with one and eight.*

31	**trentuno**	tren-toono
35	**trentacinque**	trenta-chinqueh

38	**trentotto**	trent*o*t-to
40	**quaranta**	quar*a*nta
41	**quarantuno**	quarant-*oo*no
45	**quarantacinque**	quaranta-ch*i*nqueh
48	**quarantotto**	quarant*o*t-to
50	**cinquanta**	chinqu*a*nta
55	**cinquantacinque**	chinquanta-ch*i*nqueh
60	**sessanta**	ses-s*a*nta
65	**sessantacinque**	ses-santa-ch*i*nqueh
70	**settanta**	set-t*a*nta
80	**ottanta**	ot-t*a*nta
90	**novanta**	nov*a*nta
100	**cento**	ch*e*nto
101	**centouno**	chento-*oo*no
102	**centodue**	chento-d*oo*eh
125	**centoventicinque**	chentoventee-ch*i*nqueh
150	**centocinquanta**	chento-chin-qu*a*nta
175	**centosettantacinque**	chentoset-tanta-ch*i*nqueh
200	**duecento**	d*oo*eh-ch*e*nto
300	**trecento**	treh-ch*e*nto
400	**quattrocento**	quat-tro-ch*e*nto
500	**cinquecento**	chinqueh-ch*e*nto
1000	**mille**	m*ee*l-leh
1500	**millecinquecento**	meel-leh-chinqueh-ch*e*nto
2000	**duemila**	dooeh-m*ee*la
5000	**cinquemila**	chinqueh-m*ee*la
10,000	**diecimila**	dee-echee-m*ee*la
100,000	**centomila**	chento-m*ee*la
1,000,000	**un milione**	oon meel-y*o*neh

TIME

What time is it?	**Che ora è?**
	keh ora *e*h
It's one o'clock	**È l'una**
	eh l*oo*na
It's . . .	**Sono . . .**
	s*o*nno . . .
two o'clock	**le due**
	leh d*oo*eh
three o'clock	**le tre**
	leh tr*e*h

266/Reference: **Days and months**

It's . . .

  a quarter past five

  half past five

  a quarter to six

It's . . .

  noon

  midnight

Sono . . .
sonno . . .
le cinque e un quarto
leh chinqueh eh oon quaarto
le cinque e mezza
keh chinqueh eh med-dza
le sei meno un quarto
leh say men-o oon quaarto
È . . .
eh . . .
mezzogiorno
med-dzojorno
mezzanotte
med-dzanot-teh

DAYS AND MONTHS

Monday	**lunedí**
	loon-edee
Tuesday	**martedí**
	mart-edee
Wednesday	**mercoledí**
	maircol-edee
Thursday	**giovedí**
	jov-edee
Friday	**venerdí**
	venairdee
Saturday	**sabato**
	sabato
Sunday	**domenica**
	domen-eecca
January	**gennaio**
	jen-nah-yo
February	**febbraio**
	feb-brah-yo
March	**marzo**
	martzo
April	**aprile**
	apreeleh
May	**maggio**
	mad-jo

June	**giugno**
	j**oo**n-yo
July	**luglio**
	l**oo**l-yo
August	**agosto**
	ag**o**sto
September	**settembre**
	set-t**e**mbreh
October	**ottobre**
	ot-t**o**breh
November	**novembre**
	nov**e**mbreh
December	**dicembre**
	deech**e**mbreh

Public holidays

● On these holidays offices, shops and schools are closed.

1 January	⎡ **Primo dell'anno**	New Year's Day
	⎣ **Capodanno**	
. . .	**Lunedí dell'Angelo**	Easter Monday
25 April	**Anniversario della**	Liberation Day
	Liberazione	
1 May	**Festa dei Lavoratori**	Labour Day
15 August	**Assunzione**	Assumption
1 November	⎡ **Tutti i Santi**	All Saints Day
	⎣ **I Morti**	
8 December	**Immacolata**	Immaculate
	Concezione	Conception
25 December	**Natale**	Christmas
26 December	**Santo Stefano**	Boxing Day

Index

Portuguese

D. L. Ellis, K. Sandeman McLaughlin

Pronunciation **Dr J. Baldwin**

Useful address
Portuguese National Tourist Office
548 5th Ave.
New York, NY 10036

Contents

Reference

Pronunciation hints

In Portuguese, it is important to stress or emphasize the syllables in *italics*, just as you would if we were to take as an English example: Little Jack Horner sat in the corner. Here we have ten syllables but only four stresses.
Boa sorte!

Everyday expressions

[See also 'Shop talk', p. 287]

Hello	**Olá**
	ol*a*h
Good morning ⎤	**Bom dia**
Good day ⎦	bom d*ee*-a
Good afternoon	**Boa tarde**
	b*o*a tard
Good night	**Boa noite**
	b*o*a noyt
Goodbye	**Adeus**
	ad*eh*-oosh
Yes	**Sim**
	seem
Please	**Por favor**
	poor fav*o*r
Yes, please	**Sim, por favor**
	seem poor fav*o*r
Thank you	**Obrigado/a***
	obreeg*a*h-doo/a
Thank you very much	**Muito obrigado/a***
	moo-*ee*too obreeg*a*h-doo/a
That's right	**Exactamente**
	eez*a*tam*e*nt
No	**Não**
	nown
No thanks	**Não obrigado/a***
	nown obreeg*a*h-doo/a
I disagree	**Não concordo**
	nown concordoo
Excuse me ⎤	**Desculpe**
Sorry ⎦	deshc*oo*lp
It doesn't matter	**Não faz mal**
	nown f*a*sh mal
Where's the toilet, please?	**Onde é a casa de banho, por favor?**
	awnd *e*h ah c*a*h-za der b*a*in-yoo poor fav*o*r

*First alternative for men, second for women

Do you speak English?	**Fala inglês?**
	fah-la eenglesh
What is your name?	**Como se chama?**
	comoo ser shah-ma
My name is . . .	**Chamo-me . . .**
	shamoo-meh . . .

Asking the way

ESSENTIAL INFORMATION

- Keep a look out for all these place names as you will find them on shops, maps and notices.

WHAT TO SAY

Excuse me, please	**Com licença, por favor**
	com leesen-sa poor favor
How do I get . . .	**Para ir . . .**
	para eer . . .
to Lisbon?	**a Lisboa?**
	ah leeshboo-a
to Rua Augusta?	**à Rua Augusta?**
	ah roo-a ah-oogooshta
to the (hotel) Ritz?	**ao (hotel) Ritz?**
	ah-oo (otel) reetz
to the airport?	**ao aeroporto?**
	ah-oo airoh-portoo
to the beach?	**à praia?**
	ah prah-ya
to the bus station?	**à estação de camionetas?**
	ah shtassown der cam-yoonet-ash
to the market?	**ao mercado?**
	ah-oo maircah-doo
to the police station?	**à esquadra?**
	ah shkwah-dra
to the port?	**ao porto?**
	ah-oo portoo

to the post office?	**aos correios?**
	ah-oosh cooray-oosh
to the railway station?	**à estação (de comboios)?**
	ah shtassown (der comboy-oosh)
to the sports stadium?	**ao estádio desportivo?**
	ah-oo shtah-dee-oo deshpoorteevoo
to the tourist information office?	**ao centro de informações turísticas?**
	ah-oo sentroo der eenfoor-massoynsh tooreesh-teecash
to the town centre?	**ao centro (da cidade)?**
	ah-oo sentroo da seedad
to the town hall?	**à câmara municipal?**
	ah camera mooneeseepal
Is there . . . near by?	**Há . . . aqui perto?**
	ah . . . akee pairtoo
a baker's	**uma padaria**
	ooma padayree-a
a bank	**um banco**
	oom bancoo
a bar	**um bar**
	oom bar
a bus stop	**uma paragem de autocarros**
	ooma parajaim der ah-ootoh-carroosh
a butcher's	**um talho**
	oom tal-yoo
a café	**um café**
	oom cafeh
a cake shop	**uma pastelaria**
	ooma pashtelaree-a
a campsite	**um parque de campismo**
	oom park der campeej-moo
a car park	**um parking**
	oom parking
a change bureau	**um banco com câmbio**
	oom bancoo com cambee-oo
a chemist's	**uma farmácia**
	ooma farmah-see-a
a delicatessen	**uma charcutaria**
	ooma sharcootaree-a
a dentist's	**um dentista**
	oom denteeshta

Is there . . . near by? **Há . . . aqui perto?**
ah . . . ak*ee* p*air*too

a department store **um armazém**
oom armaz*ai*m

a disco **uma discoteca**
*oo*ma deesh-cooteh-ca

a doctor's surgery **um consultório médico**
oom consooltoree-oo m*e*dicoo

a dry-cleaner's **uma tinturaria**
*oo*ma teentooraree-a

a fishmonger's **uma peixaria**
*oo*ma paysharee-a

a garage (for repairs) **uma garagem**
*oo*ma gar*a*jaim

a greengrocer's **uma frutaria**
*oo*ma frootaree-a

a grocer's **uma mercearia**
*oo*ma mersee-ar*ee*-a

a hairdresser's **um cabeleireiro**
oom cab-el-ay-r*a*yroo

a hospital **um hospital**
oom oshpeet*a*l

a hotel **um hotel**
oom ot*e*l

an ice-cream parlour **uma gelataria**
*oo*ma jelataree-a

a laundry **uma lavandaria**
*oo*ma lavandar*ee*-a

a newsagent's **uma papelaria**
*oo*ma papelar*ee*-a

a night club **uma 'boîte'**
*oo*ma boo-*a*t

a park **um parque**
oom p*a*rk

a petrol station **uma bomba de gasolina**
*oo*ma *b*omba der gazool*ee*na

a post box **uma caixa do correio**
*oo*ma k*a*h-eesha doo coor*a*yoo

a public toilet **uma casa de banho pública**
*oo*ma c*a*h-za der b*a*in-yoo p*oo*blica

a restaurant **um restaurante**
oom resht*a*h-oorant

a supermarket	**um supermercado**
	oom supermaircah-doo
a taxi stand	**um parque de taxis**
	oom park der taxeesh
a telephone	**uma cabine telefónica**
	ooma cah-been telefoneeca
a tobacconist's	**uma tabacaria**
	ooma tabacaree-a
a travel agent's	**uma agência de viagens**
	ooma ajensia der vee-ajainsh
a youth hostel	**uma pousada de juventude**
	ooma pawssah-da der jooventood

DIRECTIONS

Left/right	**Esquerda/direita**
	shkairda/derrayta
Straight on	**Sempre em frente**
	sempr aim frent
There	**Ali**
	alee
First left/right	**Primeira à esquerda/direita**
	preemayra ah shkairda/deerayta
Second left/right	**Segunda à esquerda/direita**
	segoonda ah shkairda/deerayta

Accommodation

ESSENTIAL INFORMATION

Hotel

- If you want hotel-type accommodation, all the following words in capital letters are worth looking for on signs:
  HOTEL
  MOTEL
  PENSÃO (boarding house)
  ESTALAGEM (quality inn)
  POUSADA (state-owned inns often housed in historic buildings)

Remember that:

- A list of hotels in the town or district can usually be obtained from the local tourist information office.
- Unlisted hotels are usually cheaper and probably almost as good as listed hotels.
- Not all hotels provide meals, apart from breakfast. (**A PENSÃO** always provides meals.)
- The cost is displayed in the room itself, so you can check it when having a look around before agreeing to stay.
- The displayed cost is for the room itself, per night and not per person.
- Breakfast usually consists of strong coffee with milk, or tea with no milk unless otherwise requested, fresh bread or croissants, butter and jam.
- On arrival, you will be asked to complete a registration document and the receptionist will want to see your passport.
- Tip porters, waiters and chambermaids.
- The Directorate-General for Tourism publishes a *Tourist Accommodation Guide* which contains all the basic information on hotel establishments and tourist developments and apartments.

WHAT TO SAY

I have a booking	**Tenho uma reserva** tain-yoo *oo*ma rezairva
Have you any vacancies, please?	**Tem quartos livres, por favor?** taim kwartoosh leevresh poor favor
Can I book a room?	**Posso reservar um quarto?** possoo rezairvar oom kwartoo
It's for . . .	**É para . . .** eh para . . .
one adult/one person	**um adulto/uma pessoa** oom adooltoo/*oo*ma psaw-a
two adults/two people	**dois adultos/duas pessoas** doysh adooltoosh/doo-ash psaw-ash
and one child	**e uma criança** ee *oo*ma cree-anssa
and two children	**e duas crianças** ee doo-ash cree-anssash

It's for . . .	**É para . . .** eh para . . .
one night	**uma noite** ooma noyt
two nights	**duas noites** doo-ash noytsh
one week	**uma semana** ooma semah-na
two weeks	**duas semanas** doo-ash semah-nash
I would like . . .	**Queria . . .** keree-a . . .
a room	**um quarto** oom kwartoo
two rooms	**dois quartos** doysh kwartoosh
with a single bed	**com uma cama singela** com ooma cah-ma seenjela
with two single beds	**com duas camas separadas** com doo-ash cah-mash separah-dash
with a double bed	**com uma cama de casal** com ooma cah-ma der cazal
with a toilet	**com retrete** com retret
with a bathroom	**com casa de banho** com cah-za der bain-yoo
with a shower	**com duche** com doosh
with a cot	**com uma cama de bébé** com ooma cah-ma der beh-beh
with a balcony	**com varanda** com varanda
I would like . . .	**Queria . . .** keree-a . . .
full board	**pensão completa** pensown completa
half board	**meia pensão** may-a pensown
bed and breakfast	**dormida e pequeno almoço** doormeeda ee pekenoo almawssoo

Do you serve meals?	**Servem refeições?**
	s*a*irvaim refay-s*o*ynsh
Can I look at the room?	**Posso ver o quarto?**
	p*o*ssoo vair oo kw*a*rtoo
OK. I'll take it	**Está bem. Fico com ele**
	sht*a*h baim f*ee*coo com el
No thanks, I won't take it	**Não obrigado/a, não o quero***
	nown obreeg*a*h-doo/a nown o k*e*h-roo
The bill, please	**A conta, por favor**
	a c*o*nta poor fav*o*r
Is service included?	**O serviço está incluído?**
	oo serv*ee*ssoo sht*a*h eencloo-*ee*doo
I think this is wrong	**Acho que isto está errado**
	*a*shoo ker *ee*shtoo sht*a*h err*a*h-doo
Can you give me a receipt?	**Pode-me dar um recibo?**
	pod-meh d*a*r oom res*ee*boo

Camping

- Be prepared to have to pay:
  per person
  for the car (if applicable)
  for the tent or for trailer space
  for electricity
  for hot showers

- You must provide proof of identity, such as your passport. In some parks it is necessary to show a camper's card or license, issued by a national or international organization that is officially recognized.
- City-run sites are recommended.
- There are a number of limitations regarding camping off-site – check with the tourist office in New York before departure.
- There are also a series of campsites with the **ORBITUR** sign – these provide bath, camping and bungalow facilities.
- Most of Portugal's campsites are situated along the coast – those inland are few and far between.

*First alternative for men, second for women

Youth hostels

- Look for the sign:
  POUSADA DE JUVENTUDE
- You must provide your own sleeping bag.
- You must have a YHA card.
- The charge for the night is the same for all ages, but some hostels are dearer than others.
- There are very few youth hostels in Portugal, and those that do exist provide dormitory accommodation. Few provide accommodation for girls. Cooking facilities are limited.

WHAT TO SAY

Have you any vacancies?	**Tem espaço?** taim shp*a*ssoo
How much is it . . .	**Quanto custa . . .** kw*a*ntoo c*oo*shta . . .
for the tent?	**pela tenda?** pla t*e*nda
for the caravan?	**pela roulotte?** pla rool*o*t
for the car?	**pelo carro?** ploo c*a*rroo
for the electricity?	**pela electricidade?** pla eletreeseed*a*d
per person?	**por pessoa?** poor ps*a*w-a
per day/night?	**por dia/noite?** poor d*ee*-a/noyt
May I look round?	**Posso ver?** p*o*sso v*ai*r
Do you provide anything . . .	**Fornecem alguma coisa . . .** foorn*e*ssaim alg*oo*ma c*o*yza . . .
to eat?	**para comer?** p*a*ra coom*ai*r
to drink?	**para beber?** p*a*ra beb*ai*r
Do you have . . .	**Têm . . .** t*ay*-aim . . .
a bar?	**um bar?** oom bar

Do you have . . .

Têm . . .
tay-aim . . .

   hot showers?

   duches quentes?
   dooshesh kentsh

   a kitchen?

   uma cozinha?
   ooma coozeen-ya

   a laundry?

   uma lavandaria?
   ooma lavandaree-a

   a restaurant?

   um restaurante?
   oom reshtah-oorant

   a shop?

   uma loja?
   ooma loja

   a swimming pool?

   uma piscina?
   ooma peesh-seena

   a takeaway?

   comida preparada?
   coomeeda preparahda

[*For food shopping, see p. 289, and for eating and drinking out, see p. 299*]

Problems

The toilet	**A retrete** *a retret*
The shower	**O duche** *oo doosh*
The tap	**A torneira** *a toornayra*
The razor point	**A ficha de barbear** *a feesha der barbee-ar*
The light	**A luz** *a loosh*
. . . is not working	**. . . não funciona** *. . . nown foonsee-awna*
My camping gas has run out	**O gaz do meu fogão gastou-se** *oo gash doo meh-oo foogown gashtaw-ser*

LIKELY REACTIONS

Have you an identity document?	**Tem um documento de identificação?** *taim oom doocoomentoo der eedenteefeeca-sown*

Your membership card, please	**O seu cartão de membro, por favor**
	oo seh-oo cartown der mehm-broo poor favor
What's your name? [see p. 274]	**Como se chama?**
	comoo ser shah-ma
Sorry, we're full	**Desculpe, estamos cheios**
	deshcoolp shtamoosh shay-oosh
How many people is it for?	**Para quantas pessoas é?**
	para kwantash psaw-ash eh
How many nights is it for?	**Para quantas noites é?**
	para kwantash noytsh eh
It's (50) escudos . . .	**São (cinquenta) escudos . . .**
	sown (seenkwenta) shkoodoosh . . .
per day/per night	**por dia/por noite**
	poor dee-a/poor noyt
I haven't any rooms left	**Não tenho mais quartos**
	nown tain-yoo mah-eesh kwartoosh
Do you want to have a look?	**Quer ver?**
	kair vair

General shopping

The drugstore/The chemist's

ESSENTIAL INFORMATION

- Look for the word **FARMÁCIA** (drugstore) or these signs: a cross or an 'H'.
- Medicines (drugs) are available only at a drugstore.
- Some non-drugs can be bought at a supermarket or department store.
- Normal opening times are 9.00 a.m. to 1.00 p.m. and 3.00 p.m. to 7.00 p.m. From January to November, shops close at 1.00 p.m. on Saturday.

284/General shopping: **The drugstore/The chemist's**

- If a drugstore is shut the address of a nearby pharmacist on duty should be pinned on the door; if not, ask for the nearest **PRIMEIROS SOCORROS** (first aid center). There may be an extra charge if after midnight (approx. 20%).
- Try a pharmacist before going to the doctor's as they are usually qualified to treat minor ailments.
- If you don't have insurance you'll have to pay the full rate. Keep receipts and packaging for the insurance claims.
- Some toiletries can also be bought at a **DROGARIA**.

WHAT TO SAY

I'd like . . . please	**Queria . . . por favor**
	ker*ee*-a . . .poor fav*o*r
some Alka Seltzer	**Alka Seltzer**
	alka seltzer
some antiseptic	**antiséptico**
	antees*e*ticoo
some aspirin	**aspirinas**
	aspeer*ee*nash
some baby food	**comida para bébé**
	coom*ee*da p*a*ra beh-beh
some contraceptives	**contraceptivos**
	contrasept*ee*voosh
some cotton	**algodão**
	algood*ow*n
some disposable diapers	**fraldas de papel**
	fr*a*l-dash der pap*e*l
some eye drops	**pingos para os olhos**
	p*ee*ngoosh p*a*ra oosh *o*l-yoosh
some inhalant	**inalador**
	eenalad*o*r
some insect repellent	**repelente de insectos**
	repel*e*nt der eens*e*toosh
some paper tissues	**lenços de papel**
	lens*oo*sh der pap*e*l
some sanitary napkins	**pensos higiénicos**
	p*e*nssoosh eegee-*e*n-eecoosh
some sticking plaster	**adesivo**
	ad-es*ee*voo
some suntan lotion/oil	**loção/óleo para bronzear**
	loss*ow*n/*o*lee-oo p*a*ra brawnzee-*a*r

some Tampax	**Tampax**
	t*a*mpax
some throat lozenges	**pastilhas para a garganta**
	pash*teel*-yash p*a*ra ah garg*a*nta
some toilet paper	**papel higiénico**
	pap*e*l eegee-*e*n-eecoo
I'd like something for . . .	**Queria alguma coisa para . . .**
	ker*ee*-a alg*oo*ma c*o*yza p*a*ra . . .
bites/stings	**mordidelas**
	moordeed*e*l-ash
burns/scalds	**queimaduras**
	cay-mad*oo*rash
a cold	**constipação**
	consh-teepass*ow*n
constipation	**prisão de ventre**
	preez*ow*n der v*e*ntr
a cough	**tosse**
	toss
diarrhoea	**diarreia**
	dee-arr*a*y-a
earache	**dor de ouvidos**
	d*o*r der awv*ee*doosh
flu	**gripe**
	greep
sore gums	**gengivas doridas**
	janj*ee*vash door*ee*dash
sunburn	**queimadura do sol**
	cay-mad*oo*ra doo s*o*l
toothache	**dor de dentes**
	d*o*r der d*e*ntsh
travel sickness	**enjoo de viagem**
	enj*a*w-oo der vee-*a*jaim

[*For other essential expressions, see 'Shop talk', p. 287*]

Holiday items

ESSENTIAL INFORMATION

● Places to shop at and signs to look for:
PAPELARIA-LIVRARIA (stationery store/bookshop)
FOTOGRAFIA (film)
and of course the main department stores:
GRANDELLA
ARMAZÉNS DO CHIADO

WHAT TO SAY

I'd like . . .	**Queria . . .** ker*ee*-a . . .
a bag	**um saco** oom s*a*c-oo
a beach ball	**uma bola de praia** *oo*ma b*o*l-a der pr*a*h-ya
a bucket	**um balde** oom b*a*hld
an English newspaper	**um jornal inglês** oom joorn*a*l eengl*e*sh
some envelopes	**envelopes** ainvel*o*psh
some postcards	**postais** poosht*a*h-eesh
a spade	**uma pá** *oo*ma p*a*
a straw hat	**um chapéu de palha** oom shap*e*h-oo der p*a*l-ya
some sunglasses	**óculos de sol** *o*cooloosh der s*o*l
some writing paper	**pepel de escrever** pap*e*l der shkrev*ai*r
a roll of color film [*show the camera*]	**um filme a côres** oom feelm ah c*a*wresh
a roll of black and white film	**um filme a preto e branco** oom feelm ah pr*e*t-oo ee br*a*ncoo

Shop talk

ESSENTIAL INFORMATION

• Know how to say the important weights and measures:

50 grams	**cinquenta gramas**
	seenkwenta gram-ash
100 grams	**cem gramas**
	saim gram-ash
200 grams	**duzentas gramas**
	doozent-ash gram-ash
½ kilo	**meio quilo**
	may-oo keeloo
1 kilo	**um quilo**
	oom keeloo
2 kilos	**dois quilos**
	doysh keeloosh
½ litre	**meio litro**
	may-oo leetroo
1 litre	**um litro**
	oom leetroo
2 litres	**dois litros**
	doysh leetroosh

[*For numbers, see p. 316*]

CUSTOMER

I'm just looking	**Estou só a ver**
	shtaw soh ah vair
How much is this/that?	**Quanto custa isto/aquilo?**
	kwantoo cooshta eeshtoo/akeeloo
What is that?	**O que é aquilo?**
	oo ker eh akeeloo
What are those?	**O que são aqueles?**
	oo ker sown akel-esh
Is there a discount?	**Faz desconto?**
	fash desh-cawntoo
I'd like that, please	**Queria aquilo, por favor**
	keree-a akeeloo poor favor

Not that	**Esse não**
	*e*hsse nown
Like that	**Como aquele**
	c*o*moo ak*e*l
That's enough, thank you	**Chega obrigado/a***
	sh*e*g-a obreeg*a*h-doo/a
More, please	**Mais, por favor**
	m*a*h-eesh poor fav*o*r
Less	**Menos**
	m*e*n-oosh
That's fine	**Está bem**
	shtah baim
OK	**OK**
	*o*h kay
I won't take it, thank you	**Não quero, obrigado/a***
	nown k*e*roo obreeg*a*h-doo/a
It's not right	**Não está certo**
	nown shtah s*a*irtoo
Have you got something . . .	**Tem alguma coisa . . .**
	taim alg*oo*ma c*o*yza . . .
better?	**melhor?**
	mel-y*o*r
cheaper?	**mais barata?**
	m*a*h-eesh bar*a*ta
different?	**diferente?**
	deefer*e*nt
larger?/smaller?	**maior?/mais pequena?**
	ma-y*o*r/m*a*h-eesh pek*e*na
Can I have a bag, please?	**Posso ter um saco, por favor?**
	p*o*sso tair oom s*a*c-oo poor fav*o*r
Can I have a receipt?	**Posso ter um recibo, por favor?**
	p*o*sso tair oom res*ee*boo poor favor
Do you take . . .	**Aceita . . .**
	as*a*yta . . .
English/American money?	**dinheiro inglês/americano?**
	deen-y*a*yroo eenglesh/americ*a*noo
travellers' cheques?	**cheques de viagem?**
	sh*e*h-ksh der vee-*a*jaim
credit cards?	**cartões de crédito?**
	cart*o*ynsh der cr*e*deetoo

*First alternative for men, second for women.

SHOP ASSISTANT

Can I help you?	**Deseja alguma coisa?**
	dezay-ja algooma coyza
What would you like?	**Que quer?**
	ker kair
Will that be all?	**Não é mais nada?**
	nown eh mah-eesh nah-da
Is that all?	**É tudo?**
	eh toodoo
Anything else?	**Mais alguma coisa?**
	mah-eesh algooma coyza
Would you like it wrapped?	**Quer embrulhado?**
	kair embrool-yah-doo
Sorry, none left	**Desculpe, está esgotado**
	deshcoolp shtah esh-gootah-doo
I haven't got any	**Não tenho**
	nown tain-yoo
I haven't got any more	**Não tenho mais**
	nown tain-yoo mah-eesh
How many do you want?	**Quantos quer?**
	kwantoosh kair
How much do you want?	**Quanto quer?**
	kwantoo kair
Is that enough?	**Chega?**
	sheg-a

Shopping for food

Bread

ESSENTIAL INFORMATION

- Key words to look for: **PADARIA** (bakery) **PADEIRO** (baker) **PÃO** (bread)
- Bakeries will open weekdays from 7.30 a.m. – 12.30 p.m. and from 5.30 p.m. – 8.00 p.m. They also open on Saturday mornings.

- The most characteristic bread is a small individual bread roll called **papo seco** which is sold by item.
- For any other type of loaf, say **um pão** (oom pown), and point.

WHAT TO SAY

A loaf (like that)	**Um pão de forma (assim)** oom pown deh forma (asseem)
A home-made loaf	**Um pão caseiro** oom pown cazay-roo
A French loaf	**Um cacete** oom cah-set
A bread roll	**Um papo seco** oom pap-oo sec-oo
A crescent roll	**Um croissant** oom croo-ahssan
Two loaves	**Dois pães de forma** doysh pa-eensh der forma
A sliced loaf	**Um pão às fatias** oom pown ash fatee-ash
A wholemeal loaf	**Um pão integral** oom pown eenteh-gral

[*For other essential expressions, see 'Shop talk' p. 287*]

Cakes and ice cream

ESSENTIAL INFORMATION

- Key words to look for:
  PASTELARIA (cake shop)
  CAFÉ (a place where cakes and sandwiches can be bought to be eaten on the premises or taken away – alcoholic drinks are also served)
  PADEIRO (baker – some also sell fresh cakes)
  GELADOS (ice cream)
  GELATARIA (ice-cream parlour)
  CONFEITARIA (candy shop)
  PASTELARIA (cake shop)

- **CASA DE CHÁ** (a tea shop usually open during the afternoon)

WHAT TO SAY

The types of cakes you find in shops vary from region to region but the following are the most common:

bola de Berlim	doughnut
bol-a der berl*ee*n	
duchesse	cream-filled choux pastry
doosh*e*z	
pastel de nata	custard tart
pasht*e*l der n*a*h-ta	
bolo de côco	coconut tart
b*a*wloo der c*a*wcoo	
pão de ló	sponge
p*o*wn der l*o*h	
queque	cupcake
kek	
palmier	flat, crispy pastry biscuit
palm*ee*-eh	
mil folhas	crispy pastry with fresh cream filling – mille feuilles
meel f*a*wl-yash	
suspiro	meringue (bought by weight)
soosp*ee*roo	
tarte de amêndoa	almond tart
tart der am*a*indoo-a	
bolo de noz	walnut cake
b*a*wloo der noj	
petits fours	petits fours (bought by weight)
pet*ee* foor	
queijadas de sintra	individual cheesecakes
cay-j*a*-dash der sh*i*ntra	
fios de ovos	
f*ee*-oosh der *o*voosh	very sweet, egg-based confectionery
ovos moles	
*o*voosh m*o*lesh	

A . . . ice cream, please	**Um gelado . . . por favor**
	oom gel*a*h-doo . . . poor fav*o*r
almond	**de amêndoa**
	der amaind*oo*-a

A . . . ice cream, please	**Um gelado . . . por favor**
	oom gel*ah*-doo . . . poor fav*o*r
banana	**de banana**
	der ban*a*na
chocolate	**de chocolate**
	der shookool*a*t
strawberry	**de morango**
	der moor*a*ngoo
vanilla	**de baunilha**
	der b*a*h-oon*ee*l-ya
A (ten-escudo) cone	**Um cone de (dez escudos)**
	oom con der (desh shk*oo*doosh)

Picnic food

ESSENTIAL INFORMATION

● Key words to look for:
 CHARCUTARIA (delicatessen)
 MERCEARIA (grocery)

WHAT TO SAY

Two slices of . . .	**Duas fatias de . . .**
	d*oo*-ash fat*ee*-ash der . . .
ham	**fiambre**
	fee-*a*mbr
roast pork	**carne de porco assada**
	carn der p*o*rcoo ass*ah*-da
spam	**mortadela**
	moortad*e*la
salami	**salame**
	sal*a*mee
meaty garlic sausage	**paio**
	pah-*ee*-oo
(parma) ham	**presunto**
	prez*oo*ntoo

tongue	**língua**
	leengwa

You might also like to try some of these:

salada de feijão frade	black-eyed bean salad
salah-da der fay-jown frad	
croquetes	tiny meat rolls
croketsh	
pastéis de bacalhau	cod in batter
pashtaysh der bacal-yah-oo	
rissóis de camarão	shrimp rissoles
rissoysh der camarown	
chouriço	garlic sausage
shawreesso	
chouriço de carne	beefy garlic sausage
shawreessoo der carn	
pastéis de massa folhada/de carne/de peixe	meat/fish vol-au-vent
pashtaysh der massa fool-yah-da/der carn/der paysh	
panados de galinha	chicken pieces in breadcrumbs
panah-dosh der galeen-ya	
salsichas	sausages
salseeshash	
linguiça	very thin sausage
leengoo-eessa	
farinheira	floury pork sausage
fareen-yay-ra	
tremoços	lupin seeds (served with beer in **cervejarias**)
tremossosh	
pevides	dried and salted pumpkin seeds
peveedsh	
castanhas assadas	roast chestnuts
cashtan-yash assah-dash	
favas fritas	fried broad beans (served up as cocktail 'nibbles')
favash freetash	
queijo fresco	fresh goat's cheese (unsalted)
cay-joo freshcoo	
requeijão	fresh sheep's cheese
recay-jown	
queijo da serra	tasty full-fat cheese
cay-joo da serra	

queijo das Ilhas	strong hard cheese (like Cheddar)
c*a*y-joo dash *ee*l-yash	
queijo de Serpa	melting cheese (delicacy of the
c*a*y-joo der s*a*irpa	town of Serpa)
queijo de Évora	small, round, very hard, dried
c*a*y-joo der *e*voora	cheese
ovos cozidos	hard boiled eggs
*o*voosh cooz*ee*doosh	
almôndegas	meatballs
alm*a*wndeegash	
empadas de galinha/marisco	chicken/shellfish pies
aimp*a*h-dash der gal*ee*n-ya/	
mar*ee*sh-coo	
frango no churrasco	chicken on the spit (spicy)
fr*a*ngoo noo shoorr*a*sh-coo	
ovos verdes	hard-boiled eggs with yolks
*o*voosh v*a*irdesh	mashed with parsley
arroz doce	sweet rice with lemon peel and
*a*rrawsh daws	cinnamon
pudim molotoff	egg-white pudding with caramel
p*oo*dim molot*o*f	sauce

[*For other essential expressions, see 'Shop talk', p. 287*]

Fruit and vegetables

ESSENTIAL INFORMATION

- Key words to look for:
  FRUTA (fruit)
  FRUTARIA (fruit store)
  LEGUMES (vegetables)
  FRESCO (an indication of freshness)

WHAT TO SAY

1 kilo of . . .	**Um quilo de . . .**
	oom k*ee*loo der . . .
apples	**maçãs**
	mas*a*nsh

apricots	**alperces**
	alp*air*ssesh
bananas	**bananas**
	ban*a*nash
cherries	**cerejas**
	ser*ay*-jash
grapes (white/black)	**uvas (brancas/pretas)**
	*oo*vash (br*a*ncash/pr*e*tash)
greengages	**rainhas cláudias**
	ra-*ee*n-yash cl*ou*d-ee-ash
oranges	**laranjas**
	lar*a*njash
peaches	**pêssegos**
	p*eh*-segoosh
pears	**pêras**
	p*e*rash
plums	**ameixas**
	am*ay*-shash
strawberries	**morangos**
	moor*a*ngoosh
A pineapple, please	**Um ananás . . . por favor**
	oom anan*a*sh poor fav*o*r
A grapefruit	**Uma toranja**
	*oo*ma toor*a*nja
A melon	**Um melão**
	oom mel*ow*n
A water melon	**Uma melancia**
	*oo*ma melans*ee*-a
½ kilo of . . .	**Meio quilo de . . .**
	m*ay*-oo k*ee*loo der . . .
artichokes	**alcahofras**
	alkash*oh*-frash
broad beans	**favas**
	f*a*v-ash
carrots	**cenouras**
	sen*a*wrash
green beans	**feijão verde**
	fay-j*o*wn vaird
leeks	**alhos franceses**
	*a*l-yoosh frans*e*s-esh
mushrooms	**cogumelos**
	coogoom*e*l-oosh

½ kilo of . . .	**Meio quilo de . . .**
	m*ay*-oo k*ee*loo der . . .
onions	**cebolas**
	seb*aw*lash
peas	**ervilhas**
	airv*ee*l-yash
potatoes	**batatas**
	bat*a*tash
shallots	**chalotas**
	shal*o*-tash
spinach	**espinafre**
	shpeen*a*fr
tomatoes	**tomates**
	toom*a*tsh
A bunch of . . .	**Um molho de . . .**
	oom m*aw*l-yoo der . . .
parsley	**salsa**
	s*a*lsa
radishes	**rabanetes**
	raban*e*tsh
A head of garlic	**Uma cabeça de alho**
	*oo*ma cab*eh*-sa der *a*l-yoo
A lettuce	**Uma alface**
	*oo*ma alf*a*ss
A cucumber	**Um pepino**
	oom pep*ee*noo
A turnip	**Um nabo**
	oom nab*oo*
Like that, please	**Assim, por favor**
	ass*ee*m poor fav*o*r

Meat and fish

ESSENTIAL INFORMATION

- Key words to look for:
  TALHO (butcher shop)
  PEIXARIA (fish store)
  PEIXE (fish)

- Fresh fish can be bought at the market or at the fish auctions (**lotas**) held on the fishing beaches. It can occasionally be found in the larger supermarkets too.

WHAT TO SAY

For roasts, choose the type of meat and then say how many people it is for:

Some beef, please	**Carne de vaca, por favor**
	carn der vac-a poor favor
Some lamb	**Carne de cordeiro**
	carn der coorday-roo
Some mutton	**Carne de carneiro**
	carn der carnay-roo
Some pork	**Carne de porco**
	carn der porcoo
Some veal	**Carne de vitela**
	carn der veetel-a
A roast . . .	**Uma peça . . .**
	ooma pehsa . . .
for two people	**para duas pessoas**
	para doo-ash psaw-ash
for four people	**para quatro pessoas**
	para kwatroo psaw-ash
for six people	**para seis pessoas**
	para saysh psaw-ash
Some steak, please	**Bifes, por favor**
	beefsh poor favor
Some liver	**Fígado**
	feegadoo
Some kidneys	**Rins**
	reensh
Some sausages	**Salsichas**
	salseeshash
for three people	**para três pessoas**
	para tresh psaw-ash
for five people	**para cinco pessoas**
	para seencoo psaw-ash
Two veal scallops, please	**Dois escalopes de vitela, por favor**
	doysh shcalopsh der veetel-a poor favor

Three pork chops	**Três costoletas de porco**
	tresh cooshtoolet-ash der porcoo
Four mutton chops	**Quatro costoletas de carneiro**
	kwatroo cooshtoolet-ash der carnay-roo
Five lamb chops	**Cinco costoletas de cordeiro**
	seencoo cooshtoolet-ash der coorday-roo
A chicken	**Um frango**
	oom frangoo
A rabbit	**Um coelho**
	oom co-ayl-yoo
A tongue	**Uma língua**
	ooma leengwa

Purchase large fish and small shellfish by the weight:

½ kilo of . . .	**Meio quilo de . . .**
	may-oo keeloo der . . .
cod	**bacalhau**
	bacal-yah-oo
whiting	**pescada**
	pshcah-da
dover sole	**linguado**
	leengwah-doo
sea-bream	**pargo**
	pargoo
shrimps	**camarões**
	camarownsh
prawns	**gambas**
	gambash
mussels	**mexilhões**
	mesheel-yownsh
sardines	**sardinhas**
	sardeen-yash
squid	**lulas**
	loolash
small saurel	**carapau**
	carapah-oo
salmon	**salmão**
	salmown

halibut	**alibute**
	aleeb*oo*t
fresh tuna	**atum**
	at*oo*m

For some shellfish and 'frying pan' fish, specify the number:

A crab, please	**Um caranguejo, por favor**
	oom carang*a*y-joo poor fav*o*r
A lobster	**Uma lagosta**
	*oo*ma lag*a*wshta
A female crab	**Uma santola**
	*oo*ma sant*o*l-a
A big lobster	**Um lavagante**
	oom lavag*a*nt
A trout	**Uma truta**
	*oo*ma tr*oo*ta
A mackerel	**Uma cavala**
	*oo*ma cav*a*l-a
A hake	**Uma garoupa**
	*oo*ma gar*a*wpa

Eating and drinking out

Ordering a drink and a snack

ESSENTIAL INFORMATION

- By law, the price list of drinks (**TARIFAS DE CONSUMO**) must be displayed outside or in the window.
- There is waiter service in all cafés, but you can drink at the bar or counter if you wish – same price, but no service charge.
- Always leave a tip of 10% to 15% unless you see **SERVICO INCLUÍDO** (service included) printed on the bill or on a notice.
- Cafés serve non-alcoholic drinks and alcoholic drinks, and are normally open all day.

- Most cafés and 'beer houses' (**CERVEJARIAS**) also serve reasonably priced snacks and some also have a good à la carte service.
- A number of popular local snacks are often served free with beer/lager: **tremoços** (lupin seeds), **pevides** (salted and dried pumpkin seeds) and **favas ricas** (salted and fried beans).
- It is best to drink Portuguese tea on its own as milk impairs its flavour.

WHAT TO SAY

I'll have . . . please	**Queria . . . por favor** ker*ee*-a . . . poor fav*o*r
a small espresso black coffee	**uma bica** *oo*ma b*ee*ca
a small milky coffee	**um garoto** oom gar*a*wtoo
a diluted black coffee	**um carioca** oom car*ee*-*o*ca
a large milky coffee	**um galão** oom gal*o*wn
a tea	**um chá** oom shah
——with milk	**com leite** com late
with lemon	**com limão** com leem*o*wn
a glass of milk	**um copo de leite** oom k*o*poo der late
two glasses of milk	**dois copos de leite** doysh k*o*poosh der late
a hot chocolate	**um chocolate quente** oom shookool*a*t kent
a mineral water	**uma água mineral** *oo*ma *a*h-gwa meener*a*l
a lemonade (fizzy)	**uma limonada (com gás)** *oo*ma leemoon*a*da (com gash)
an orangeade (fizzy)	**uma laranjada (com gás)** *oo*ma laranj*a*da (com gash)
an orange juice	**um sumo de laranja** oom s*oo*moo der lar*a*nja

a grape juice	**um sumo de uva**
	oom soomoo der oova
a pineapple juice	**um sumo de ananás**
	oom soomoo der ananash
a fruit milkshake	**um batido de fruta**
	oom bateedoo der froota
a lager	**uma cerveja**
	ooma servay-ja
a glass of draught lager	**uma imperial**
	ooma eemperee-al
a pint of draught lager	**uma caneca**
	ooma kaneka
a brown ale	**uma cerveja preta**
	ooma servay-ja preta
I'll have . . . please	**Queria . . . por favor**
	keree-a . . . poor favor
a cheese sandwich	**uma sandes de queijo**
	ooma sandsh der cay-joo
a ham sandwich	**uma sandes de fiambre**
	ooma sandsh der fee-ambr
a cheese and ham sandwich	**uma sandes mista**
	ooma sandsh meeshta

These are some other snacks you may like to try:

uma sandes de paio	a garlic sausage sandwich
ooma sandsh der pah-ee-oo	
um cachorro	a hot dog
oom cashaw-rroo	
um prego	a hot beefsteak roll
oom preg-oo	
uma bifana	a hot pork steak roll
ooma beefana	
uma sandes de presunto	a local parma-type ham sandwich
ooma sandsh der prezoontoo	
um bitoque	a small steak with fried egg and
oom beetoc	chips
um pacote de batatas fritas	a packet of crisps
oom pacot der batatash	
freetash	
uma tosta	a toasted sandwich
ooma tosh-ta	

uma tosta mista
*oo*ma t*o*sh-ta m*ee*shta   cheese and ham toasted sandwich

um chouriço assado
oom shawr*ee*ssoo ass*ah*-doo   a roasted garlic sausage

uma dose de mariscos
*oo*ma d*o*z deh mar*ee*sh-coosh   a portion of shellfish

In a restaurant

ESSENTIAL INFORMATION

- You can eat at these places:
  RESTAURANTE
  CAFÉ
  CERVEJARIA (beer house)
  SNACK BAR
  SELF-SERVICE
  ESTALAGEM (quality inn)
  POUSADA (state owned inn)
- By law, the menus must be displayed outside or in the window
  – and that is the *only* way to judge if a place is right for your
  needs.
- Self-service exists, but most places have waiter service.
- Tip approximately 10% unless service is included.
- Half portions (**meia dose**) can be ordered for adults as well as
  children.
- Eating times are flexible – approximately 12.00 p.m. to 3.00 p.m.
  and 7.00 p.m. to 11.00 p.m.

WHAT TO SAY

May I book a table?   **Posso reservar uma mesa?**
                       p*o*ssoo rezairv*a*r *oo*ma m*e*z-a

I've booked a table   **Tenho uma mesa reservada**
                       t*ai*n-yoo *oo*ma m*e*z-a rez*ai*rvah-da

A table . . .   **Uma mesa . . .**
                       *oo*ma m*e*z-a . . .

  for one   **para uma pessoa**
                       para *oo*ma ps*aw*-a

for three	**para três pessoas**
	pa*r*a tresh psaw-ash
The à la carte menu, please	**O menu à la carte, por favor**
	oo mehn*oo* *a*h la cart poor fav*o*r
The fixed-price menu	**O menu de preço fixo**
	oo mehn*oo* de*r* press*oo* feecsoo
The tourist menu	**O menu turístico**
	oo mehn*oo* tooreeshtic*oo*
Today's special menu	**Os pratos do dia**
	oosh pr*a*t-oosh doo d*ee*-a
What's this, please? [*point to menu*]	**O que é isto, por favor?**
	oo ker eh *ee*shtoo poor fav*o*r
The wine list	**A lista das vinhos**
	a leeshta doosh v*ee*n-yoosh
A carafe of wine, please	**Um jarro de vinho, por favor**
	oom j*a*rroo de*r* v*ee*n-yoo poor favor
A half	**Meio jarro**
	m*a*y-oo j*a*rroo
A glass	**Um copo**
	oom c*o*p-oo
A (half) bottle	**Uma (meia) garrafa**
	*oo*ma (m*a*y-a) garr*a*fa
A litre	**Um litro**
	oom l*ee*troo
Red/white/rosé/house wine	**Vinho da casa tinto/branco/rosé**
	v*ee*n-yoo da c*a*h-za t*ee*ntoo/ branc*o*o/rozeh
Some more bread, please	**Mais pão, por favor**
	mah-*ee*sh pown poor fav*o*r
Some more wine	**Mais vinho**
	mah-*ee*sh v*ee*n-yoo
Some oil	**Óleo**
	ol-ee-oo
Some olive oil	**Azeite**
	az*a*yt
Some vinegar	**Vinagre**
	veen*a*gr
Some salt/pepper	**Sal/pimenta**
	sahl/peem*e*nta
Some water	**Água**
	*a*h-gwa

With/without garlic	**Com/sem alho**
	com/saym al-yoo
How much does that come to?	**Quanto é tudo?**
	kwantoo eh toodoo
Is service included?	**Tem serviço incluído?**
	taim serveessoo eencloo-eedoo
Where is the toilet, please?	**A casa de banho, por favor?**
	a cah-za der bain-yoo poor favor
The bill, please	**A conta, por favor**
	a conta poor favor

Key words for courses, as seen on some menus: [*Only ask the question if you want the waiter to remind you of the choice*]

What have you got in the way of . . .	**O que tem de . . .**
	oo ker taim der . . .
starters?	**entradas?**
	entrah-dash
soup?	**sopa?**
	sawpa
egg dishes?	**ovos?**
	ovoosh
fish?	**peixe?**
	paysh
meat?	**carne?**
	carn
game?	**caça?**
	cassa
fowl?	**aves?**
	ahvsh
vegetables?	**legumes?**
	legoomsh
cheese?	**queijo?**
	cay-joo
fruit?	**fruta?**
	froota
ice-cream?	**gelados?**
	gelah-doosh
dessert?	**sobremesa?**
	sawbr-mehza

UNDERSTANDING THE MENU

- You will find the names of the principal ingredients of most dishes on these pages:

  Starters see p. 292   Fruit see p. 294
  Meat see p. 297   Dessert see p. 291
  Fish see p. 298   Cheese see p. 293
  Vegetables see p. 295 Ice-cream see p. 291

- Used together with the following lists of cooking and menu terms, they should help you to decode the menu.

Cooking and menu terms

em açorda	in breadcrumbs (but not fried)
à alentejana	with garlic, clams and coriander
com alho	with garlic
assado	roasted
com azeite	with olive oil
bem passado	well done
na brasa	barbecued
à Bráz	with onions and potatoes in egg
à Bulhão-Pato	with garlic, olive oil and coriander
caldo	broth
na cataplana	cooked on a griddle
no churrasco	on the spit
com coentros	with fresh coriander
cozido	boiled
cozido a vapor	steamed
cru	raw
doce	sweet
de escabeche	marinated
escalfado	poached
à espanhola	with onions and tomato
no espeto	on the spit
estrelado	fried (egg)
estufado	cooked in its own juices
fervido	boiled
no forno	in the oven
frio	cold
frito	fried
fumado	smoked
em geleia	in aspic

à Gomes de Sá	with olives, potatoes and egg
gratinado	au gratin
guisado	stewed
com limão	with lemon
com Madeira	with Madeira
com manteiga	with butter
médio	medium done
meio cru	rare
mexido	scrambled
com molho	with sauce
com molho da casa	with the house sauce
com molho de vinagrete	with vinaigrette sauce
com molho picante	with spicy sauce
ao natural	plain
com ovo a cavalo	with fried egg on top
panado	fried in breadcrumbs
passado por água	blanched
à portuguesa	with tomatoes, onions, olive oil
recheado	stuffed
com salsa	with parsley
salteado	sautéed
com tinta	in its own ink (squid)
com tomate	with tomato
à transmontana	with cabbage

Further words to help you understand the menu

açorda à alentejana	very rich coriander soup with egg and bread
almôndegas	meatballs
ameijoas à Bulhão-Pato	clams in garlic sauce
arroz à portuguesa	vegetable rice
bacalhau	salted dried cod served in numerous ways
bife	steak
borrego	lamb
cabrito	kid
caranguejo	crab
carne de porco à alentejana	pork with clams
carnes frias	cold meats
chispalhada	pigs' trotters stew
chocos com tinta	squid in their own ink

codorniz	quail
coelho guisado	stewed rabbit
dobrada	tripe stew
empadas de galinha	chicken pies
enchidos	garlic sausages
ervilhas guisadas	stewed peas
favas	broad beans
feijoada	bean and sausage stew
fígado	liver
gambas al iajilho	king prawns fried in olive oil with garlic
gaspacho	cold vegetable soup (usually tomato)
linguado	dover sole
lulas	squid
mexilhão	mussels
miolas	brains
pastéis de massa folhada	vol-au-vents
peixe espada	swordfish
peixinhos da horta	runner beans in batter
perdizes	partridges
perna de porco	leg of pork
pombo	pigeon
rins	kidneys
salada de atum	tuna salad
salsichas	sausages
sopa de marisco	shellfish soup
torta	type of Swiss roll sponge with filling
tripas	tripe

Health

ESSENTIAL INFORMATION

● It is *essential* to have proper medical insurance. A policy can be bought through a travel agent, a broker or a motoring organization.

- Take your own first-aid kit with you.
- For minor disorders and treatment at a drugstore, see p. 283.
- For finding your way to a doctor, dentist or drugstore, see p. 276.
- In an emergency, dial 115 for ambulance service.

What's the matter?

I have a pain here [*point*]	**Tenho uma dor aqui** t*ai*n-yoo *oo*ma dor ak*ee*
I have a toothache	**Tenho uma dor de dentes** t*ai*n-yoo *oo*ma dor der d*e*ntsh
I have broken . . .	**Parti . . .** part*ee* . . .
my dentures	**a minha dentadura** ah m*ee*n-ya dentad*oo*ra
my glasses	**os meus óculos** oosh m*e*h-oosh *o*cooloosh
I have lost . . .	**Perdi . . .** perd*ee* . . .
my contact lenses	**as minhas lentes de contacto** ash m*ee*n-yash lentsh der cont*a*ctoo
a filling	**um chumbo** oom sh*oo*mboo
My child is ill	**O meu filho/a minha filha está doente** oo m*e*h-oo f*ee*l-yoo/a m*ee*n-ya f*ee*l-ya shtah doo-*e*nt

Already under treatment for something else?

I take . . . regularly [*show*]	**Tomo . . . regularmente** t*o*moo . . . regoolarm*e*nt
this medicine	**este medicamento** *e*sht medeecam*e*ntoo
these pills	**estes comprimidos** *e*shtsh compreem*ee*doosh
I have . . .	**Sofro . . .** s*a*wfroo . . .
a heart condition	**do coração** doo coorass*ow*n
haemorrhoids	**das hemorroidas** dash em-oorroydash

rheumatism	**de reumático**
	der reh-oomaticoo
I am . . .	**Sou . . .**
	saw . . .
diabetic	**diabético/a***
	dee-abetico/a
asthmatic	**asmático/a***
	ash-maticoo/a
allergic to penicillin	**alérgico/a à penicilina***
	alairjicoo/a ah pehnee-seeleena
I am pregnant	**Estou grávida**
	shtaw grav-eeda

*First alternative for men, second for women.

Problems: loss, theft

ESSENTIAL INFORMATION

- If worse comes to worst, find the police station. To ask the way, see p. 274.
  Look for:
  POLÍCIA
  GNR (Guarda Nacional Republicana – National Guard)
- If you lose your passport go to the nearest U.S. consulate.
- In an emergency, dial 322222 (Fire) or 364141/372131 (Police).

LOSS
[*See also 'Theft' below: the lists are interchangeable*]

I have lost . . .	**Perdi . . .**
	perdee
my camera	**a minha máquina fotográfica**
	ah meenya mac-eena footoografeeca
my car keys	**as chaves do meu carro**
	ash shavsh doo meh-oo carroo
my car registration	**o livrete do meu carro**
	oo leevret doo meh-oo carroo

I have lost . . .	**Perdi . . .**
	perd*ee*
my driving licence	**a minha carta de condução**
	ah m*ee*n-ya c*a*rta der cawndoos*o*wn
my insurance certificate	**o meu certificado de seguro**
	oo m*e*h-oo serteefee-c*a*h-do der seg*oo*roo

THEFT

Someone has stolen . . .	**Roubaram-me . . .**
	rawbar*o*wn meh . . .
my car	**o meu carro**
	oo m*e*h-oo c*a*rroo
my luggage	**a minha bagagem**
	ah m*ee*n-ya bagaj*ai*m
my money	**o meu dinheiro**
	oo m*e*h-oo deen-y*a*y-roo
my purse	**o meu porta-moedas**
	oo m*e*h-oo p*o*rta-m*oo*edash
my tickets	**os meus bilhetes**
	oosh m*e*h-oosh beel-y*e*tsh
my travellers' cheques	**os meus travellers' cheques**
	oosh m*e*h-oosh travellers' sk*e*h-ksh
my wallet	**a minha carteira**
	ah m*ee*n-ya cart*a*y-ra

The post office and phoning home

ESSENTIAL INFORMATION

- Key words to look for:
  CORREIOS
  CTT – CORREIOS, TELEGRAFOS E TELEFONES
- Look for the letters **CTT** on a blue sign.
- Unless you read and speak Portuguese well, it's best not to make phone calls by yourself. Go to a post office and write the town and number you want on a piece of paper.

- For the UK dial 0744 and the number you require.
- For the USA dial 17 and ask the operator for the number you require.
- Tourist information (in English) is available on this number in Lisbon: 706341.

WHAT TO SAY

To England, please	**Para Inglaterra, por favor**
	para eenglatairra poor favor
[Hand letters, cards or parcels over the counter]	
To Australia	**Para a Austrália**
	para a ah-oosh-trahlia
To the United States	**Para os Estados Unidos**
	para oosh shtah-doosh ooneedoosh
I'd like to send a telegram	**Queria enviar um telegrama**
	keree-a envee-ar oom telegrama
I'd like this number . . .	**Queria este número . . .**
[show number]	keree-a esht noomeroo . . .
in England	**na Inglaterra**
	na eenglatairra
in Canada	**no Canadá**
	noo canadah
Can you dial it for me, please?	**Podia-me marcar por favor?**
	poodee-a-meh marcar poor favor

Cashing checks and changing money

ESSENTIAL INFORMATION

- Look for these words on buildings:
  BANCO (bank)
  CRÉDITO
  CÂMBIO-EXCHANGE (exchange bureau)
- To cash checks, exactly as at home, use your bank card where you see the Eurocheque sign.
- Have your passport handy.

WHAT TO SAY

I'd like to cash . . .	**Queria trocar . . .** ker*ee*-a troo*car* . . .
this travellers' cheque	**este cheque de viagem** esht shek de vee-*a*jaim
I'd like to change this . . .	**Queria trocar isto . . .** ker*ee*-a troo*car ee*shtoo . . .
into Portuguese escudos	**por escudos portugues** poor shk*oo*doosh poortoog*e*sh
into French francs	**por francos franceses** poor fr*a*ncoosh frans*ez*-esh
into Spanish pesetas	**por pesetas espanholas** poor pez*et*-ash shpan-y*o*l-ash

Car travel

ESSENTIAL INFORMATION

- Grades of gasoline:
  SUPER
  NORMAL (regular)
  GASÓLEO (diesel)
- 1 gallon is about 3¾ liters.
- Types of garages: Often 'all in one' called **GARAGEM**, but sometimes separate under **BATE CHAPAS** (body repairs); **GARAGEM DE SERVIÇO** (mechanical repairs and service); **REPARAÇÕES ELÉCTRICAS** (for electrical repairs); and **PNEUS** (tires).
- Most garages are open 8.00 a.m. to 12.00 p.m. and 2.00 p.m. to 7.00 p.m. but not Saturdays. If driving inland, remember to fill up as gas stations may be closed or hard to find.

WHAT TO SAY

[*For numbers, see p. 316*]

(9) litres of . . .	**(Nove) litros de . . .**
	(nov) l*e*etroosh der . . .
(200) escudos of . . .	**(Duzentos) escudos de . . .**
	(doozentoosh) shk*oo*doosh der . . .
standard/premium/diesel	**normal/super/gasóleo**
	norm*a*l/s*oo*per/gazol-ee-oo
Fill it up, please	**Pode encher, por favor**
	pod *a*inchair poor fav*o*r
Will you check . . .	**Pode verificar . . .**
	pod vereefeec*a*r . . .
the oil?	**o nível do óleo?**
	oo n*ee*evel doo *o*l-ee-oo
the battery?	**a água da bateria?**
	a *a*h-gwa da bater*ee*-a
the radiator?	**a água do radiador?**
	a *a*h-gwa doo radee-ad*o*r
the tyres?	**a pressão dos pneus?**
	a press*o*wn doosh pn*e*h-oosh
I've run out of petrol	**Acabou-se a gasolina**
	acab*a*w-seh a gazool*ee*na
Can you help me, please?	**Pode ajudar-me, por favor?**
	pod aj*oo*dar-meh poor fav*o*r
Do you do repairs?	**Faz reparações?**
	fash reparas*o*ynsh
I have a puncture	**Tenho um pneu furado**
	t*a*in-yoo oom pneh-oo foor*a*h-doo
I have a broken windscreen	**Tenho o pára-brisas partido**
	t*a*in-yoo oo p*a*ra-br*e*ezash part*ee*doo
I think the problem is here . . . [*point*]	**Penso que o problema está aqui . . .**
	p*e*nsoo ker oo probl*e*ma shtah ak*ee* . . .

LIKELY REACTIONS

I don't do repairs	**Não faço reparações**
	nown f*a*ssoo reparas*o*ynsh

Where is your car? **Onde está o seu carro?**
awnd shtah oo seh-oo carroo

What make is it? **De que marca é?**
der ker marca eh

Come back tomorrow/on **Volte amanhã/na segunda-feira**
Monday volt aman-yan/na segoonda fayra

[*For days of the week, see p. 318*]

Public transport

ESSENTIAL INFORMATION

- Frequent fast electric trains connect Lisbon with the tourist zones of Sintra and Cascais. The **CP** (Portuguese Railways) keep two steam trains in circulation during the high season for tourists.
- Lisbon is serviced by trams, buses and a small subway network. If you are spending a couple of days in the capital, buy a *tourist ticket* at any of the City Transport Company's information booths (they can only be used for surface public transport).
- The Portuguese often do not wait in line to enter buses, trams, etc.
- Booklets of tickets are also available for subway travel – you will have to pay more if you buy each ticket separately.
- Key words on signs:
  BILHETES (tickets)
  ENTRADA (entrance)
  PROIBIDO (forbidden)
  CAIS (platform)
  INFORMAÇÕES (information)
  SAÍDA (exit)
  DEPÓSITO DE BAGAGEM (left-luggage)
  PARAGEM DE AUTOCARRO (bus stop)
  HORÁRIO (timetable)

WHAT TO SAY

Where does the train for (Lisbon) leave from?	**De onde parte o comboio para (Lisboa)?** der awnd part oo comboy-oo para (leeshboo-a)
Is this the train for (Lisbon)?	**É este o comboio para (Lisboa)?** eh esht oo comboy-oo para (leeshboo-a)
Where does the bus for (Coimbra) leave from?	**De onde parte a camioneta para (Coimbra)?** der awnd part a kam-yoonet-a para (coo-eembra)
Is this the bus for (Coimbra)?	**É esta a camioneta para (Coimbra)?** eh eshta a kam-yoonet-a para (coo-eembra)
Do I have to change?	**Tenho que fazer mudança?** tain-yoo ker fazair moodansa
Can you put me off at the right stop, please?	**Pode dizer-me onde devo descer, por favor?** pod deezair-meh awnd devoo desh-sehr poor favor
Where can I get a taxi?	**Onde posso arranjar um taxi?** awnd possoo arranjar oom taxi
Can I book a seat?	**Posso reservar um lugar?** possoo rezervar oom loogar
A single	**Uma ida** ooma eeda
A return	**Uma ida e volta** ooma eeda ee volta
First class	**Em primeira classe** aim preemay-ra klas
Second class	**Em segunda classe** aim segoonda klas
One adult	**Para um adulto** para oom adooltoo
Two adults	**Para dois adultos** para doysh adooltoosh
and one child	**e uma criança** ee ooma cree-ansa
How much is it?	**Quanto custa?** kwantoo cooshta

Reference

NUMBERS

0	**zero**	zeh-roo
1	**um**	oom
2	**dois**	doysh
3	**três**	tresh
4	**quatro**	kwatroo
5	**cinco**	seencoo
6	**seis**	saysh
7	**sete**	set
8	**oito**	oytoo
9	**nove**	nov
10	**dez**	desh
11	**onze**	awnz
12	**doze**	dawz
13	**treze**	trez
14	**catorze**	catorz
15	**quinze**	keenz
16	**dezasseis**	dez-asaysh
17	**dezassete**	dez-aset
18	**dezoito**	dez-oytoo
19	**dezanove**	dez-anov
20	**vinte**	veent
21	**vinte e um**	veent ee oom
22	**vinte e dois**	veent ee doysh
23	**vinte e três**	veent ee tresh
24	**vinte e quatro**	veent ee kwatroo
25	**vinte e cinco**	veent ee seencoo
26	**vinte e seis**	veent ee saysh
27	**vinte e sete**	veent ee set
28	**vinte e oito**	veent ee oytoo
29	**vinte e nove**	veent ee nov
30	**trinta**	treenta
31	**trinta e um**	treenta ee oom
32	**trinta e dois**	treenta ee doysh
33	**trinta e três**	treenta ee tresh
34	**trinta e quatro**	treenta ee kwatroo
35	**trinta e cinco**	treenta ee seencoo

40	**quarenta**	kwarenta
41	**quarenta e um**	kwarenta ee oom
45	**quarenta e cinco**	kwarenta ee seencoo
50	**cinquenta**	seenkwenta
55	**cinquenta e cinco**	seenkwenta ee seencoo
60	**sessenta**	sessenta
66	**sessenta e seis**	sessenta ee saysh
70	**setenta**	set-enta
77	**setenta e sete**	set-enta ee set
80	**oitenta**	oytenta
88	**oitenta e oito**	oytenta ee oytoo
90	**noventa**	nooventa
99	**noventa e nove**	nooventa ee nov
100	**cem**	saim
101	**cento e um**	sentoo ee oom
102	**cento e dois**	sentoo ee doysh
125	**cento e vinte cinco**	sentoo ee veent ee seencoo
150	**cento e cinquenta**	sentoo ee seenkwenta
175	**cento e setenta e cinco**	sentoo ee set-enta ee seencoo
200	**duzentos**	doozentoosh
300	**trezentos**	trez-entoosh
400	**quatrocentos**	kwatrosentoosh
500	**quinhentos**	keen-yentoosh
1,000	**mil**	meel
2,000	**dois mil**	doysh meel
10,000	**dez mil**	desh meel
100,000	**cem mil**	saim meel
1,000,000	**um milhão**	oom meel-yown

TIME

What time is it?	**Que horas são?** ker orash sown	
It's one o'clock	**É uma hora** eh ooma ora	
It's . . .	**São . . .** sown . . .	
two o'clock	**duas horas** doo-ash orash	
three o'clock	**três horas** tresh orash	

It's . . .	É . . .
	eh . . .
noon	**meio-dia**
	m*a*y-oo d*ee*-a
midnight	**meia-noite**
	m*a*y-a noyt
a quarter past five	**cinco e um quarto**
	s*ee*ncoo ee oom kw*a*rtoo
half past five	**cinco e meia**
	s*ee*ncoo ee m*a*y-a
a quarter to six	**um quarto para as seis**
	oom kw*a*rtoo p*a*ra ash saysh

DAYS AND MONTHS

Monday	**segunda-feira**
	seg*oo*nda f*a*yra
Tuesday	**terça-feira**
	t*a*irsa f*a*yra
Wednesday	**quarta-feira**
	kw*a*rta f*a*yra
Thursday	**quinta-feira**
	k*ee*nta f*a*yra
Friday	**sexta-feira**
	s*a*yshta f*a*yra
Saturday	**sábado**
	s*a*b-adoo
Sunday	**domingo**
	doom*ee*ngoo
January	**janeiro**
	jan*a*y-roo
February	**fevereiro**
	fev-er*a*y-roo
March	**março**
	m*a*rsoo
April	**abril**
	abr*ee*l
May	**maio**
	m*a*h-ee-oo
June	**junho**
	j*oo*n-yoo

July	**julho**
	jool-yoo
August	**agosto**
	agawshtoo
September	**setembro**
	set-embroo
October	**outubro**
	awtoobroo
November	**novembro**
	noovembroo
December	**dezembro**
	dez-embroo

Public holidays

● Offices, shops and schools are all closed on the following dates.

1 January	**Ano Novo**	New Year's Day
. . .	**Fexta Feira Santa**	Good Friday
25 April	**Vinte e cinco de Abril**	Freedom Day (date of 1974 revolution)
1 May	**Dia do Trabalhador**	Labour Day
. . .	**Corpo de Deus**	Corpus Christi
10 June	**Dia de Portugal**	National Day
15 August	**Assunção**	Assumption Day
5 October	**Proclamação da Republíca**	Proclamation of the Republic
1 November	**Todos os Santos**	All Saints' Day
1 December	**Restauração da Independência**	Restoration of Independence
8 December	**Imaculada Conceição**	Immaculate Conception
25 December	**Natal**	Christmas Day

Index

Serbo-Croat
for Yugoslavia

D. L. Ellis, E. Spong

Pronunciation **Dr J. Baldwin**

Useful address
Yugoslav National Tourist Office
630 5th Ave. – Ste. 210
New York, NY 10020

Contents

Pronunciation hints

In Serbo-Croat, it is important to stress or emphasize the syllables
in *italics*, just as you would if we were to take as an English example:
Little Jack Horner sat in the corner. Here we have ten syllables but
only four stresses.

For interest, you will find below the characters of the Cyrillic
alphabet which you will probably not need but which is used throughout Yugoslavia – except in Slovenia and Croatia where the Roman
alphabet is in use. The columns on the left show the printed capital
and small letters, and the one on the right the corresponding letter
in the Roman alphabet (as used in this book).

А	а	a	Г	г	g	О	о	o
Б	б	b	Х	х	h	П	п	p
Ц	ц	c	И	и	i	Р	р	r
Ч	ч	č	Ј	ј	j	С	с	s
Ћ	ћ	ć	К	к	k	Ш	ш	š
Д	д	d	Л	л	l	Т	т	t
Џ	џ	dž	Љ	љ	lj	У	у	u
Ђ	ђ	dj	М	м	m	В	в	v
Е	е	e	Н	н	n	З	з	z
Ф	ф	f	Њ	њ	nj	Ж	ж	ž

Dobra zabava!

Everyday expressions

[*See also 'Shop talk', p. 338*]

Hello (informal)	**Zdravo** zdra-fo
Good morning	**Dobro jutro** dob-ro yootro
Good day (hello)	**Dobar dan** dob-ar dun
Good night	**Laku noć** la-koo noch
Goodbye	**Zbogom** zbog-om
Yes	**Da** da
Please	**Molim** mol-im
Yes, please	**Da, Molim** da mol-im
Thank you	**Hvala vam** fa-la vum
Thank you very much	**Puno vam hvala** poono vum fa-la
That's right	**Točno** toch-no
No	**Ne** neh
I disagree	**Ne slažem se** neh sla-shem seh
Excuse me } Sorry }	**Oprostite/pardon** aprost-eet-eh/par-don
It doesn't matter	**Ne smeta** neh smeh-ta
Where's the toilet, please?	**Gdje je toaleta, molim?** gd-yeh twa-leh-ta mol-im
Do you speak English?	**Govorite li engleski?** gov-oree-teh lee en-glesky
What's your name?	**Kako se zovete?** ka-ko seh zov-et-eh
My name is . . .	**Ja se zovem . . .** ya seh zov-em . . .

Asking the way

ESSENTIAL INFORMATION

- Keep a look out for all these place names as you will find them on shops, maps and notices.

WHAT TO SAY

Excuse me, please
Oprostite, molim
oprost-eet-eh mol-im

Which is the way . . .
Koji je put . . .
koyee yeh poot . . .

to Belgrade?
za Beograd?
za beh-ograd

to (Republic) street?
za ulicu (Republike)?
za ooleetsoo (repoob-leekeh)

to the Hotel Lapad?
za Hotel Lapad?
za hotel lap-ad

to the airport?
za aerodrom?
za ah-airodrom

to the beach?
za plažu?
za plash-oo

to the bus station?
za autobusnu stanicu?
za ah-ooto-boosnoo stan-eetsoo

to the market?
za tržnicu?
za ter-shnee-tsoo

to the police station?
za miliciju?
za meel-eets-yoo

to the port?
za luku?
za loo-koo

to the post office?
za poštu?
za posh-too

to the railway station?
za željezničku stanicu?
za shel-yezneech-koo stan-eetsoo

to the sports stadium?
za športski stadion?
za shport-skee stad-ee-on

to the tourist information office?
za turistički ured?
za toorist-eech-kee oo-red

to the town centre?	**za centar grada?**
	za tsen-tar gra-da
to the town hall?	**za gradsku općinu?**
	za grat-skoo op-chee-noo
Excuse me, please	**Oprostite, molim**
	oprost-eet-eh mol-im
Is there . . . near by?	**Ima li ovdje blizu . . .?**
	eema lee ovd-yeh blee-zoo . . .
a baker's	**pekarna**
	pek-arna
a bank	**banka**
	ban-ka
a bus stop	**autobusna stanica**
	ah-ooto-boosna stan-eetsa
a butcher's	**mesarnica**
	mesar-neetsa
a café	**kavana**
	kava-na
a cake shop	**slastičarna**
	slastee-charna
a campsite	**autokamp**
	ah-ooto-kamp
a car park	**parkiralište**
	par-kee-ral-eeshteh
a change bureau	**mjenjačnica**
	m-hyen-yach-neetsa
a chemist's	**apoteka**
	apotek-ah
a concert hall	**dvorana za koncerte**
	dvora-na za kon-tsairteh
a delicatessen	**delikatesna radnja**
	delikates-na radn-ya
a dentist's	**zubar**
	zoobar
a department store	**robna kuća**
	robna koocha
a disco	**disko klub**
	disko cloob
a doctor's surgery	**liječnička ordinacija**
	lee-yech-neechka ordeen-atsee-ya
a dry cleaner's	**kemijska čistiona**
	kem-eeska cheest-yona

Is there . . . near by?   **Ima li ovdje blizu . . .?**
eema lee ovd-yeh blee-zoo . . .

a fishmonger's	**ribarnica**
	reebar-neetsa
a garage (for repairs)	**garaža**
	gara-sha
a hairdresser's	**frizer**
	friz-air
a greengrocer's	**voćarna**
	voch-arna
a grocer's	**dućan mješovite robe**
	doochan m-yesh-oveeteh robeh
a hospital	**bolnica**
	bol-nitsa
a hotel	**hotel**
	hotel
an ice-cream parlour	**slastičarna**
	slasti-charna
a laundry	**praonica**
	pra-on-eetsa
a newsagent's	**prodavaona novina**
	prodava-ona novee-na
a night club	**noćni lokal**
	nochni lok-al
a park	**park**
	park
a petrol station	**benzinska stanica**
	benzeen-ska stan-eetsa
a post box	**poštanski sandučić**
	poshtan-skee sand-oochitch
a restaurant	**restoran**
	rest-oran
a supermarket	**supermarket/robna kuća**
	supermarket/robna koocha
a taxi stand	**stajalište taksija**
	sta-yaleesh-teh tak-see-ya
a telephone	**telefon**
	telephon
a tobacconist's	**trafika**
	traf-eeka
a toilet	**toaleta**
	twa-leh-ta

a travel agent's	**putna agencija**
	pootna agentsee-ya
a youth hostel	**omladinski dom**
	omlad-een-skee dom

DIRECTIONS

Left	**Lijevo**
	lee-yev-o
Right	**Desno**
	desno
Straight on	**Ravno**
	ravno
There	**Tamo**
	tamo
First left/right	**Prva na lijevo/na desno**
	perva na lee-yev-o/na desno
Second left/right	**Druga na lijevo/na desno**
	drooga na lee-yev-o/na desno

Accommodation

ESSENTIAL INFORMATION

Hotel

- If you want hotel-type accommodation, all the following words in capital letters are worth looking for on signs:
  HOTEL
  MOTEL
  PANSION (superior boarding house)
- Houses which rent rooms privately usually have signs in French, English, German or Italian.
  CHAMBRES/ROOMS/ZIMMER/CAMERE
  Remember that:
- A list of hotels in the town or district can usually be obtained at the local tourist information office.
- Hotels are divided into five classes, pensions into three.

- Not all hotels provide meals, apart from breakfast. (A pension always provides meals). However, for stays of more than three days, hotels and pensions have fixed prices which include accommodation, three meals a day and whatever services are available.
- The cost is displayed in the room itself so you can check it when having a look around before agreeing to stay.
- The displayed cost is for the room itself, per night and not per person.
- Breakfast usually consists of coffee, milk, tea or cocoa with rolls or toast, butter and jam or honey.
- On arrival you will be asked to complete a registration document and the receptionist will want to see your passport and travel documents.
- Tipping is not obligatory but 10% is usual.

WHAT TO SAY

I have a booking	**Imam rezervirano**
	*ee*m-am rezair-*veer*-ano
Have you any vacancies, please?	**Imate li praznu sobu, molim?**
	*ee*mat-eh lee pr*a*z-noo s*o*-boo m*o*l-im
Can I book a room?	**Mogu li rezervirati sobu?**
	m*o*g-oo lee rezair-*veer*-atee s*o*-boo
It's for . . .	**To je za . . .**
	toh yeh za . . .
one adult	**jednu osoby**
	yed-noo *o*s-oboo
two adults	**dvije osobu**
	dv*ee*-yeh *o*s-obeh
and one child	**i jedno dijete**
	ee yedno dee-yet-eh
and two children	**i dvoje djece**
	ee dvo-yeh dee-yetseh
It's for . . .	**To je za . . .**
	toh yeh za . . .
one night	**jednu noć**
	yed-noo noch
two nights	**dvije noći**
	dv*ee*-yeh n*o*chee
one week	**jednu sedmicu**
	yed-noo sedmee-tsoo

two weeks	**dvije sedmice**
	dv*ee*-yeh s*e*dmee-tseh
I would like . . .	**Želio/željela* bih . . .**
	sh*e*l-yo/sh*e*l-yel-ah beeh . . .
one room	**jednu sobu**
	y*e*d-noo s*o*-boo
two rooms	**dvije sobe**
	dv*ee*-yeh s*o*-beh
with a single bed	**jednokrevetnu**
	y*e*d-nokr*e*v-et-noo
with two single beds	**dvokrevetnu sa odvojenim krevetima**
	dvo-kr*e*v-et-noo sa odv*o*-yen-eem
	kr*e*v-et-eema
with a double bed	**dvokrevetnu**
	dvo-kr*e*v-et-noo
with a toilet	**sa toaletom**
	sa tw*a*-leh-tom
with a bathroom	**sa kupatilom**
	sa koo-p*a*t-eelom
with a shower	**sa tušom**
	sa t*oo*-shom
with a cot	**sa dječjim krevetom**
	sa dee-y*e*ch-eem kr*e*v-et-om
with a balcony	**sa balkonom**
	sa balk*o*n-om
I would like . . .	**Želio/željela* bih . . .**
	sh*e*l-yo/sh*e*l-yeh-ah beeh . . .
full board	**sa punim pansionom**
	sa p*oo*n-eem pans*ee*-onom
bed and breakfast	**sobu i doručak**
	s*o*-boo ee d*o*roo-chak
Do you serve meals?	**Servirate li jela?**
	s*ai*rv-eerat-eh lee yel-ah
Can I look at the room?	**Mogu li da vidim sobu?**
	m*o*g-oo lee da v*ee*-deem s*o*-boo
OK, I'll take it	**Dobro je, uzeti ću je**
	d*o*bro yeh *oo*z-et-ee ch*oo* yeh
No thanks, I won't take it	**Ne hvala, neću je uzeti**
	neh f*a*-la neh-choo yeh *oo*z-etee

*Men use the first alternative, women the second

The bill, please	**Račun, molim**
	rach-oon mol-im
Is service included?	**Je li servis uračunat?**
	yeh lee sairvis oorach-oonat
I think this is wrong	**Mislim da ovo nije točno**
	meeslim da o-vo nee-yeh toch-no
May I have a receipt?	**Želio/željela* bih priznanicu**
	shel-yo/shel-yeh-ah beeh preeznan-
	eetsoo

*Men use the first alternative, women the second

Camping

- Look for the words: **KAMPING** or **AUTO-CAMP**.
- Be prepared for the following charges
  per person
  for the car (if applicable)
  for the tent or for trailer space
  for electricity
  for hot showers
- You must provide proof of identity, such as your passport.
- All campsites are state owned and state controlled.
- If you wish to camp off-site, you must obtain a permit from the local tourist office or the municipality.
- On some sites, accommodation is also available in chalets.

Youth hostels

- Look for the word: **OMLADINSKI DOM**
- You must have a YHA card.
- Accommodation is usually provided in small dormitories and you should take your own sleeping bag lining with you.
- Food and cooking facilities vary from place to place and you may also have to help with the domestic chores.
- Accommodation is also available in the student hotels to be found in larger towns which are run by **FERIJALNI SAVEZ** (Yugoslav Youth School Organization).
- **NAROMTRAVEL** which specializes in travel and holidays for young people and students in Yugoslavia also runs its own international youth centres in Dubrovnik, Rovinj and Bečići (near Budva).

WHAT TO SAY

Have you any vacancies?	**Imate li mjesta?** *ee*mat-eh lee m-y*e*sta
How much is it . . .	**Koliko je . . .** k*o*l-eeko yeh . . .
for the tent?	**za šator?** za sh*a*-tor
for the caravan (trailer)?	**za karavanu?** za karav*a*noo
for the car?	**za kola?** za k*o*la
for the electricity?	**za struju?** za str*oo*-yoo
per person?	**po osobi?** po *o*s-obee
per day/night?	**na dan/noć?** na d*u*n/n*o*ch
May I look round?	**Mogu li pogledati okolo?** m*o*g-oo lee p*o*gleh-da-tee *o*kolo
Do you provide anything . . .	**Mogu li nabaviti nešto . . .** m*o*g-oo lee n*a*-bav-eetee n*e*sh-to . .
to eat?	**za jesti?** za y*e*s-tee
to drink?	**za piti?** za p*ee*tee
Do you have . . .	**Imate li . . .** *ee*mat-eh lee . . .
a bar?	**bar?** bar
hot showers?	**vrući tuš?** vr*oo*-chee toosh
a kitchen?	**kuhinju?** k*oo*-heen-yoo
a laundry?	**praonicu?** pra-*o*nee-tsoo
a restaurant?	**restoran?** rest-oran
a shop?	**dućan?** d*oo*ch-an
a swimming pool?	**bazen?** b*a*z-en

Do you have . . .   **Imate li . . .**
                 *ee*mat-eh lee . . .

   a takeaway?   **snak-bar?**
                 snack bar

[*For food shopping, see p. 341, and for eating and drinking out, see p. 351*]

Problems

The toilet	**Toaleta**
	tw*a*-leh-ta
The shower	**Tuš**
	to*o*sh
The tap	**Slavina**
	sl*a*v-eena
The electric point	**Utikač**
	*oo*teek-ach
The light	**Svijetlo**
	svee-y*e*tlo
. . . is not working	**. . . ne radi**
	neh r*a*-dee
My camping gas has run out	**Nestalo mi je plina**
	n*e*h-stalo mee yeh pl*ee*-na

LIKELY REACTIONS

Have you an identity document?	**Imate li legitimaciju?**
	*ee*mat-eh lee leg-eetee-m*a*tsee-yoo
Your membership card, please	**Vašu člansku kartu, molim**
	v*a*shoo chl*a*n-skoo k*a*rtoo m*o*l-im
What's your name, please?	**Vaše ime molim?**
[*see p. 325*]	v*a*sheh *ee*meh m*o*l-im
Sorry, we're full	**Žao mi je ali smo puni**
	sh*a*-o mee yeh *ah*-lee smo p*oo*nee
How many people is it for?	**Za koliko osoba?**
	za k*o*l-eeko *o*s-oba
How many nights is it for?	**Za koliko noći?**
	za k*o*l-eeko n*o*chee
It's . . . dinars	**To je . . . dinara**
	toh yeh . . . d*ee*na-ra
per day/per night	**na dan/na noć**
[*For numbers, see p. 368*]	na d*u*n/na n*o*ch

I haven't any rooms left	**Nemam niti jednu sobu praznu**
	neh-mum neetee yed-noo so-boo praz-noo
Do you want to have a look?	**Hoćete li da vidite?**
	hoch-et-eh lee da veed-eet-eh

General shopping

The drugstore/The chemist's

ESSENTIAL INFORMATION

- Look for the words **APOTEKA** or **LJEKARNA**, a large cross or this sign:
- Medicines can also be bought at supermarkets or department stores.
- Try a pharmacist *before* going to a doctor: they are usually qualified to treat minor injuries.
- Drugstores are normally open between 8.00 a.m. and 9.00 p.m. However, some drugstores are open twenty-four hours, look for **DEŽURNA APOTEKA** on the shop door or in the local newspaper.
- Some toiletries can also be bought at a **PARFUMERIJA** but they will be more expensive.

WHAT TO SAY

I'd like . . .	**Želio/željela* bih . . .**
	shel-yo/shel-yel-ah beeh . . .
some Alka Seltzer	**Alku Seltzer**
	alkoo seltzer
some antiseptic	**antiseptičnu mast**
	anti-septeech-noo must
some aspirin	**aspirinu**
	aspee-ree-noo

*Men use the first alternative, women the second

I'd like . . .	**Želio/željela* bih . . .**
	shel-yo/shel-yel-ah beeh . . .
some baby food	**diječija hrana**
	dee-yech-eeya he-rana
some contraceptives	**kontraceptivno sredstvo**
	kontra-tsep-teev-no sret-stvo
some cotton	**vatu**
	va-too
some disposable diapers	**papirne pelene**
	pap-eer-neh pel-en-eh
some eye drops	**kapi za oči**
	kap-ee za ochee
some inhalant	**nešto za udisanje**
	neshto za oodee-san-yeh
some insect repellent	**sredstvo protiv insekata**
	sret-stvo prot-eev insek-ata
some paper tissues	**papirne maramice**
	pap-eer-neh ma-ram-eetseh
some sanitary napkins	**mjesečne uloške**
	m-yesech-neh oolosh-keh
some sticking plaster	**flaster**
	fluster
some suntan lotion/oil	**losion/ulje za sunčanje**
	lotion/ool-yeh za soon-chan-yeh
some Tampax	**Tampax**
	tampax
some throat lozenges	**tablete za grlo**
	tablet-eh za gher-lo
some (soft) toilet paper	**(mekani) toaletni papir**
	(mek-anee) twa-let-nee pap-eer
I'd like something for . . .	**Želio/željela* bih nešto za . . .**
	shel-yo/shel-yel-ah beeh neshtoo
	za . . .
bites	**ubode**
	oobod-eh
burns	**opekotine**
	opek-ot-eeneh
a cold	**nahladu**
	na-hladoo
constipation	**tvrdu stolicu**
	tver-doo stol-eetsoo

*Men use the first alternative, women the second

a cough	**kašalj**
	k*a*sh-eye
diarrhoea	**proljev**
	pr*o*l-yev
earache	**bol uha**
	b*o*hl *oo*ha
flu	**gripu**
	gr*ee*-poo
scalds	**oparenje**
	opar*e*n-yeh
sore gums	**upalu desni**
	*oo*p-aloo d*e*h-snee
stings	**ubode**
	*oo*bod-eh
sunburn	**opeklinu od sunca**
	*o*pek-lee-noo od s*oo*n-tsa
travel sickness	**protiv mučnine**
	pr*o*t-eev m*oo*ch-neen-eh

[*For other essential expressions, see 'Shop talk' p. 338*]

Holiday items

ESSENTIAL INFORMATION

- Places to shop at and signs to look for:
  PAPIRNICA (stationery store)
  KNJIŽARA (bookshop)
  FOTO STUDIO (films)
  and main department stores like: **ROBNA KUĆA**
- If you wish to buy local crafts look for the following sign
  NARODNA RADINOST. These shops, to be found in larger
  towns and tourist resorts, specialize in hand-made embroidery,
  filigree jewellery and ceramics.

WHAT TO SAY

I'd like . . .	**Želio/željela* bih . . .** shel-yo/shel-yel-ah beeh . . .
a bag	**torbu** torboo
a beach ball	**loptu za plažu** lop-too za pla-shoo
a bucket	**kantu** kan-to
an English newspaper	**engleske novine** en-gleskeh nov-eeneh
some envelopes	**koverta** kovair-ta
some postcards	**dopisnica** doh-pees-neetsa
a spade	**lopatu** lop-atoo
a straw hat	**slamnat šešir** slam-nat shesheer
some sunglasses	**naočale za sunce** na-och-al-eh za soon-tseh
some writing paper	**papira za pisanje** papeera za pee-san-yeh
a colour film [*show the camera*]	**film u boji** film oo boyee
a black and white film	**film crno bijeli** film tser-no beeyeh-lee

*Men use the first alternative, women the second

Shop talk

ESSENTIAL INFORMATION

- Know how to say the important weights and measures:
  [*For numbers, see p. 368*]

50 grams	**Pedeset grama** peh-deh-set gra-ma
100 grams	**Sto grama** sto gra-ma

200 grams	**Dvjesta grama**
	dvee-yeh-sta gra-ma
½ kilo	**Pola kila**
	pol-a keela
1 kilo	**Kilo**
	keelo
2 kilos	**Dva kila**
	dva keela
½ litre	**Pola litre**
	pol-a leetreh
1 litre	**Litra**
	leetra
2 litres	**Dvije litre**
	dvee-yeh leetreh

CUSTOMER

I'm just looking	**Samo gledam**
	sa-mo gled-am
How much is this/that?	**Koliko košta ovo/to?**
	kol-eeko koshta ov-o/toh
What is that?	**Što je to?**
	shto yeh toh
What are those?	**Što su te?**
	shto soo teh
Is there a discount?	**Ima li popusta?**
	eema lee pop-oosta
I'd like that, please	**Želio/željela* bih to, molim**
	shel-yo/she-yel-ah beeh toh mol-im
Not that	**Ne to**
	neh toh
Like that	**Onako**
	on-a-ko
That's enough, thank you	**To je dosta, hvala**
	toh yeh dosta fa-la
More please	**Više, molim**
	veesheh mol-im
Less	**Manje od toga**
	man-yeh od tog-a
That's fine	**To je dobro**
	toh yeh dob-ro

*Men use the first alternative, women the second

OK
Dobro je
dob-ro yeh

I won't take it, thank you
Deću to, hvala vam
nech-oo toh fa-la vum

It's not right
Nije točno
nee-yeh toch-no

Have you got something . . .
Imate li nešto . . .
eemat-eh lee neshto . . .

better?
bolje?
bol-yeh

cheaper?
jevtinije?
yeft-een-yeh

different?
različitije?
razleech-eet-yeh

larger?/smaller?
veće?/manje?
veh-cheh/man-yeh

Can I have a bag, please?
Mogu li da dobijem kesicu, molim?
mog-oo lee da dob-ee-yem
kes-eetsoo mol-im

Can I have a receipt?
Mogu li da dobijem priznanicu?
mog-oo lee da dob-ee-yem
preeznan-eetsoo

Do you take . . .
Primate li . . .
preemat-eh lee . . .

English/American money?
engleski/amerikanski novac?
en-gleskee/amerikan-skee nov-ats

travellers' cheques?
putne čekove?
poot-neh check-oveh

credit cards?
kreditne karte?
cred-eetneh karteh

SHOP ASSISTANT

Can I help you?
Mogu li vam pomoći?
mog-oo lee vum pom-ochee

What would you like?
Što želite?
shto shel-eeteh

Is that all?
Je li to sve?
yeh lee toh sveh

Anything else?
Nešto drugo?
neshto droogo

Would you like it wrapped?
Želite li da vam zamotam?
shel-eeteh lee da vum zamot-an

Sorry, none left	**Žao mi je nemamo više**
	sha-o mee yeh nem-amo veesheh
I haven't got any	**Nemam ni jedan**
	nem-am nee yed-an
I haven't got any more	**Nemam više**
	nem-am veesheh
How many do you want?	**Koliko želite?**
	kol-eeko shel-eeteh
Is that enough?	**Je li to dosta?**
	yeh lee toh dosta?

Shopping for food

Bread

ESSENTIAL INFORMATION

- Key words to look for:
  PRODAVAONICA KRUHA
  PEKARNA
  TRGOVINA KRUHA
- Opening times: 7.00/7.30 a.m. – 12.00 p.m. and 5.00 p.m. – 8.00 p.m. Saturday: 7.00/7.30 a.m. to 12.00 p.m.
- The most characteristic type of loaves in Croatia are **pogača** which are large, flat and round. However, the words for the various types of bread differ throughout Yugoslavia and you should be prepared to point to what you want.

WHAT TO SAY

One loaf (like that)	**Jednu pogaču (kao tu)**
	yed-noo pog-achoo (kow too)
A large one	**Veliku**
	vel-eekoo
A small one	**Malu**
	mal-oo
One bread roll	**Jednu rusicu**
	yed-noo roo-see-tsoo

½ kilo of . . .	**Pola kile . . .**
	pol-a keeleh . . .
1 kilo of . . .	**Kilo . . .**
	keelo . . .
white bread	**bijelog kruha**
	bee-yel-og krooha
wholemeal bread	**crnog kruha**
	tser-nog krooha

[*For other essential expressions, see 'Shop talk', p. 338*]

Cakes and ice cream

ESSENTIAL INFORMATION

- Key words to look for:
  SLASTIČARNA (cake shop)
  SLADOLED (ice cream)
- **KAVANA** is a place where cakes can be bought to be eaten on the premises or taken away – alcoholic drinks are also served.
- Ordering a drink and a snack see p. 351.

WHAT TO SAY

The type of cakes you find in the shops varies from region to region but the following are some of the most common.

doboš torta	chocolate layer cake with glazed
doh-bosh torta	sugar topping
hladna krema	custard pie
ladna krem-a	
krafen	doughnut
kraf-en	
krem pita	custard cake
krem peeta	
išler	éclair
eesh-ler	

marcapan	marzipan
marTsapan	
pita od jabuka	apple strudel
peeta od ya-booka	
pita od sira	cheese cake
peeta od seera	
princes krafne	cream doughnut
princes kraf-neh	
trokut	mille feuilles
trok-oot	
šampita	tart with whipped cream and
shampeeta	meringue mixture

A . . . ice cream, please	**Sladoled . . . molim**
	sla-doh-led . . . mol-im
banana	**od banana**
	od banan
chocolate	**ok čokolade**
	od chokola-deh
hazelnut	**od lješnjaka**
	od l-yeh-shen-yaka
raspberry	**od malina**
	od ma-leena
strawberry	**od jagoda**
	od ya-goda
vanilla	**od vanilje**
	od vaneel-yeh
A single	**Jedan**
	yed-an
Two singles	**Dva**
	dva
A double	**Jedan dupli**
	yed-an doop-lee
Two doubles	**Dva dupla**
	dvadoopla
A cone	**Kornet**
	kor-net

[*For other essential expressions, see 'Shop talk', p. 338*]

Picnic food

ESSENTIAL INFORMATION

● Key words to look for:
  DELIKATESNA RADNJA (delicatessen)
  MESARNICA (butcher shop)
  ŽIVEŽNE NAMIRNICE (grocery)

WHAT TO SAY

Two slices of . . .	Dva odreska . . .
	dva od-res-ka . . .
roast beef	**govedjeg pečenja**
	gov-ed-yeg pech-en-ya
roast pork	**svinjskog pečenja**
	sveen-skog pech-en-ya
tongue	**jezika**
	yez-eeka
ham	**šunke**
	shoonkeh
paté	**paštete**
	pash-teh-teh
garlic sausage	**kobasica**
	kobas-eetsah
salami	**salame**
	salam-eh

You might also like to try some of these:

dalmatinski pršut	ham from Dalmatia
dalmat-eenskee per-shoot	
dimljeni sir	smoked cheese
diml-yen-ee seer	
domaće kobasice	homemade sausages
domacheh kobas-eetseh	
domaći sir	local cheese
domachee seer	
jastog	lobster
yast-og	

kajmak	rich soft cheese made from scalded
ka-eemuk	milk
kamenice	oysters
kamen-eetseh	
kranjske kobasice	sausages from Slovenia
kran-yes-keh kobas-eetseh	
kuhana šunka	cooked ham
koohana shoon-ka	
marinirana riba	marinated fish
marin-eerana reeba	
mliječni sir	milk cheese
mlee-yech-nee seer	
pašteta od džigerice	liver paté
pash-teh-ta od jeeg-eritseh	
pašteta od mesa	meat paté
pash-teh-ta od meh-sa	
paški sir	cheese from Pag island
pash-kee seer	
pečena guska	roast goose
pech-ena gooska	
pečena patka	roast duck
pech-ena patka	
pečeno pile	roast chicken
pech-eno peeleh	
pečena teletina	roast veal
pech-ena teh-leh-teena	
pohano meso	fried meat in breadcrumbs
po-hano meh-soh	
pohano pile	fried chicken in breadcrumbs
po-hano peeleh	
punjena jaja	stuffed eggs
poon-yen-ah ya-ya	
sardine	sardines
sardeeneh	
sir sa vrhnjem	curd cheese with sour cream
seer sa verhen-yem	
sušene haringe	smoked herrings
sooshen-eh har-een-gheh	
trapist	ewe's milk cheese (firm and mild)
trap-eest	
tunjevina	tuna fish
toon-yev-eena	

[*For other essential expressions, see 'Shop talk', p. 338*]

Fruit and vegetables

ESSENTIAL INFORMATION

- Key words to look for:
  VOĆE (fruit)
  VOĆARNA (fruit shop)
  POVRĆE (vegetables)
- It is customary for you to choose your own fruit and vegetables at the market (and in some shops) and for the vendor to weigh and price them. You must take your own shopping bag: paper and plastic bags are not normally provided.

WHAT TO SAY

1 kilo of . . .	**Kilo . . .**
	keelo . . .
apples	**jabuka**
	ya-booka
apricots	**marelica**
	mar-el-eetsa
bananas	**banana**
	banana
cherries	**trešanja**
	treshan-ya
figs	**smokve**
	smok-veh
grapes (white/black)	**groždja (bijeloga/crnoga)**
	grosh-ja (bee-yeloga/tsernoga)
oranges	**naranača**
	naran-acha
pears	**krušaka**
	kroosha-ka
peaches	**breskava**
	bresk-ava
plums	**šljiva**
	shl-eeva
strawberries	**jagoda**
	ya-goda
A pineapple, please	**Ananas, molim**
	ananas mol-im

A grapefruit	**Grejpfrut**
	grapefruit
A melon	**Dinju**
	deen-yoo
A water melon	**Lubenicu**
	looben-eetsoo
½ kilo of . . .	**Pola kila . . .**
	pol-a keela . . .
aubergines	**melancane**
	melan-tsaneh
beans	**graha**
	gra-ha
carrots	**mrkve**
	merk-veh
courgettes	**tikvice**
	teek-veetseh
green beans	**mahuna**
	mahoo-na
leeks	**poriluka**
	poreel-ooka
mushrooms	**gljiva**
	gleeva
onions	**luka**
	looka
peas	**graška**
	grashka
potatoes	**krompira**
	kromp-eera
spinach	**spanaća**
	spanacha
tomatoes	**paradajza**
	parada-eeza
A bunch of . . .	**Kitu . . .**
	keetoo . . .
parsley	**peršuna**
	persh-oona
radishes	**rotkvica**
	kot-kvee-tsa
A head of garlic	**Glava češnjaka**
	glava cheshn-ya-ka
A lettuce	**Salata**
	sal-ata

A cucumber	**Krastavac**
	kras-tavats
A turnip	**Repa**
	rep-a
Like that, please	**Tako, molim vas**
	tak-o mol-im vus

[*For other essential information, see 'Shop talk' p. 338*]

Meat and fish

ESSENTIAL INFORMATION

- Key words to look for:
  MESARNICA or **MESNICA** (butcher shop)
  MESAR (butcher shop)
  RIBARNICA (fish store)
- The meat is not displayed in the same way as in the US, nor should you expect to find the same cuts. However, you should tell the butcher whether you intend to boil, grill or roast the meat so that he will know what to give you.
- It is not normal practice in Yugoslavia to fillet fish, and you may find that some fish-store employees will not clean fish, so check beforehand.

WHAT TO SAY

For a roast, choose the type of meat and then say how many people it is for and how you intend to cook it:

Some beef, please	**Komad govedine, molim**
	kom-ad gov-ed-eeneh mol-im
Some lamb	**Komad janjetine**
	kom-ad yan-yet-eeneh
Some mutton	**Komad ovčetine**
	kom-ad ov-chet-eeneh
Some pork	**Komad svinjetine**
	kom-ad sveen-yet-eeneh

Some veal	**Komad teletine**
	kom-ad teh-leh-teeneh
A roast . . .	**Komad . . .**
	kom-ad . . .
for two people	**za dvije osobe**
	za dvee-yeh os-obeh
for four people	**za četiri osobe**
	za chet-eeree os-obeh
for six people	**za šest osoba**
	za shehst os-oba
to boil	**za kuhati**
	za koo-hat-ee
to grill	**za na roštilju**
	za nah rosh-teel-yoo
to roast	**za peći**
	za pech-ee

For steak, liver or kidneys, do as above

Some steak, please	**Biftek, molim**
	beeftek mol-im
Some liver	**Jetre**
	yet-reh
Some kidneys	**Bubrega**
	boob-reg-ah
Some sausages	**Kobasice**
	kobas-eetseh
for three people	**za tri osobe**
	za tree os-obeh
for five people	**za pet osoba**
	za pet os-obah
Two veal scallops, please	**Dvije teleće šnicle, molim**
	dvee-yeh teh-lech-eh shnits-leh mol-im
Three pork chops	**Tri svinjska kotleta**
	tree sveen-ska kot-leh-ta
Four mutton chops	**Četiri ovčja kotleta**
	chet-eeree ov-chee-ya kot-leh-ta
Five lamb chops	**Pet janjećih kotleta**
	peht yan-yech-eeh kot-leh-ta
A chicken	**Pile**
	peeleh

A rabbit	**Kunić**
	koonich
A tongue	**Jezik**
	yez-eek

Purchase large fish and small shellfish by weight:

½ kilo of . . .	**Pola kila . . .**
	pol-a keela . . .
bass	**brancina**
	bran-tseena
carp	**šarana**
	shar-ana
squid	**liganja**
	leegan-ya
cod (dried)	**bakalara**
	bakalar-ah
cod (fresh)	**svježog bakalara**
	svye-shog bakalar-ah
eels	**jegulja**
	yeg-ool-ya
grey mullet	**cipola**
	tseep-ola
lobster	**jastoga**
	yas-tog-ah
mussels	**mušula**
	moosh-oola
oysters	**kamenica**
	kamen-eetsa
prawns	**gambora**
	gambora
red mullet	**barbuna**
	barboona
scampi	**škampija**
	shkam-peea
sole	**listova**
	leestova
pilchards	**sardela**
	sard-ela
salmon	**lososa**
	los-os-a
fresh tuna	**tunjevine**
	toon-jev-eeneh

For some shellfish and 'frying pan' fish, say the name and then
specify the number you want [*For numbers, see p. 368*]

A crab	**Rak**
	rak
A lobster	**Jastog**
	yastog
An ink fish	**Sipa**
	seepa
An octopus	**Hobotnica**
	hob-otneetsah
A sole	**List**
	leest
A trout	**Pastrva**
	past-erva
A mackerel	**Lokarda**
	lok-arda
A herring	**Haringa**
	har-eenga
A pike	**Štuka**
	shtooka
Please can you . . .	**Molim vas možete li . . .**
	mol-im vus mosh-et-eh lee . . .
clean them?	**očistiti ih?**
	ocheest-eetee

Eating and drinking out

Ordering a drink and a snack

ESSENTIAL INFORMATION

- The places to ask for: **KAVANA BIFE BAR**
- By law, the price list of drinks must be displayed outside or in
  the window.
- There is waiter service in all cafés, but you can drink at the bar
  or counter if you wish (cheaper).
- Always leave a tip of 10%–15% of the bill unless you see **SERVIS
  UKLJUČEN** (service included) printed on the bill or on a notice.

- Cafés serve non-alcoholic drinks and alcoholic drinks, and are normally open all day. Children may accompany their parents into bars.
- Local mineral water is available.
- The following list of drinks are all local brandies which you may like to try: **kajsjevača** (apricot brandy), **komovica** (brandy made from grape-pressings), **orahovica** (brandy made from grape pressings with green shells of walnuts in it), **rakija** (brandy from fruit pressings), **šljivovica** (plum brandy).

WHAT TO SAY

I'll have . . .	**Htio/htjela* bih . . .**
	htee-o/ht-yelah beeh . . .
a black coffee	**crnu kavu**
	tser-noo ka-voo
a coffee with cream	**kavu sa šlagom**
	ka-voo sa shlag-om
a tea	**čaj**
	cha-ee
with milk/lemon	**sa mlijekom/limunom**
	sa mlee-yek-om/leemoon-om
a glass of milk	**čašu mlijeka**
	chash-oo mlee-yek-a
two glasses of milk	**dvije čaše mlijeka**
	dvee-yeh chash-eh mlee-yek-a
a hot chocolate	**kakao**
	kaka-o
a mineral water	**mineralnu vodu**
	meenairal-noo vod-oo
a lemonade	**limunadu**
	leemoona-doo
a lemon squash	**sok limuna**
	soak leemoona
an orangeade	**oranžadu**
	oranja-doo
an orange juice	**sok od naranče**
	soak od naran-cheh
a grape juice	**sok od grožđja**
	soak od grosh-ja

*Men use the first alternative, women the second

a pineapple juice	**sok od ananasa**
	soak od ananasa
a small bottle of beer	**malu bocu pive**
	ma-loo botsoo peeveh
I'll have . . . please	**Molim vas htio/htjela* bih . . .**
	molim vus htee-o/ht-yelah beeh . . .
a cheese sandwich	**sendvič od sira**
	send-wich od seera
a ham sandwich	**sendvič od šunke**
	send-wich od shoonkeh
a pancake	**palačinku**
	palach-inkoo
a packet of crisps	**paketić krispsa**
	pack-et-ich krisp-sa

*Men use the first alternative, women the second

These are some other snacks you may like to try:

sendvič od budžole	a pork sausage sandwich – a
send-wich od boojol-eh	speciality
sendvič od čajne kobasice	a sandwich of smoked sausage
send-wich od chaee-neh kobas-eetseh	
sendvič od dalmatinske šunke	a Parma ham sandwich
send-wich od dalmat-eenskeh shoonkeh	
sendvič od Gavrilović salame	a salami sandwich (Gavrilovic is
send-wich od gavril-ovich sala-meh	Yugoslavia's best known salami)
sendvič od gušče pastete	a goose paté sandwich
send-wich od goosh-cheh pash-tet-eh	
sendvič od livanskog sira	a Serbian cheese sandwich
send-wich od leevan-skog seera	
sendvič od mortadele	a mortadella sandwich
send-wich od mortadel-eh	
sendvič od piletine	a chicken sandwich
send-wich od peelet-eeneh	

Chips are not available as snacks. They can only be ordered as part of a meal in a restaurant when you should ask for '**pom frit**'.

In a restaurant

ESSENTIAL INFORMATION

- You can eat at these places:
  RESTORAN
  BIFE
  (light snacks, alcoholic and soft drinks)
  EKSPRES RESTORAN
  (self-service, available only in large towns)
  GOSTIONA
  (modest restaurant)
  KAVANA
  (ice-creams, cakes, tea, coffee and alcoholic drinks)
  MLIJEČNI RESTORAN
  (dairy bar)
  RIBLJI RESTORAN
  (principally for fish dishes)
- By law, the menus must be displayed outside or in the window: and that is the *only* way to judge if a place is right for your needs.
- Self-service restaurants do exist, but most places have waiter service.
- Tipping is not obligatory but even where service is included, it is customary to tip 10% of the bill.
- Children's portions (**POLA PORCIJE**) are not commonly available, but it may be worth asking.
- Eating times are flexible and vary between 12.00 p.m. to 13.00 p.m. and 7.00 p.m. to 11.00 p.m.

WHAT TO SAY

May I book a table?	**Mogu li rezervirati jedan stol?**
	m*o*g-oo lee rezair-*vee*r-atee yed-an stol
I've booked a table	**Imam rezervirani stol**
	*ee*m-um rezair-*vee*r-anee stol
A table . . .	**Stol . . .**
	stol . . .

for one	**za jedno**
	za yed-no
for three	**za troje**
	za troy-eh
The menu, please	**Jelovnik, molim**
	yelov-neek mol-im
The fixed-price menu	**Pansionski jelovnik**
	pansion-skee yelov-neek
The tourist menu	**Turistički jelovnik**
	toorist-ich-kee yelov-neek
Today's special menu	**Današnji specijalni jelovnik**
	dan-ashn-yee spetsial-nee yelov-neek
What's this, please?	**Što je ovo, molim?**
[*point to the menu*]	shto yeh ov-o mol-im
The wine list	**Vinska karta**
	veen-ska karta
A carafe of wine, please	**Bocu vina, molim**
	botsoo veena mol-im
A quarter (25 cc)	**Četvrt litre vina**
	chet-vert leetreh veena
A half (50 cc)	**Pola litre vina**
	pol-a leetreh veena
A glass	**Cašu**
	cha-shoo
A bottle	**Bocu**
	botsoo
A half-bottle	**Pola boce**
	pol-a botseh
A litre	**Litru**
	leet-roo
Red/white/rosé/house wine	**Crnog/bijelog/ružičastog/domaćeg vina**
	tser-nog/bee-yel-og/roosh-ichastog domach-eg veena
Some more bread, please	**Malo više kruha, molim**
	ma-lo veesheh krooha mol-im
Some more wine	**Malo više vina**
	ma-lo veesheh veena
Some oil	**Malo ulja**
	ma-lo ool-ya

Some vinegar	**Malo octa**
	ma-lo ots-ta
Some salt	**Malo soli**
	ma-lo sol-ee
Some pepper	**Malo bibera**
	ma-lo beeb-era
Some water	**Malo vode**
	ma-lo vod-eh
How much does that come to?	**Koliko to košta?**
	kol-eeko to koshta
Is service included?	**Da li je servis uračunat?**
	da lee yeh sair-vis oorach-oonat
Where is the toilet, please?	**Gdje je toaleta, molim?**
	gd-yeh yeh twa-leh-ta mol-im
Miss!/Waiter!	**Gospodjice!/Konobar!**
	gospoj-yeetseh/kon-obar
The bill, please	**Račun, molim**
	rach-oon mol-im

Key words for courses as seen on some menus

[*Only ask this question if you want the waiter to remind you of the choice*]

What have you got in the way of . . .	**Što imate za . . .**
	shto eemat-eh za . . .
starters?	**predjelo?**
	pred-ee-yelo
soup?	**juhu?**
	yoo-hoo
egg dishes?	**jaja?**
	ya-ya
fish?	**ribu?**
	reeboo
meat?	**meso?**
	meh-so
game?	**divljač?**
	deev-leeach
fowl?	**piletinu?**
	peelet-eenoo
vegetables?	**povrće?**
	pov-ercheh

cheese?	**sir?**
	s*ee*r
fruit?	**voće?**
	vo*ch*-eh
ice-cream?	**sladoled?**
	sl*a*-doh-led
dessert?	**dezert?**
	dez*ai*rt

UNDERSTANDING THE MENU

- You will find that most menus in Yugoslavia are in one or more European languages and the names of the various dishes will differ all over the country.
- You will find the names of the principal ingredients of most dishes on these pages:

  Starters see p. 344   Fruit see p. 346
  Meat see p. 348   Dessert see p. 342
  Fish see p. 350   Cheese see p. 345
  Vegetables see p. 347   Ice-cream see p. 343
- Used together with the following list of cooking and menu terms, they should help you to decode the menu.

Cooking and menu terms

banjo marija	bain marie
na dalmatinsku	Dalmatian
dimljeno	smoked
dinstovano	stewed
dobro kuvano ⎤	well done
dobro pečeno ⎦	
faširano	minced
filovano	stuffed
frigano	fried
garnirano	garnished
na gradele	grilled
gusta juha	thick soup
hladno	cold
juha	broth
sa kiselim vrhnjem	with sour cream
kuvano	boiled
kuvano u pari	steamed

na maslu	with butter
meso u hladetini	meat in aspic jelly
minestrun	vegetable soup
mljeveno	ground
sa mušulama	with mussels
pasirano	creamed
u peć	in the oven
pečeno	roast
pirjano (podušeno)	poached
pire	purée
polupečeno	rare
u prosulju	in the frying pan
punjeno	stuffed
na puteru	with butter
prženo	fried
ragu	stew
na ražnju	on the spit
na roštilju	grilled
seckano	diced
slatko/kiselo	sweet/sour
srednje pečeno	medium done
ukiseljeno (meso/riba)	marinated (meat/fish)
u umaku	with sauce
na žaru	grilled on charcoal

Further words to help you understand the menu

bubrezi	kidneys
ćevapčići	kebab of minced meat
djuveč	a vegetable dish of tomatoes with peppers and aubergines, sometimes part of a meat stew – the menu will specify
dvopek u kremi	trifle
faširano meso	minced meat
fazan	pheasant
file steak	fillet steak
gavuni	sprats
girice	small Adriatic fish (sprats)
golub	pigeon
govedje pečenje	roast beef
janjeće pečenje	roast lamb

jarebica	partridge
jetra	liver
jezik	tongue
juha od paradajza	tomato soup
kobasice	sausages
kolač	cake
krezle	sweetbreads
kunić	rabbit
marinirane glijive	marinated mushrooms
mozak	brain
musaka	moussaka: layers of minced meat and sliced aubergines with a topping of eggs and sour milk
omleti	omelets
palačinke	pancakes
patka	duck
piletina na ražnju	chicken on the spit
piletina pržena	fried chicken
piletina pohana	chicken fried in breadcrumbs
punjena jaja	stuffed eggs
punjeni patlidžan	stuffed aubergines
punjeni paradajz	stuffed tomatoes
punjene paprike	stuffed peppers in tomato sauce
punjene tikvice	stuffed courgettes
puran	turkey
razne salate	various salads
razni sladoledi	various ice-creams
ražnjići	pieces of pork/veal on skewers – shish kebab
riblja juha	fish soup
rižot	risotto
salama	salami
sarma	stuffed and pickled cabbage leaves in tomato sauce
škampi na žaru	scampi grilled on charcoal
slanina	bacon
srce	heart
šunka	ham
svinjska glava	pig's head
svinjska kiljenica	pig's trotters
svinjsko pečenje	roast pork
teleće pečenje	roast veal

zelena menestra	green leaf soup with ham
zec (divlji)	hare (wild)
zubatac	a large delicately flavoured fish (dentex)

Health

ESSENTIAL INFORMATION

- Be sure to have medical insurance.
- For minor disorders and treatment at a pharmacy, see p. 335.
- For finding your way to a doctor, dentist and pharmacy, see p. 327.

What's the matter?

I have a pain here [*point*]	**Boli me ovdje** bol-ee meh ovd-yeh
I have toothache	**Boli me zub** bol-ee meh zoob
I have broken . . .	**Slomio/slomila* sam . . .** slom-ee-o/slom-eela sum . . .
my dentures	**moju protezu** moyoo protez-oo
my glasses	**moje naočale** moyeh now-cha-leh
I have lost . . .	**Izgubio/izgubila* sam . . .** *eez*-goobee-o/*eez*-goobee-la sum . . .
my contact lenses	**moja kontaktna stakla** moya contact-na stak-la
a filling	**plombu** plom-boo
My child is ill	**Moje je dijete bolesno** moyeh yeh dee-yet-eh bol-esno

*Men use the first alternative, women the second

Already under treatment for something else?

I take . . . regularly [*show*]	**Uzimum redovito . . .**
	*oo*zee-mum red*ov*-eetoh . . .
this medicine	**ovaj lijek**
	ov-oy lee-y*ek*
these pills	**ove pilule**
	ov-eh p*ee*lool-eh
I have . . .	**Bolujem od . . .**
	b*o*loo-yem od . . .
a heart condition	**srca**
	s*er*-tsa
haemorrhoids	**hemoroida**
	h*em*-oroyda
rheumatism	**reumatizma**
	reh-oomat-*ee*zma
I am . . .	**Ja sam . . .**
	ya sum . . .
diabetic	**dijabetičar**
	dee-*a*-bet-eechar
asthmatic	**astmatičar**
	asm*a*t-eechar
pregnant	**očekujem bebu**
	*o*chek-ooyem b*eb*-oo
I'm allergic to penicillin	**Ja sam alergičan/alergična* na penicilin**
	ya sum *a*lairg-ichan/*a*lairg-ich-na na penitsil-*ee*noo

*Men use the first alternative, women the second

Problems: loss, theft

ESSENTIAL INFORMATION

● If worse comes to worst, find the police station. To ask the way, see p. 326.

- Look for:
  MILICIJA (police)
  SAOBRAĆAJNA MILICIJA (traffic police)
  POGRANIČNA MILICIJA (border police)
  LUČKA KAPETANIJA (port authority)
- If you lose your passport, go to the nearest U.S. consulate.
- In an emergency dial 94 for an ambulance, 93 for the fire brigade and 92 for the police.

LOSS

[*See also 'Theft' below: the lists are interchangeable*]

I have lost . . .	**Izgubio/izgubila sam*** . . .
	eez-goobee-o/*eez*-goobee-la sum . . .
my camera	**moj fotoaparat**
	moy photo-*a*parat
my car keys	**ključeve mojih kola**
	klee-y*oo*ch-eh-veh m*o*yeeh k*o*la
my car registration	**saobraćajnu knijižicu**
	sa-*o*bracha-eenoo kn-y*ee*-shee-tsoo
my driver's license	**moju vozačku dozvolu**
	m*o*y-oo voz*a*ch-koo d*o*z-vol-oo
my insurance certificate	**moju potvrdu osiguranja**
	m*o*y-oo p*o*t-ver-doo oseegoo-r*a*n-yah

THEFT

Someone has stolen . . .	**Ukrali su mi** . . .
	*oo*kra-lee soo mee . . .
my car	**moja kola**
	m*o*ya k*o*la
my money	**moj novac**
	moy n*o*v-ats
my tickets	**moje karte**
	m*o*y-eh k*a*rteh
my travellers' cheques	**moje putne čekove**
	m*o*y-eh p*oo*t-neh ch*e*k-oveh
my wallet	**moj novčanik**
	moy nov-ch*a*n-ik

*Men use the first alternative, women the second

my luggage	**moju prtljagu** m*oy*-oo pertl-*ya*-goo

The post office and phoning home

ESSENTIAL INFORMATION

- Key words to look for **POŠTA, TELEGRAF I TELEFON**
- For stamps look for the word **MARKE** on a post office counter.
- Stamps are also sold at tobacco shops, newsstands, and stationery stores.
- Mail boxes are yellow and fixed to the walls.
- Unless you read and speak Serbo-Croat well, it's best not to make phone calls by yourself. Go to a post office and write the town and number you want on a piece of paper.
- The code for the UK is 9944 followed by the UK subscriber's own telephone number. Calls to the USA have to go through the operator.

WHAT TO SAY

To England, please	**Za Englesku, molim** za *e*n-gles-koo m*o*l-im
[Hand letters, card or parcels over the counter]	
To Australia	**Za Australiju** za *ah*-oostralee-yoo
To the United States	**Za Ameriku** za *a*merik-oo
I'd like to send a telegram	**Želim da pošaljem telegram** sh*e*l-im da p*o*shal-yem t*e*legram
I'd like this number . . . *[show number]*	**Želim ovaj broj . . .** sh*e*l-im *o*v-eey br*o*y . . .
in England	**za Englesku** za *e*n-gles-koo
in Canada	**za Kanadu** za k*a*nadoo
Can you dial it for me, please?	**Možete li vi nazvati za mene, molim?** m*o*sh-et-eh lee vee n*a*z-va-tee za m*e*h-neh m*o*l-im

Cashing checks and changing money

ESSENTIAL INFORMATION

- Look for these words on buildings:
  BANKA (bank)
  MJENJAČNICA (money changed)
  NARODNA BANKA (national bank)
  TURISTIČKA AGENCIJA (most travel agencies will change money)
- Money can also be changed at some post offices. It is illegal to change foreign currency other than in official exchange offices. Avoid all approaches to change money – particularly on trains.
- To cash checks, exactly as at home, use your bank card where you see the Eurocheque sign. Write in English.
- Have your passport handy.

WHAT TO SAY

I'd like to cash . . .	**Želim da promjenim . . .** shel-im da prom-yen-im . . .
these travellers' cheques	**ove putne čekove** ov-eh poot-neh check-oveh
this cheque	**ovaj ček** ov-aee check
I'd like to change this . . .	**Želim da promjenim ovo . . .** shel-im da prom-yen-im ov-o . . .
into dinars	**u dinare** oo deen-areh
into Austrian schillings	**u austrijske šilinge** oo ah-oos-tree-skeh shee-leen-geh
into Hungarian forint	**u madžarske forinte** oo mad-jar-skeh foreen-teh
into Rumanian leu	**u rumunjske leje** oo roomoon-skeh leh-yeh
into Bulgarian lev	**u bugarske leve** oo boogar-skeh lev-eh

into Italian lira	**u talijanske lire**
	oo tal*ee*-yan-skeh l*ee*reh
into Greek drachma	**u grčke drahme**
	oo g*e*rch-keh dr*a*-hmeh
into Albanian lek	**u albanske leke**
	oo *a*lban-skeh l*e*k-eh

Car travel

ESSENTIAL INFORMATION

- Grades of petrol:
  NORMAL (86 octane)
  MJEŠAVINA (mixed)
  SUPER (98 octane)
  NAFTA/DIZL (gas oil/diesel)
- 1 gallon is about 3¾ liters.
- For general repairs, look for the sign
  AUTOMEHANIKA
  Other garages with the proprietor's name in front of the sign
  SERVIS undertake general repair work.
- Opening times: 6.00 a.m. – 12.00 p.m.
- You will find 24-hour service stations along the main roads.
- The Yugoslav Automobile Association (**AMSJ**) runs some 120
  assistance/information centers which are manned by mechanics
  and open between 8.00 a.m. and 8.00 p.m. Some of these stations
  still have individual telephone numbers, but many of them can be
  contacted by dialling 987.
- Members of foreign motor and touring clubs may get free legal
  advice from lawyers associated with the Yugoslav Automobile
  Association (particularly applicable in larger towns).

WHAT TO SAY

[*For numbers, see p. 368*]

(9) litres of . . .	**(Devet) litara . . .**
	d*e*h-vet l*ee*t-ara . . .

(150) dinars of . . .
(Sto pedeset) dinara . . .
sto peh-deh-set deen-ara . . .

standard/premium
normala/supera
normal-ah/sooper-ah

diesel
mješavine/nafte
mee-yesha-veeneh/nafteh

Fill it up, please
Napunite, molim
napoo-neeteh mol-im

Will you check . . .
Molim vas provjerite . . .
mol-im vus prov-yair-eeteh . . .

the oil?
ulje?
ool-yeh

the battery?
akumulator?
akoomoola-tor

the radiator?
radijator?
rad-ya-tor

the tyres?
gume?
goomeh

I've run out of petrol
Ostao sam bez benzine
osta-o sum bez benzeeneh

Can you help me, please?
Možete li mi pomoći, molim vas?
mosh-et-eh lee mee pom-ochee mol-im vus

Do you do repairs?
Da li pravite popravke?
da lee pra-veeteh pop-rav-keh

I have a puncture
Imam probušenu gumu
eem-am pro-booshenoo goomoo

I have a broken windscreen
Imam razbijeno predje staklo
eem-am raz-bee-yen-o pred-yeh staklo

I think the problem is here . . . [point]
Mislim da je problem ovdje . . .
meeslim da yeh problem ovd-yeh . . .

LIKELY REACTIONS

I don't do repairs
Ne vršim popravke
neh ver-sheem poprav-keh

Where is your car?
Gdje su vaša kola?
gd-yeh soo vasha kola

What make is it?
Koja je marka Vaših kola?
koya yeh marka vash-eeh kola

Come back tomorrow/on
  Monday

Povratite se sutra/u ponedjeljak
pov-rat-eeteh seh sootra/oo
  poned-yel-yak

[*For days of the week, p. 371*]

Public transport

ESSENTIAL INFORMATION

- Key words on signs:
  ŽELJEZNIČKA STANICA (railway station)
  PRODAJA KARTA (tickets, ticket office)
  ULAZ (entrance)
  ZABRANJENO JE (forbidden)
  ULAZ (entrance, for buses)
  PERON (platform)
  URED ZA INFORMACIJE (information, information office)
  ČEKAONICA (waiting room)
  ŽTP JŽ (initials for Yugoslav railways)
  IZLAZ (exit)
  GARDEROBA (left luggage)
  AUTOBUSNA STANICA (bus stop)
  RED VOŽNJE (timetable)

WHAT TO SAY

Where does the train for
  (Belgrade) leave from?

Odakle polazi vlak za (Beograd)?
od-akleh pol-azee vlak za
  (beh-ograd)

Is this train for (Belgrade)?

Da li je ovo vlak za (Beograd)?
da lee yeh ov-o vlak za
  (beh-ograd)?

Where does the bus for (Split)
  leave from?

Odakle polazi autobus za (Split)?
od-akleh pol-azee ah-ooto-boos za
  (spleet)?

Is this the bus for (Split)?

Da li je ovo autobus za (Split)?
da lee yeh ov-o ah-ooto-boos za
  (spleet)?

Do I have to change?	**Moram li da presjedim?**	
	mor-am lee da pres-yeh-dim	
Can you put me off at the right stop, please?	**Hoćete li mi reći kad treba da se iskrcam, molim vas?**	
	hoch-et-eh lee mee rech-ee kad treb-ah da seh is-ker-tsam mol-im vus	
Where can I get a taxi?	**Gdje mogu uzeti taksi?**	
	gd-yeh mog-oo oozet-ee taxi?	
Can I book a seat?	**Mogu li rezervirati jedno mjesto?**	
	mog-oo lee rezairv-eer-atee yed-no m-yesto	
A single	**Jednosmjernu kartu**	
	yed-no-smee-yair-noo kartoo	
A return	**Jednu povratnu kartu**	
	yed-noo povrat-noo kartoo	
First class	**Prvi razred**	
	per-vee raz-red	
Second class	**Drugi razred**	
	droo-ghee raz-red	
One adult	**Za jednu osobu**	
	za dvee-yeh os-obeh	
and one child	**i jedno dijete**	
	ee yed-no dee-yet-eh	
and two children	**i dvoje djece**	
	ee dvoyeh dee-yetseh	
How much is it?	**Koliko košta?**	
	kol-eeko koshta	

Reference

NUMBERS

0	**nula**	noolah
1	**jedan**	yed-an
2	**dva**	dva
3	**tri**	tree
4	**četiri**	chet-eeree
5	**pet**	peht
6	**šest**	shehst

7	**sedam**	s*eh*-dam
8	**osam**	*o*sam
9	**devet**	d*eh*-vet
10	**deset**	d*eh*-set
11	**jedanaest**	y*eh*-d*a*-na-est
12	**dvanaest**	dv*ah*-na-est
13	**trinaest**	tr*ee*-na-est
14	**četrnaest**	chet-er-na-est
15	**petnaest**	p*eh*t-na-est
16	**šesnaest**	sh*eh*st-na-est
17	**sedamnaest**	seh-d*a*m-na-est
18	**osamnaest**	o-s*a*m-na-est
19	**devetnaest**	deh-v*e*t-na-est
20	**dvadeset**	dv*a*-deh-set
21	**dvadeset jedan**	dv*a*-deh-set y*e*d-an
22	**dvadeset dva**	dv*a*-deh-set dv*a*
23	**dvadeset tri**	dv*a*-deh-set tr*ee*
24	**dvadeset četiri**	dv*a*-deh-set chet-eeree
25	**dvadeset pet**	dv*a*-deh-set p*eh*t
26	**dvadeset šest**	dv*a*-deh-seh sh*eh*st
27	**dvadeset sedam**	dv*a*-deh-set s*eh*-dam
28	**dvadeset osam**	dv*a*-deh-set *o*-sam
29	**dvadeset devet**	dv*a*-deh-set d*eh*-vet
30	**trideset**	tr*ee*-deh-set
31	**trideset jedan**	tr*ee*-deh-setyed-an
32	**trideset dva**	tr*ee*-des-set dv*a*
40	**četrdeset**	chet-er-d*eh*-set
41	**četrdeset jedan**	chet-er-d*eh*-set y*e*d-an
42	**četrdeset dva**	chet-er-d*eh*-set dv*a*
50	**pedeset**	peh-d*eh*-set
51	**pedeset jedan**	peh-d*eh*-set y*e*d-an
52	**pedeset dva**	peh-d*eh*-set dv*a*
60	**šezdeset**	shehz-d*eh*-set
61	**šezdeset jedan**	shehz-d*eh*-set y*e*d-an
62	**šezdeset dva**	shehz-d*eh*-set dv*a*
70	**sedamdeset**	seh-dam-d*eh*-set
71	**sedamdeset jedan**	seh-dam-d*eh*-set y*e*d-an
72	**sedamdeset dva**	seh-dam-d*eh*-set dv*a*
80	**osamdeset**	o-sam-d*eh*-set
81	**osamdeset jedan**	o-sam-d*eh*-set y*e*d-an
82	**osamdeset dva**	o-sam-d*eh*-set dv*a*
90	**devedeset**	deh-vet-d*eh*-set

91	**devedeset jedan**	deh-vet-deh-set yed-an
92	**devedeset dva**	deh-vet-deh-set dva
100	**sto**	sto
101	**sto jedan**	sto yed-an
110	**sto deset**	sto deh-set
120	**sto dvadeset**	sto dva-deh-set
200	**dvjesta**	dvee-yeh-sta
300	**trista**	tree-sta
400	**cetrsto**	chet-er-sto
500	**petsto**	peht-sto
600	**šesto**	sheh-sto
700	**sedamsto**	seh-dam-sto
800	**osamsto**	o-sam-sto
900	**devetsto**	deh-vet-sto
1,000	**hiljada/tisuća**	heel-ya-da/tees-oocha
2,000	**dvije hiljade**	dvee-yeh heel-ya-deh
3,000	**tri hiljade**	tree heel-ya-deh
10,000	**deset hiljada**	deh-set heel-yada
100,000	**sto hiljada**	sto heel-ya-da
1,000,000	**milijun**	meelee-yoon

TIME

What time is it?	**Koliko je sati?**	
	kol-eeko yeh sa-tee	
It's . . . (this is not translated in Serbo-Croat)		
one o'clock	**jedan sat**	
	yed-an sat	
two o'clock	**dva sata**	
	dva sa-ta	
three o'clock	**tri sata**	
	tree sa-ta	
noon	**podne**	
	pod-neh	
midnight	**ponoć**	
	po-noch	
a quarter past five	**pet i petnaest**	
	peht ee peht-na-est	
half past five	**pola šest**	
	po-la shehst	
a quarter to six	**petnaest do šest**	
	peht-na-est doh shehst	

DAYS AND MONTHS

Monday	**ponedjeljak**
	pon*e*d-yel-yak
Tuesday	**utorak**
	*oo*to-rak
Wednesday	**srijeda**
	sree-y*e*da
Thursday	**četvrtak**
	chet-v*e*r-tak
Friday	**petak**
	p*e*h-tak
Saturday	**subota**
	s*oo*-bota
Sunday	**nedjelja**
	n*e*d-yel-ya
January	**januar**
	y*a*-noo-ar
February	**februar**
	f*e*h-broo-ar
March	**mart**
	m*a*rt
April	**april**
	*a*p-reel
May	**maj**
	m*a*-ee
June	**juni**
	y*oo*-nee
July	**juli**
	y*oo*-lee
August	**august**
	ah-oo-goost
September	**septembar**
	sep-tem-bar
October	**oktobar**
	okt*o*-bar
November	**novembar**
	nov*e*m-bar
December	**decembar**
	deh-ts*e*m-bar

Public holidays

Offices, shops and schools are all closed on the following dates.

1–2 January	**Nova godina**	New Year holiday
1–2 May	**Prvi Maj**	Labour Day
4 July	**Dan borca**	Fighter's Day
29–30 November	**Dan Republike**	Days of the Republic

Republican national holidays

Serbia 7 July
Montenegro 13 July
Slovenia 22 July
Croatia, Bosnia and Herzegovina 27 July
Macedonia 2 August and 11 October

Index

Spanish

D. L. Ellis, R. Ellis

Pronunciation **Dr J. Baldwin**

Useful addresses

Spanish National Tourist Office
665 5th Ave.
New York, NY 10022

Mexican Government Tourist Office
405 Park Ave.
New York, NY 10022

Venezuelan Government Tourist Bureau
450 Park Ave.
New York, NY 10022

Argentina Consulate Tourist Department
1600 N. Hampshire Ave.
Washington, D.C. 20009

Contents

Pronunciation hints

In Spanish it is important to stress or emphasize the syllables in italics, just as you would if we were to take as an English example: *li*ttle Jack *Hor*ner *sat* in the *cor*ner. Here we have ten syllables but only four stresses.
¡Suerte!

Everyday expressions

[See also 'Shop Talk', p. 392]

Hello	**Hola** *o*-la
Good morning	**Buenos días** bwen-os dee*as*
Good afternoon	**Buenas tardes** bwen-as tard-es
Goodnight	**Buenas noches** bwen-as noch-es
Good-bye	**Adiós** ad-yos
Yes	**Sí** see
Please	**Por favor** por fab-or
Yes, please	**Sí, por favor** see por fab-or
Thank you	**Gracias** grath-yas
Thank you very much	**Muchas gracias** moochas grath-yas
That's right	**Exacto** exacto
No	**No** no
No, thank you	**No, gracias** no grath-yas
I disagree	**No estoy de acuerdo** no estoy deh acwaido
Excuse me ⎤ Sorry ⎦	**Perdone** pairdon-eh
It doesn't matter	**No importa** no importa
Where's the toilet, please?	**¿Dónde están los servicios, por favor?** dondeh estan los sairbith-yos por fab-or
Do you speak English?	**¿Habla usted inglés?** abla oosted in-gles

What is your name?	**¿Cómo se llama?**
	com-o seh yama
My name is . . .	**Me llamo . . .**
	meh yamo . . .

Asking the way

ESSENTIAL INFORMATION

- Keep a look out for all these place names as you will find them on shops, maps and notices.

WHAT TO SAY

Excuse me, please	**Perdone, por favor**
	pairdon-eh por fab-or
How do I get . . .	**¿Para ir . . .**
	para eer . . .
to Madrid?	**a Madrid?**
	ah madreed
to Alfonso Primero street?	**a la calle Alfonso Primero?**
	ah la ca-yeh alfonso prim-airo
to the Hotel Castilla?	**al hotel Castilla?**
	al ot-el castee-ya
to the airport?	**al aeropuerto?**
	al airo-pwairto
to the beach?	**a la playa?**
	ah la pla-ya
to the bus station?	**a la estación de autobuses?**
	ah la estath-yon deh ah-ooto-booses
to the market?	**al mercado?**
	al maircad-o
to the police station?	**a la comisaría de policía?**
	ah la comisareea deh politheea
to the port?	**al puerto?**
	al pwairto
to the post office?	**a correos?**
	ah cor-reh-os

Is there . . . near by?	**¿Hay . . . cerca?**
	ah-ee . . . thairca
to the railway station?	**a la estación de tren?**
	ah la estath-yon deh tren
to the sports stadium?	**al estadio de deportes?**
	al estad-yo deh dep-ort-es
to the tourist information office?	**a la oficina de información y turismo?**
	ah la ofitheena deh informath-yon ee too-rismo
to the town centre?	**al centro de la ciudad?**
	al thentro deh la thee-oodad
to the town hall?	**al ayuntamiento?**
	al a-yoontam-yento
Is there . . . near by?	**¿Hay . . . cerca?**
	ah-ee . . . thairca
a baker's	**una panadería**
	oona panad-ereeah
a bank	**un banco**
	oon banco
a bar	**un bar**
	oon bar
a bus stop	**una parada de autobús**
	oona parad-ah deh ah-ooto-boos
a butcher's	**una carnicería**
	oona carnith-ereea
a café	**una cafetería**
	oona cafet-ereea
a cake shop	**una pastelería**
	oona pastel-ereea
a campsite	**un camping**
	oon camping
a car park	**un aparcamiento**
	oon aparcam-yento
a change bureau	**una oficina de cambio**
	oona ofitheena deh camb-yo
a chemist's	**una farmacia**
	oona farmath-ya
a delicatessen	**una mantequería**
	oona mantek-ereea
a dentist's	**un dentista**
	oon dentista

a department store	**unos almacenes**
	*oo*nos almath-*en*-es
a disco	**una discoteca**
	oona discotec-ah
a doctor's surgery	**un consultorio médico**
	oon consooltorio medic-o
a dry cleaner's	**una tintorería**
	*oo*na tintor-er*ee*a
a fishmonger's	**una pescadería**
	*oo*na pescad-er*ee*a
a garage (for repairs)	**un garaje**
	oon ga-*ra*heh
a greengrocer's	**una verdulería**
	*oo*na berdool-er*ee*a
a grocer's	**una tienda de comestibles**
	oona tee-*en*da deh com-est*ee*-bles
a hairdresser's	**una peluquería**
	*oo*na pelook-er*ee*a
a Health and Social Security Office	**una oficina de la Seguridad Social**
	*oo*na ofith*ee*na deh la segoo-reed*ad* soth-y*al*
a hospital	**un hospital**
	oon ospit*al*
a hotel	**un hotel**
	oon ot-*el*
an ice-cream parlour	**una heladería**
	*oo*na ellad-er*ee*a
a laundry	**una lavandería**
	*oo*na laband-er*ee*a
a newsagent's	**una tienda de periódicos**
	*oo*na tee-*en*da deh peri-*o*dicos
a nightclub	**una sala de fiestas**
	*oo*na s*al*-ah deh fee-*es*tas
a petrol station	**una gasolinera**
	*oo*na gasolin-*er*ra
a post box	**un buzón**
	oon booth*on*
a public garden	**un jardín público**
	oon hard*een* p*oo*blico
a public toilet	**unos servicios públicos**
	*oo*nos sairb*ith*-yos p*oo*blicos
a restaurant	**un restaurante**
	oon resta-oor*an*teh

Is there . . . near by?	**¿Hay . . . cerca?**
	*a*h-ee . . . th*ai*rca
a supermarket	**un supermercado**
	oon supermairc*a*d-o
a taxi stand	**una parada de taxis**
	*oo*na par*a*d-ah deh t*a*xis
a telephone	**un teléfono**
	oon tel*e*f-ono
a tobacconist's	**un estanco**
	oon est*a*nco
a travel agent's	**una agencia de viajes**
	*oo*na ah*e*nth-ya deh bee-*a*h-hes
a youth hostel	**un albergue juvenil**
	oon alb*ai*r-geh hooben-*ee*l

DIRECTIONS

Left	**Izquierda**
	ithk-y*ai*rda
Right	**Derecha**
	der*e*ch-ah
Straight on	**Todo recto**
	t*o*do r*e*cto
There	**Allí**
	ay*ee*
First left/right	**La primera a la izquierda/derecha**
	la prim-*ai*ra ah la ithk-y*ai*rda/
	der*e*ch-a
Second left/right	**La segunda a la izquierda/derecha**
	la seg-*oo*nda ah la ithk-y*ai*rda/
	der*e*ch-a

Accommodation

ESSENTIAL INFORMATION
Hotel

- If you want hotel-type accommodation, all the following words in capital letters are worth looking for on signs:
  HOTEL (accommodation with all facilities, the quality depending on the star rating)
  HOTEL-RESIDENCIA (similar to the above but often for longer stays)

PENSION (small, privately run hotel)
HOSTAL
FONDA (a modest form of **pensión**)
MOTEL
ALBERGUE (often picturesque type of hotel situated in the countryside)
PARADOR (converted palaces and castles in recognized beauty spots – relatively expensive)

- The last two are run by the **Secretaria de Estado de Turismo** (Secretary of State for Tourism).
- In some places, you will find the following: **CAMAS** (beds), **HABITACIONES** (rooms), **CASA** (house) followed by the owner's name or **CASA DE HUESPEDES** (guest house) – these are all alternatives to a **pensión**.
- Hotels are divided into five classes (from luxury to tourist class) and **pensiones** into three.
- A list of hotels and **pensiones** in the town or district can usually be obtained at the local tourist information office.
- The cost is displayed in the room itself, so you can check it when having a look around before agreeing to stay.
- The displayed cost is for the room itself, per night and not per person. Breakfast is extra and therefore optional.
- Service and VAT is always included in the cost of the room, so tipping is voluntary. In Spain, however, it is normal practice to tip porters and waiters.
- Not all hotels provide meals, apart from breakfast. A **pensión** always provides meals. Breakfast is continental style: coffee/tea with rolls and jam.
- When registering you will be asked to leave your passport at the reception desk and to complete a form.

WHAT TO SAY

I have a booking	**Tengo una reserva** tengo *oo*na res-*air*ba
Have you any vacancies, please?	**¿Tiene habitaciones libres, por favor?** tee-*en*-eh abeetath-y*on*-es *lee*-bres por fab-*or*
Can I book a room?	**¿Puedo reservar una habitación?** pw*ed*-o res-airb*ar oo*na abeetath-y*on*

It's for . . .	**Es para . . .**
	es p*a*ra . . .
one adult/one person	**un adulto/una persona**
	oon ad*oo*lto/*oo*na pairs*o*n-ah
two adults/two people	**dos adultos/dos personas**
	d*o*s ad*oo*ltos/d*o*s pairs*o*n-as
and one child	**y un niño**
	ee *oo*n n*ee*n-yo
and two children	**y dos niños**
	ee d*o*s n*ee*n-yos
It's for . . .	**Es para . . .**
	es p*a*ra . . .
one night	**una noche**
	*oo*na n*o*ch-eh
two nights	**dos noches**
	d*o*s n*o*ch-es
one week	**una semana**
	*oo*na sem-*a*nna
two weeks	**dos semanas**
	d*o*s sem-*a*nnas
I would like . . .	**Quiero . . .**
	kee-*airo* . . .
a (quiet) room	**una habitación (tranquila)**
	*oo*na abeetath-y*o*n (trank*ee*-ya)
two rooms	**dos habitaciones**
	d*o*s abeetath-y*o*n-es
with a single bed	**con una cama individual**
	con *oo*na c*a*m-ah indibid-w*a*l
with two single beds	**con dos camas individuales**
	con d*o*s c*a*m-as indibid-w*a*l-es
with a double bed	**con una cama doble**
	con *oo*na c*a*m-ah d*o*bleh
with a toilet	**con servicio**
	con sairb*i*th-yo
with a bathroom	**con baño**
	con b*a*n-yo
with a shower	**con ducha**
	con d*oo*cha
with a cot	**con una cuna**
	con *oo*na c*oo*na
with a balcony	**con balcón**
	con balc*o*n

I would like . . .	**Quiero . . .** kee-*air*o . . .
full board	**pensión completa** pens-*y*on compl*e*t-ah
half board	**media pensión** med-ya pens-*y*on
bed and breakfast [*see essential information*]	**desayuno incluido** desa-*y*oono incloo-*ee*do
Do you serve meals?	**¿Sirven comidas?** seerben com-*ee*das
Can I look at the room?	**¿Puedo ver la habitación?** pwed-o b*air* la abeetath-y*on
OK, I'll take it	**Está bien, la tomo** esta bee-*e*n la t*o*m-o
No thanks, I won't take it	**No gracias, no la tomo** no gr*a*th-yas no la t*o*m-o
The bill, please	**La cuenta, por favor** la cwenta por fab-*o*r
Is service included?	**¿Está incluido el servicio?** esta incloo-*ee*do el sairb*i*th-yo
I think this is wrong	**Creo que esto está mal** creh-o keh *e*sto esta m*a*l
Can you give me a receipt?	**¿Puede darme un recibo?** pwed-eh d*a*rmeh oon reth*ee*bo

Camping

- Look for the word: **CAMPING**
- Be prepared to have to pay:
  per person
  for the car (if applicable)
  for the tent or for trailer space
  for electricity
  for hot showers
- You must provide proof of identity such as your passport.
- In Spain, most campsites are situated along the coast and those inland are few and far between. You can camp off-site with the permission of the authorities and/or the landowner; however, there are a number of regulations governing where you can or cannot camp – the Spanish Tourist Office in New York has details so check with them before travelling abroad.

- Camping carnets are no longer essential but advisable as they do provide third-party insurance for those camping off-site.
- During the high season it is advisable to book in advance by writing direct to the campsite.
- Persons under the age of sixteen are not admitted on a site unless accompanied by an adult.

Youth hostels

- Look for the words: **ALBERGUE JUVENIL**.
- You will be asked for a YHA card and passport on arrival.
- Food and cooking facilities vary from hostel to hostel and you may have to help with the domestic chores.
- You must take your own sleeping bag lining but bedding can sometimes be rented on arrival.
- In the high season it is advisable to book beds in advance, and your stay will be limited to a maximum of three consecutive nights per hostel.
- Apply to the Spanish Tourist Office in New York or local tourist offices in Spain for lists of youth hostels and details of regulations for hostellers.

WHAT TO SAY

Have you any vacancies?	**¿Tiene plazas libres?** tee-en-eh pl*a*thas l*ee*-bres
It's for . . .	**Es para . . .** *e*s p*a*ra . . .
one adult/one person	**un adulto/una persona** oon ad*oo*lto/*oo*na pairson-ah
two adults/two people	**dos adultos/dos personas** d*o*s ad*oo*ltos/d*o*s pairson-as
and one child	**y un niño** ee *oo*n n*ee*n-yo
and two children	**y dos niños** ee d*o*s n*ee*n-yos
How much is it . . .	**¿Cuánto es . . .** cw*a*nto *e*s . . .
for the tent?	**por la tienda?** por la tee-*e*nda

for the caravan?	**por la caravana?** por la carab*a*n-ah
for the car?	**por el coche?** por el c*o*ch-eh
for the electricity?	**por la electricidad** por la electrithee-d*a*d
per person?	**por persona?** por pairs*o*n-ah
per day/night?	**por día/noche?** por d*ee*a/n*o*ch-eh
May I look round?	**¿Puedo mirar?** pw*e*d-o mee-r*a*r
Do you provide anything . . .	**¿Dan ustedes algo . . .** d*a*n oost*e*d-es *a*lgo . . .
to eat?	**de comer?** deh com-*air*
to drink?	**de beber?** deh beb-*air*
Is there/are there . . .	**¿Hay . . .** *a*h-ee . . .
a bar?	**bar?** b*a*r
hot showers?	**duchas calientes?** d*oo*chas cal-y*e*ntes
a kitchen?	**cocina?** coth*ee*na
a laundry?	**lavandería?** laband-er*ee*a
a restaurant?	**restaurante?** resta-oor*a*nteh
a shop?	**tienda?** tee-*e*nda
a swimming pool?	**piscina?** pis-th*ee*na
a takeaway?	**tienda de comidas preparadas?** tee-*e*nda deh com-*ee*das prepa-r*a*d-as

[*For food shopping, see p. 394, and for eating and drinking out, see p. 405*]

I would like a counter for the shower	**Quiero una ficha para la ducha** kee-*airo* *oo*na f*ee*cha para la d*oo*cha

Problems

The toilet	**El servicio**
	el sairb*i*th-yo
The shower	**La ducha**
	la d*oo*cha
The tap	**El grifo**
	el gr*ee*fo
The razor point	**El enchufe de la maquinilla de afeitar**
	el ench*oo*feh deh la makin*ee*-ya deh affayt*a*r
The light	**La luz**
	la l*oo*th
. . . is not working	**. . . está roto/a**
	. . . est*a* r*o*t-o/ah
My camping gas has run out	**Mi camping gas se ha acabado**
	mee c*a*mping g*a*s seh *a*h acab*a*d-o

LIKELY REACTIONS

Have you an identity document?	**¿Tiene usted un documento de identidad?**
	tee-*e*n-eh oost*e*d oon docoom*e*nto deh id-entid*a*d
Your membership card, please	**Su carnet, por favor**
	soo carn*e*t por fab-*o*r
What's your name? [see p. 379]	**¿Cómo se llama?**
	c*o*m-o seh y*a*ma
Sorry, we're full	**Lo siento, está lleno**
	lo see-*e*nto est*a* y*e*n-o
How many people is it for?	**¿Para cuántas personas es?**
	p*a*ra cw*a*ntas pairs*o*n-as *e*s
How many nights is it for?	**¿Para cuántas noches es?**
	p*a*ra cw*a*ntas n*o*ch-es *e*s
It's (100) pesetas . . .	**Son (cien) pesetas . . .**
	son (thee-*e*n) pes-*e*t-as . . .
per day/per night	**por día/por noche**
	por d*ee*a/por n*o*ch-eh
I haven't any rooms left	**No me quedan habitaciones**
	n*o* meh k*e*d-an abeetath-y*o*n-es
Do you want to have a look?	**¿Quiere ver la habitación?**
	kee-*ai*reh b*ai*r la abeetath-y*o*n

General shopping

The drugstore/The chemist's

ESSENTIAL INFORMATION

- Look for the word **FARMACIA** (drugstore), or these signs.
- Medicines (drugs) are available only at a drugstore.
- Some non-drugs can be bought at a supermarket or department store, of course.
- Try a pharmacist *before* going to a doctor: they are usually qualified to treat minor injuries.
- Normal opening times are 9 a.m. – 1 p.m. and 4 p.m. – 8 p.m.
- If a drugstore is closed, a notice on the door headed **FARMACIAS DE GUARDIA** gives the address of the nearest pharmacist on duty.
- Some toiletries can also be bought at a **PERFUMERIA**, but they will probably be more expensive.

WHAT TO SAY

I'd like . . .	**Quiero . . .**
	kee-*airo* . . .
some antiseptic	**antiséptico**
	antis*e*ptico
some aspirin	**aspirinas**
	aspir*in*-as
some baby food	**comida para niños**
	com-*ee*da *p*ara n*ee*n-yos
some contraceptives	**anticonceptivos**
	anti-conthept-*ee*bos
some cotton	**algodón**
	algod-*on*
some disposable diapers	**pañales de papel**
	pan-y*al*-es deh pap-*el*
some eye drops	**gotas para los ojos**
	g*o*t-as para los *o*-hos

I'd like . . .	**Quiero . . .**
	kee-*airo* . . .
some inhalant	**inhalante**
	in-al*a*nteh
some insect repellent	**loción contra los insectos**
	loth-y*o*n c*o*ntra los ins*e*ctos
some paper tissues	**tisús**
	tis*oo*s
some sanitary napkins	**compresas**
	compr*e*s-as
some sticking plaster	**esparadrapo**
	esparadr*a*ppo
some suntan lotion/oil	**loción/aceite bronceador**
	loth-y*o*n/ath*ay*-teh bronteh-ad*o*r
some Tampax	**Tampax**
	t*a*mpax
some (soft) toilet paper	**papel higiénico (suave)**
	pap-*e*l eehi-y*e*nnico (sw*a*-beh)
I'd like something for . . .	**Quiero algo para . . .**
	kee-*airo a*lgo p*a*ra . . .
bites/stings	**las picaduras**
	las pic-ad*oo*ras
burns	**las quemaduras**
	las kem-ad*oo*ras
a cold	**el catarro**
	el cat*a*rro
constipation	**el estreñimiento**
	el estren-yee-mee-*e*nto
a cough	**la tos**
	la t*o*s
diarrhoea	**la diarrea**
	la dee-ah-r*e*h-ah
ear-ache	**el dolor de oido**
	el dol-*o*r deh o-*ee*do
flu	**la gripe**
	la gr*ee*p-eh
scalds	**las escaldaduras**
	las escald-ad*oo*ras
sunburn	**las quemaduras de sol**
	las kem-ad*oo*ras deh s*o*l
travel sickness	**el mareo**
	el ma-r*e*yo

[*For other essential expressions, see 'Shop talk', p. 392*]

Holiday items

ESSENTIAL INFORMATION

- Places to shop at and signs to look for:
  LIBRERIA-PAPELERIA (bookshop/stationery store)
  FOTOGRAFIA (films)
  MATERIAL FOTOGRAFICO (films)
  and the main department stores:
  GALERIAS PRECIADOS
  SEPU
  EL CORTE INGLES

WHAT TO SAY

I'd like . . .	**Quiero . . .** kee-*air*o . . .
a bag	**un bolso** oon b*o*lso
a beach ball	**una pelota para la playa** *oo*na pel*o*ta p*a*ra la pl*a*-ya
a bucket	**un cubo** oon c*oo*bo
an English newspaper	**un periódico inglés** oon peri-*o*d-ico in-gl*e*s
some envelopes	**sobres** sob-res
some postcards	**postales** post*a*l-es
a spade	**una pala** *oo*na p*a*l-ah
a straw hat	**un sombrero de paja** oon sombr*air*o deh p*a*-ha
some sunglasses	**unas gafas de sol** *oo*nas g*a*f-as deh s*o*l
some writing paper	**papel de escribir** pap-*e*l deh escrib-*ee*r
a roll of color film [*show the camera*]	**un rollo en color** oon r*o*-yo en col-*o*r
a roll of black and white film	**un rollo en blanco y negro** oon r*o*-yo en bl*a*nco ee n*e*g-ro

[*For other essential expressions, see 'Shop talk', p. 392*]

Shop talk

ESSENTIAL INFORMATION

- Know how to say the important weights and measures

50 grams	**cincuenta gramos**	
	thin-cwenta gram-os	
100 grams	**cien gramos**	
	thee-en gram-os	
200 grams	**doscientos gramos**	
	dos-thee-entos gram-os	
½ kilo	**medio kilo**	
	med-yo kilo	
1 kilo	**un kilo**	
	oon kilo	
2 kilos	**dos kilos**	
	dos kilos	
½ litre	**medio litro**	
	med-yo litro	
1 litre	**un litro**	
	oon litro	
2 litres	**dos litros**	
	dos litros	

[*For numbers, see p. 424*]

CUSTOMER

I'm just looking	**Sólo estoy mirando**
	sol-o estoy mirrando
How much is this/that?	**¿Cuánto es esto/eso?**
	cwanto es esto/es-o
What is that?	**¿Qué es eso?**
	keh es es-o
What are those?	**¿Qué son esos?**
	keh son es-os
Is there a discount?	**¿Hay descuento?**
	ah-ee des-cwento
I'd like that, please	**Quiero eso, por favor**
	kee-airo es-o por fab-or

Not that	**Eso no**
	es-o no
Like that	**Así**
	asee
That's enough, thank you	**Basta, gracias**
	basta grath-yas
More, please	**Más, por favor**
	mas por fab-or
Less, please	**Menos, por favor**
	men-os por fab-or
That's fine	**Eso está bien**
	es-o está bien
OK	**Está bien**
	esta bee-en
I won't take it, thank you	**No lo tomo, gracias**
	no lo tom-o grath-yas
It's not right	**No está bien**
	no esta bee-en
Have you got something . . .	**¿Tiene algo . . .**
	tee-en-eh algo . . .
better?	**mejor?**
	meh-hor
cheaper?	**más barato?**
	mas ba-rat-o
different?	**diferente?**
	diffair-enteh
larger?/smaller?	**más grande?/pequeño?**
	mas grandeh/peken-yo
Can I have a bag, please?	**¿Puedo tener una bolsa, por favor?**
	pwed-o ten-air oona bolsa por
	fab-or
Can you give me a receipt?	**¿Puede darme un recibo?**
	pwed-eh darmeh oon retheebo
Do you take . . .	**¿Toman ustedes . . .**
	tom-an oosted-es . . .
English/American money?	**dinero inglés/americano?**
	din-airo in-gles/americano
travellers' cheques?	**cheques de viaje?**
	chek-es deh bee-ah-heh
credit cards?	**tarjetas de crédito?**
	tarhet-as deh credit-o

SHOP ASSISTANT

Can I help you?	**¿En qué puedo servirle?** en keh pwed-o sairbeer-leh
What would you like?	**¿Qué desea/quiere?** keh des-eh-ah/kee-aireh
Will that be all?	**¿Será eso todo?** serra es-o tod-o
Is that all?	**¿Eso es todo?** es-o es tod-o
Anything else?	**¿Algo más?** algo mas
Would you like it wrapped?	**¿Quiere que se lo envuelva?** kee-aireh keh seh lo enbwelba
Sorry, none left	**Lo siento, no queda ninguno** lo see-ento no ked-ah nin-goono
I haven't got any	**No tengo** no tengo
I haven't got any more	**No tengo más** no tengo mas
How many do you want?	**¿Cuántos quiere?** cwantos kee-aireh
How much do you want?	**¿Cuánto quiere?** cwanto kee-aireh
Is that enough?	**¿Basta?** basta

Shopping for food

Bread

ESSENTIAL INFORMATION

- Key words to look for:
  HORNO (bakery)
  PANADERIA (bakery)
  PANADERO (baker)
  PAN (bread)

- **Panaderías**, as well as other shops, are open from 9 a.m. – 1 p.m. and from 4 p.m. – 8 p.m. closing at lunchtime. In popular resorts, the shops often remain open all day.
- The most characteristic type of loaf is the **barra** which is a wider version of the 'french stick', and comes in different sizes according to the weight.
- For any other type of loaf, say **un pan** (oon p*a*n), and point.
- In some bakeries you can buy milk; look for this sign: **LECHERIA-PANADERIA**. Soft drinks, sweets and ice-creams can also be bought here.
- It's quite usual in Spain to have your bread delivered; if you wish to take advantage of this service, simply have a word with your local baker. You only have to say: **¿Puede traer el pan a casa?** (pw*e*d-eh tra-*air* el p*a*n ah c*a*s-a).

WHAT TO SAY

A loaf (like that)	**Un pan (así)** oon p*a*n (as*ee*)
One long loaf	**Una barra** *oo*na b*a*rra
Three loaves	**Tres panes** tres p*a*n-es
A bread roll	**Un panecillo** oon panneth*ee*-yo
Four crescent rolls	**Cuatro croissants** cw*a*tro crw*a*ssans
A packet of . . .	**Un paquete de . . .** oon pak*e*t-eh deh . . .
English bread	**pan de molde** p*a*n deh m*o*ldeh
toasted bread	**pan tostado** p*a*n tost*a*d-o
brown bread	**pan integral** p*a*n inteh-gr*a*l

[*For other essential expressions, see 'Shop talk', p. 392*]

Cakes and ice cream

ESSENTIAL INFORMATION

- Key words to look for:
  PASTELERIA (cake shop)
  CONFITERIA (candy shop, they also sell cakes)
  PASTELERO (cake/pastry maker)
  PASTELES (cakes)
  PASTAS (pastries)
  HELADOS (ice creams)
  HELADERO (ice-cream maker/seller)
  HELADERIA (ice-cream shop/parlour)
  HORCHATERIA (ice-cream shop which also sells soft ice drinks)
- **CHURRERIA**: a place to buy **churros**, a kind of fritter that can
  be eaten on its own or dipped in hot thick chocolate. You have to
  ask for: **chocolate con churros.**
- **CAFETERIA**: a place where you can buy cakes, as well as drinks.
  You can also have chocolate and **churros**. See p. 405 'Ordering
  a drink and a snack'.

WHAT TO SAY

The type of cakes you find in the shops varies from region to region
but the following are some of the most common.

un churro oon ch*oo*ro	a finger-size fritter
un buñuelo oon boon-yoo-*e*l-o	a round fritter
magdalenas magda-len-as	madeleines (small sponge teacakes)
una ensaimada oona en-sa-ee-m*a*d-ah	a bun made of puff pastry covered with sugar icing and filled with cream
el mantecado el manteh-c*a*d-o	shortbread
turrón too-r*o*n	nougat (can be hard or soft)
el mazapán el matha-p*a*n	marzipan

una yema oona yem-ah	a candied egg yolk
una rosquilla oona ros-kee-ya	a ring-shaped roll (like a doughnut)
un merengue oon meh-ren-geh	a meringue

A . . . ice cream, please	**Un helado de . . ., por favor** oon elad-o deh . . . por fab-or
chocolate	**chocolate** chocolat-eh
pistachio	**mantecado** manteh-cad-o
raspberry	**frambuesa** frambwessa
strawberry	**fresa** fressa
vanilla	**vainilla** banee-ya
nougat flavour	**turrón** too-ron
hazelnut	**avellana** ab-el-yanna
mint	**menta** menta
A single [*specify flavour as above*]	**Uno sencillo** oono senthee-yo

Picnic food

ESSENTIAL INFORMATION

● Key words to look for:
CHARCUTERIA (delicatessen)
EMBUTIDOS (cold meat sausages)
FIAMBRES (cold meat, cold cuts)
TIENDA DE ULTRAMARINOS (grocery)
MANTEQUERIA (delicatessen)
CARNECERIA (butcher shop)

- In these shops you can buy a wide variety of food such as ham, salami, cheese, olives, appetizers, sausages and freshly made takeout dishes. Specialties differ from region to region.

WHAT TO SAY

Two slices of . . .	**Dos rodajas de . . .** dos rod-*a*has deh . . .
salami	**salchichón** salcheech*o*n
spicy hard sausage	**chorizo** chor-*ee*tho
pâté	**paté** pat*e*h
ham	**jamón de york** ham-*o*n deh york
cured ham, thinly sliced	**jamón serrano** ham-*o*n serr*a*nno
pork and beef cold meat	**mortadela** morta-d*e*lla
stuffed turkey	**pavo trufado** p*a*b-o troofad-*o*

You may also like to try some of these:

pizza p*i*zza	pizza
salchicha de frankfurt salcheecha deh fr*a*nkfort	frankfurter
pollo asado p*o*l-yo asad-*o*	roast chicken
morcilla morth*ee*-ya	black pudding
palitos de queso pal*ee*tos deh k*e*s-o	cheese sticks
cortezas cort*e*th-as	pork crackling/scratchings
puntas de espárragos p*oo*ntas deh esp*a*rragos	asparagus tips
salmón ahumado sal-m*o*n ah-oomad-*o*	smoked salmon
butifarra booti-f*a*rra	spiced sausage

longaniza	highly-seasoned sausage made with
longa-n*ee*tha	pork and herbs
olivas rellenas	stuffed olives
ol*ee*bas reh-yen-as	
olivas negras	black olives
ol*ee*bas n*e*g-ras	
patatas fritas	crisps
pat*a*t-as fr*ee*tas	
pepinillos	gherkins
peppin*ee*-yos	
galletas saladas	crackers
ga-y*e*t-as sal*a*d-as	
sardinas en aceite	sardines in oil
sard*ee*nas en ath*ay*-teh	
sardinas rancias	dry salty sardines
sard*ee*nas r*a*nth-yas	
atún	tuna
at*oo*n	
queso de Burgos	soft, creamy cheese
k*e*s-o deh b*oo*rgos	
queso manchego	hard cheese from ewe's milk
k*e*s-o mancheg-o	
queso de roncal	salted, smoked cheese made from
k*e*s-o deh roncal	ewe's milk
queso de bola	a round-shaped, mild cheese
k*e*s-o deh b*o*l-ah	
queso de cabra	goat cheese
k*e*s-o deh c*a*bra	
queso de teta	a firm, bland cheese made from
k*e*s-o deh t*e*ta	cow's milk

[*For other essential expressions, see 'Shop talk', p. 392*]

Fruit and vegetables

ESSENTIAL INFORMATION

● Key words to look for:
VERDURA (vegetables)   **FRUTA** (fruit)
LEGUMBRES (vegetables)   **FRUTERO** (fruit seller)
VERDULERIA (vegetable shop)   **FRUTERIA** (fruit shop)

FRESCO (an indication of freshness)

● It is customary for you to choose your own fruit and vegetables in the market (and in some shops) and for the vendor to weigh and price them. You must take your own shopping bag: paper and plastic bags are not normally provided.

WHAT TO SAY

1 kilo of . . .	**Un kilo de . . .** oon k*i*lo deh . . .
apples	**manzanas** manth*a*nas
bananas	**plátanos** pl*a*ttan-os
cherries	**cerezas** ther*e*th-as
figs	**higos** *ee*-gos
grapes (black/white)	**uvas (blancas/negras)** *oo*bas (bl*a*ncas/n*e*g-ras)
oranges	**naranjas** na-r*a*ng-has
pears	**peras** p*e*rras
peaches	**melocotones** mellocot*o*n-es
plums	**ciruelas** theer-rw*e*llas
strawberries	**fresas** fr*e*ssas
A pineapple, please	**Una piña, por favor** *oo*na p*ee*n-ya por fab-*o*r
A grapefruit	**Un pomelo** oon pom*e*llo
A melon	**Un melón** oon mel*o*n
A water-melon	**Una sandía** *oo*na sand*ee*a
½ kilo of . . .	**Medio kilo de . . .** med-yo k*i*lo deh . . .
artichokes	**alcachofas** alkach*o*ffas

asparagus	**esparrago**
	esp*a*rrago
broad beans	**habas**
	*a*bbas
carrots	**zanahorias**
	thanna-*o*ree-as
green beans	**judías verdes**
	hood*ee*-as b*air*-des
leeks	**puerros**
	pw*e*rros
mushrooms	**champiñones**
	champin-y*o*n-es
onions	**cebollas**
	theb*o*l-yas
peas	**guisantes**
	ghiss*a*nt-es
potatoes	**patatas**
	pat*a*t-as
shallots	**chalotes**
	chall*o*t-es
spinach	**espinacas**
	espin*a*c-as
tomatoes	**tomates**
	tom*a*t-es
A bunch of . . .	**Un puñado de . . .**
	oon poon-y*a*d-o deh . . .
parsley	**perejil**
	perreh*i*l
radishes	**rábanos**
	r*a*b-annos
A head of garlic	**Una cabeza de ajo**
	*oo*na cabeth-ah deh *a*h-ho
A lettuce	**Una lechuga**
	oona lech*oo*ga
A cucumber	**Un pepino**
	oon pep*ee*no
Like that, please	**Así, por favor**
	as*ee* por fab-*o*r

Meat and fish

ESSENTIAL INFORMATION

- Key words to look for:
  CARNICERIA (butcher shop)
  CARNICERO (butcher)
  PESCADERIA (fish store)
  MARISCOS (seafood)
- The diagrams opposite are to help you make sense of labels on counters and supermarket displays, and decide which cut or roast to choose. Translations do not help, and you don't need to say the Spanish word involved.
- Markets and large supermarkets usually have a fresh-fish counter.

WHAT TO SAY

For a roast, choose the type of meat and then say how many people it is for:

Some beef, please	**Buey, por favor**
	bway por fab-or
Some lamb/young lamb	**Cordero/ternasco**
	cordairo/tairnasco
Some mutton	**Carnero/oveja**
	carnairo/obeh-ha
Some pork	**Cerdo**
	thairdo
Some veal	**Ternera**
	tairnaira
A roast . . .	**Un asado . . .**
	oon asado . . .
for two people	**para dos personas**
	para dos pairson-as
for four people	**para cuatro personas**
	para cwatro pairson-as
for six people	**para seis personas**
	para seys pairson-as
Some steak, please	**Bistec, por favor**
	bistec por fab-or

Some liver	**Hígado**
	*ee*ga-do
Some kidneys	**Riñones**
	rin-yon-es
Some sausages	**Salchichas**
	salch*ee*chas
Some mince	**Carne picada**
	c*a*rneh peec*a*da
Two veal escalopes	**Dos escalopes de ternera**
	dos escal*o*p-es deh tairn*ai*ra
Three pork chops	**Tres chuletas de cerdo**
	tres chool*e*ttas deh th*ai*rdo
Four mutton chops	**Cuatro chuletas de oveja**
	cw*a*tro chool*e*ttas deh ob*e*h-ha
Five lamb chops	**Cinco chuletas de cordero**
	th*i*nko chool*e*ttas deh cord*ai*ro
A chicken	**Un pollo**
	oon p*o*l-yo
A rabbit	**Un conejo**
	oon conn*e*h-ho
A tongue	**Una lengua**
	*oo*na len-gwa

Purchase large fish and small shellfish by weight:

½ kilo of . . .	**Medio kilo de . . .**
	m*e*d-yo k*i*lo deh . . .
clams	**almejas**
	alm*e*h-has
cod	**bacalao**
	bakkal*a*-o
fresh tuna	**bonito**
	bon*ee*to
hake	**merluza**
	mairl*oo*tha
mussels	**mejillones**
	mehee-y*o*n-es
prawns	**gambas**
	g*a*mbas
salmon	**salmon**
	sal-m*o*n

½ kilo of . . .	**Medio kilo de . . .**
	med-yo kilo deh . . .
sardines	**sardinas**
	sardeenas
sea bream	**besugo**
	besoogo
shrimps (two names)	**camarones/quisquillas**
	cammaron-es/kiskee-yas
sprats	**sardinetas**
	sardinettas
turbot	**rodaballo**
	roddaba-yo
whitebait	**boquerones**
	bokeh-ron-es

For some shellfish and 'frying pan' fish, specify the number:

A crab, please	**Un cangrejo, por favor**
	oon cangreh-ho por fab-or
A lobster	**Una langosta**
	oona lan-gosta
A plaice	**Un gallo**
	oon gal-yo
A whiting	**Una pescadilla**
	oona pescadee-ya
A trout	**Una trucha**
	oona troocha
A sole	**Un lenguado**
	oon len-gwaddo
A mackerel	**Una caballa**
	oona cabal-ya
A herring	**Un arenque**
	oon arrenkeh
An octopus	**Un pulpo**
	oon poolpo
A carp	**Una carpa**
	oona carpa

Eating and drinking out

Ordering a drink and a snack

ESSENTIAL INFORMATION

- The places to ask for:
  UNA CAFETERIA (a more luxurious and modern café)
  UN CAFÉ
  UN BAR
- If you want to try Spanish wine and **tapas** in a typically Spanish atmosphere the places to go are: **UNA TASCA, UNA BODEGA, UN MESON** or **UNA TABERNA**. Usually you'll find all these places in the same area and it is the custom to make a tour of several local bars having one or two drinks in each.
- By law, the price list of drinks (**TARIFA** or **LISTA DE PRECIOS**) must be displayed outside or in the window.
- There is waiter service in all cafés, but you can drink at the bar or counter if you wish (cheaper).
- Always leave a tip of 10% to 15% of the bill unless you see **SERVICIO INCLUIDO**, although it is still common practice to leave a few pesetas for these bills also.
- Cafés serve non-alcoholic drinks and alcoholic drinks, and are normally open all day.
- You will find plates of assorted food, e.g. cheese, fish, olives, salads etc. on the bar, usually before lunchtime or dinner time. These are called **tapas**, and you can either have a portion (**una ración** rath-yon) or food skewered on sticks (**banderillas,** bande*ree*-yas). You have them as a snack with your drink. As with drinks you pay for **tapas** on leaving the bar, though some offer small **tapas** free.

WHAT TO SAY

I'd like . . . please	Quiero . . . por favor
	kee-*airo* . . . por fab-*or*
a black coffee	**un café solo**
	oon caf*eh* sol-o
a white coffee	**un café con leche**
	oon caf*eh* con lech-eh

I'd like . . . please	**Quiero . . . por favor** kee-*air*o . . . por fab-*or*
a black coffee with a dash of milk	**un cortado** oon cort*a*d-o
a tea	**un té** oon t*e*h
with milk/lemon	**con leche/limón** con l*e*ch-eh/lim-*o*n
a glass of milk	**un vaso de leche** oon b*a*sso deh l*e*ch-eh
a hot chocolate (thick)	**un chocolate** oon chocol*a*t-eh
a mineral water	**un agua mineral** oon *a*gwa miner*a*l
a lemonade	**una limonada** oona lim-onn*a*d-ah
an orangeade	**una naranjada** oona na-rang-h*a*dda
an orange juice	**un zumo de naranja** oon th*oo*mo deh na-r*a*ng-ha
a grape juice	**un mosto** oon m*o*sto
a pineapple juice	**un zumo de piña** oon th*oo*mo deh p*i*n-ya
a milkshake	**un batido** oon bat*ee*do
a beer	**una cerveza** *oo*na thairb*e*th-ah
a draught beer	**una caña** *oo*na c*a*n-ya
a cider	**una sidra** *oo*na s*i*dra
I'd like . . . please	**Quiero . . . por favor** kee-*air*o . . . por fab-*or*
a cheese sandwich	**un bocadillo de queso** oon boccad*ee*-yo deh k*e*s-o
a ham sandwich	**un bocadillo de jamón de york** oon boccad*ee*-yo deh ham-*o*n deh york
a smoked ham sandwich	**un bocadillo de jamón serrano** oon boccad*ee*-yo deh ham-*o*n serr*a*nno

These are some other snacks you may like to try:

albondigas con tomate	spiced meatballs in tomato sauce
albondeegas con tomat-eh	
banderillas	savouries on sticks
bandere*e*-yas	
berberechos	cockles in vinegar
bairbehrech-os	
callos	tripe, usually in hot paprika suace
c*a*-yos	
caracoles	snails
carracol-es	
empanadillas	small pastries with a variety of
empannade*e*-yas	fillings
patatas bravas	fried potatoes in spicy sauce
pat*a*t-as br*a*b-as	
pimientos rellenos	stuffed peppers
pim-y*e*ntos rel-y*e*nos	
pinchitos	grilled kidneys or spicy sausages
pinch*ee*tos	(usually on skewers)
tortilla de patata	Spanish omelet, made of potatoes
tort*ee*-ya deh pat*a*t-ah	and onions

In a restaurant

ESSENTIAL INFORMATION

* You can eat at these places:
  RESTAURANTE
  CAFETERIA (luxurious café)
  HOSTERIA
  MESON
  PARADOR　　　　　(regional cooking)
  POSADA
  ALBERGUE DE CARRETERA (roadside inn)
  FONDA (cheap simple food)
  MERENDERO (on the outskirts of a town suitable for meals or snacks during the early evening)
  CASA DE COMIDAS (a simple restaurant with typical Spanish food)

- You may also find **CASA** plus the name of the owner.
- Tipping is very common in Spain and it is usual to leave 10% of the bill for the waiter.
- By law, the menus must be displayed outside or in the window and that is the only way to judge if a place is right for your needs.
- Self-service restaurants (**AUTOSERVICIOS**) are not unknown, but all other places have waiter service.
- Restaurants are usually open from 1 p.m. – 3/3.30 p.m. and from 9 p.m. – 11.30 p.m. but this can vary. It's not difficult to get a meal before 9 p.m. as lots of restaurants, especially **CASAS DE COMIDAS** or **MESONES** provide meals in the early evening (**meriendas**). And if you want to eat before 1 p.m. you can always try some **tapas** which can be a meal in themselves.
- By law, **Hojas de Reclamaciones** (Complaint Forms) must be kept in restaurants as well as in hotels, bars and gas stations. All complaints are investigated by the Tourist Authority.

WHAT TO SAY

May I book a table?	**¿Puedo reservar una mesa?**
	pwed-o res-airbar oona mes-ah
I've booked a table	**He reservado una mesa**
	eh res-airbad-o oona mes-ah
A table . . .	**Una mesa . . .**
	oona mes-ah . . .
for one	**para uno**
	para oono
for three	**para tres**
	para tres
The à la carte menu, please	**El menú a la carta, por favor**
	el menoo ah la carta por fab-or
The fixed-price menu	**El menú de precio fijo**
	el menoo deh preth-yo fee-ho
The (300) pesetas menu	**El menú de (trescientas) pesetas**
	el menoo deh (tres-thee-entas) pes-et-as
The tourist menu	**El menú turístico**
	el menoo tooristico
Today's special menu	**El menú del día**
	el menoo del deea
The wine list	**La lista de vinos**
	la leesta deh beenos

What's this, please? [*point to menu*]	**¿Qué es eso, por favor?** keh es es-o por fab-or
A carafe of wine, please	**Una jarra de vino, por favor** oona harra deh beeno por fab-or
A quarter (25cc)	**Un cuarto** oon cwarto
A half (50cc)	**Medio** med-yo
A glass	**Un vaso** oon basso
A (half) bottle	**Una (media) botella** oona (med-ya) botel-ya
A litre	**Un litro** oon litro
Red/white/rosé/house wine	**Tinto/blanco/rosado/vino de la casa** tinto/blanco/rosad-o/beeno deh la cas-ah
Some more bread, please	**Más pan, por favor** mas pan por fab-or
Some more wine	**Más vino** mas beeno
Some oil	**Aceite** athay-teh
Some vinegar	**Vinagre** beenag-reh
Some salt/pepper	**Sal/pimienta** sal/pim-yenta
Some water	**Agua** agwa
With/without garlic	**Con/sin ajo** con/sin aho
How much does that come to?	**¿Cuánto es?** cwanto es
Is service included?	**¿Está incluído el servicio?** esta incloo-eedo el sairbith-yo
Where is the toilet, please?	**¿Dónde está el servicio, por favor?** dondeh esta el sairbith-yo por fab-or
Miss!/Waiter	**¡Señorita!/¡Camarero!** sen-yoreeta/camma-rairo
The bill, please	**La cuenta, por favor** la cwenta por fab-or

Key words for courses, as seen on some menus:
[*Only ask this question if you want the waiter to remind you of the choice.*]

What have you got in the way of . . .	¿Qué tienen de . . .
	keh tee-*en*-en deh . . .
starters?	**entremeses?**
	entreh-m*ess*-es
soup?	**sopas?**
	s*o*pas
egg dishes?	**huevos?**
	w*e*b-os
fish?	**pescados?**
	pesc*a*d-os
meat?	**carnes?**
	c*a*rnes
game?	**caza?**
	c*a*tha
fowl?	**aves?**
	*a*bes
vegetables?	**verduras/legumbres?**
	bairdo*o*-ras/leh-g*oo*m-bres
cheese?	**quesos?**
	k*e*s-os
fruit?	**frutas?**
	fr*oo*tas
ice-cream?	**helados?**
	el*a*ddos
dessert?	**postres?**
	p*o*s-tres

UNDERSTANDING THE MENU

- You will find the names of the principal ingredients of most dishes on these pages:

Starters p. 398	Fruit p. 400
Meat p. 402	Cheese p. 399
Fish p. 403	Ice-cream p. 397
Vegetables p. 401	Dessert p. 396

- Used together with the following lists of cooking and menu terms, they should help you to decode the menu.

Cooking and menu terms

con aceite	in oil
en adobo	marinated in red wine
al ajillo	in garlic sauce
con ajolio (allioli)	in garlic mayonnaise
ahumado	smoked
en almíbar	in syrup
asado (al ast)	roasted
a la barbacoa	barbecued
a la brasa	grilled on an open fire
en cacerola	casserole
caldo	stock
caliente	hot
cocido	boiled
crudo	raw
a la chilindrón	with tomatoes, peppers and onion
dulce	sweet
en dulce	in sweet sauce
duro	hard boiled
empanado	fried in breadcrumbs
en escabeche	marinated
escalfado	poached
estofado	braised/stewed
flameado	flamed
a la francesa	with milk, flour and butter
frio	cold
frito	fried
gratinado	browned with breadcrumbs or cheese
guisado	stewed
hervido	boiled
horneado	baked
al horno	baked
al jerez	in sherry
en su jugo	pot roasted
con mantequilla	with butter
marinado (a la marinera)	marinated
a minuto	prepared in a very short time
a la parrilla	grilled
pasado por agua	soft boiled
con perejil	with parsley

a la pescadora	with egg, lemon, wine and vinegar
a la plancha	grilled
rehogado	fried in oil with garlic and vinegar
relleno	stuffed
a la romana	deep fried
salado	salted
en salazón	cured
en salsa	in a sauce
en salsa blanca	in a white sauce
salsa mahonesa	in a mayonnaise sauce
salsa verde	sauce made from white wine, herbs, onion and flour
salsa vinagreta	sauce made from salt, vinegar and oil
salteado	sautéed
tostado	toasted
trufado	stuffed with truffles
al vapor	steamed
a la vasca	with asparagus, peas, egg, herbs, garlic, onion and flour
en vinagre	in vinegar

Further words to help you understand the menu:

anguilas	eels
arroz a la cubana	rice, fried eggs, bananas and tomato sauce
arroz a la milanesa	rice with 'chorizo' (spicy sausage), ham, cheese and peas
atún	tuna
brazo de gitano	cake filled with cream or marmalade
buñuelos (buñuelitos)	small fritters with a variety of fillings
cabeza (de cordero)	lamb's head
caldereta	fish or lamb stew
callos (a la madrileña)	tripe in piquant sauce
cocido (madrileño)	vegetable and meat stew with beans or chick-peas
codorniz	quail
cochinillo asado	suckling pig, roasted
congrio	conger eel

conejo a la aragonesa	rabbit cooked with onion, garlic, almonds and herbs
consomé	clear soup
criadillas	sweetbreads
cuajada	coagulated milk, similar to yogurt
empanada gallega	tenderloin of pork, onions and chilli pepper as filling
fabada	beans, black pudding, ham, pig's ear, onion and garlic in a stew
flan	cream caramel
gallina en pepitoria	chicken casserole with almonds and saffron
ganso	goose
garbanzos	chick-peas
gazpacho	cold spicy soup made of onion, tomatoes, peppers, bread, garlic, oil and vinegar
huevos a la flamenca	eggs baked with tomato, ham, onion, asparagus and peppers
huevos al plato	fried eggs
huevos revueltos	scrambled eggs
lentejas	lentils
lengua aragonesa	tongue with vegetables
liebre	hare
lomo	loin
magras con tomate	smoked ham fried with tomatoes
menestra (de verduras, de carne o pollo)	mixed (vegetable, or meat, or chicken) stew
mero (lubina)	sea bass
migas	bits of bread fried with garlic, spicy sausages, bacon and ham
natillas	custard
paella catalana	spicy pork sausages, pork, squid, tomato, chilli pepper and peas
paella marinera	fish and seafood only
paella valenciana	the classic paella with chicken, mussels, shrimp, prawns, peas, tomato, peppers and garlic
parrillada	boned and shelled fish, shellfish, chicken and meat, fried
pastel de carne	meat pie
pato	duck

pavo	turkey
perdiz	partridge
pimientos a la riojana	sweet peppers stuffed with minced meat
pisto	fried mixed vegetables
pollo a la chilindrón	chicken fried with tomatoes, peppers and smoked ham or bacon
potaje	vegetable stew
pote gallego	beans, meat, potatoes and cabbage
puchero de gallina	stewed chicken
salmonete	red mullet
sesos	brains (of lamb)
solomillo	tenderloin steak (of pork)
sopa Juliana	shredded vegetable soup
ternasco a la aragonesa	young lamb roasted with potatoes and garlic
tocino	bacon
toro de lidia	beef from the bullring
torrijas	bread soaked in milk and egg and then fried, sprinkled with sugar (french toast)
tortilla francesa	plain omelet
tortilla de patatas/española	typical Spanish omelet made with potatoes
trucha a la navarra	trout filled with smoked ham
zarzuela	savoury stew of assorted fish and shellfish

Health

ESSENTIAL INFORMATION

- Be sure to have health insurance.
- For minor disorders and treatment at a pharmacy, see p. 389.
- For finding your way to a doctor, dentist or pharmacy, see p. 380.

- In case of sudden illness or an accident, you can go to a **CASA DE SOCORRO.** These are emergency first-aid centers open to the general public and are free. If you have a serious accident, the same free service is provided by an **equipo quirúrgico.** If you are on the road there are **PUESTOS DE SOCORRO** (first-aid centers) run by the **CRUZ ROJA** (Red Cross).
- To find a doctor in an emergency, look for:
  Médicos (in the Yellow Pages of the telephone directory)
  Urgencias (emergency ward)

Casas de Socorro	
Puestos de Socorro	(first-aid centers)
H	
Hospital	(hospital)

What's the matter?

I have a pain here [*point*]	**Me duele aquí**
	meh dwel-eh ak-*ee*
I have a toothache	**Me duelen las muelas**
	meh dwel-en las mwel-as
I have broken . . .	**Me he roto . . .**
	meh *eh* rot-o . . .
my dentures	**la dentadura**
	la dentado*o*ra
my glasses	**las gafas**
	las gaf-as
I have lost . . .	**He perdido . . .**
	eh pairde*e*do . . .
my contact lenses	**mis lentes de contacto**
	mees lent-es deh contacto
a filling	**un empaste**
	oon emp*a*steh
My child is ill	**Mi hijo/a está enfermo/a***
	mee *ee*ho/ah esta enf*air*mo/ah

*For boys use **'o'**, for girls use **'a'**.

Already under treatment for something else?

I take . . . regularly [*show*]	**Tomo . . . regularmente**
	tom-o . . . regoolarmenteh
this medicine	**esta medicina**
	esta meditheena

I take . . . regularly [*show*]	**Tomo . . . regularmente**
	tom-o . . . regoolarmenteh
these pills	**estas píldoras**
	*e*stas *pí*ldor-as
I have . . .	**Tengo . . .**
	t*e*ngo . . .
haemorrhoids	**hemorroides**
	emmoro-*ee*d-es
rheumatism	**reuma**
	reh-*oo*ma
I am . . .	**Soy . . .**
	s*o*y . . .
diabetic	**diabético/a***
	dee-abet-*ee*co/ah
asthmatic	**asmático/a***
	asm*a*tico/ah
I am allergic to (penicillin)	**Soy alérgico/a a (la penicilina)***
	s*o*y al*air*-heeco/ah ah (la penni-thil*ee*na)
I am pregnant	**Estoy embarazada**
	est*o*y embarrath*a*d-ah
I have a heart condition	**Estoy del corazón**
	est*o*y del corath*o*n

*Men use '**o**', women use '**a**'.

Problems: loss, theft

ESSENTIAL INFORMATION

- If worse comes to worst, find the police station. To ask the way, see p. 379.
- Look for:
  COMISARIA DE POLICIA (police station)
  CUARTEL DE LA GUARDIA CIVIL
  (Civil Guard – in small towns and villages)
  OFICINA DE OBJETOS PERDIDOS (lost-and-found office)
- If you lose your passport, go to the nearest U.S. consulate.

• In an emergency dial 091 for the police. The numbers for Fire and Ambulance differ according to region. Remember, however, that the ambulance service is not free and nor are emergency calls from public phones.

LOSS
[*See also 'Theft' below, the lists are interchangeable*]

I have lost . . .	**He perdido . . .**
	eh pairdeedo . . .
my camera	**mi cámara**
	mee camara
my car keys	**las llaves de mi coche**
	las yab-es deh mee coch-eh
my car registration	**mi cartilla de propriedad**
	mee cartee-ya deh prop-yed-ad
my driver's license	**mi carnet de conducir**
	mee carnet deh condootheer
my insurance certificate	**mi certificado del seguro**
	mee thair-tificad-o del segoo-ro

THEFT

Someone has stolen . . .	**Alguien ha robado . . .**
	alg-yen ah robbad-o . . .
my car	**mi coche**
	mee coch-eh
my money	**mi dinero**
	mee din-airo
my tickets	**mis billetes**
	mees bee-yet-es
my travellers' cheques	**mis cheques de viaje**
	mees check-es deh bee-ah-heh
my wallet	**mi cartera**
	mee cartaira
my luggage	**mi equipaje**
	mee ek-ee-pa-heh

The post office and phoning home

ESSENTIAL INFORMATION

- Key words to look for:
  CORREOS
  CORREOS Y TELEGRAFOS
  SERVICIO POSTAL
- It is best to buy stamps at the tobacconist's. Only go to the post office for more complicated transactions, like telegrams.
- Unless you read and speak Spanish well, it's best not to make phone calls by yourself. Go to **CENTRAL TELEFONICA (CTNE)** which in large towns are open twenty-four hours a day and write the town and number you want on a piece of paper and hand it over to the operator.
- In Spain the telephone network operates independently of the post office, so don't expect to find phones in post offices.

WHAT TO SAY

To England, please	**Para Inglaterra, por favor** para ingla-terra por fab-or
[Hand letters, cards or parcels over the counter]	
To Australia	**Para Australia** para ah-oostral-ya
To the United States	**Para los Estados Unidos** para los estad-os ooneedos
I'd like to send a telegram	**Quiero enviar un telegrama** kee-airo embee-ar oon telegramma
I'd like this number . . .	**Quiero este número . . .** kee-airo esteh noomairo . . .
[show number]	
in England	**en Inglaterra** en ingla-terra
in Canada	**en Canadá** en canada
Can you dial it for me, please?	**¿Puede usted marcar por mí, por favor?** pwed-eh oosted marcar por mee por fab-or

Cashing checks and changing money

ESSENTIAL INFORMATION

- Look for these words:
  BANCO (bank)
  CAJA DE AHORROS (savings bank)
  CAMBIO (exchange)
  CAJA DE CAMBIO (exchange teller in a bank)
  OFICINA DE CAMBIO (exchange bureau)
- To cash checks, exactly as at home, use your bank card where you see the Eurocheque sign. Write in English.
- Have your passport handy and remember that in Spain banks open at 9 a.m. and close at 2 p.m. and on Saturdays at 1 p.m.

WHAT TO SAY

I'd like to cash . . .	**Quiero cobrar . . .**
	kee-*airo* cobrar . . .
these travellers' cheques	**estos cheques de viaje**
	*e*stos check-es deh bee-*ah*-heh
this cheque	**este cheque**
	*e*steh check-eh
I'd like to change this . . .	**Quiero cambiar esto . . .**
	kee-*airo* camb-yar esto . . .
into pesetas	**en pesetas**
	en pes-*et*-as
into French francs	**en francos franceses**
	en franc-os franth*es*-es
into lire	**en liras**
	en l*ee*-ras
into escudos	**en escudos**
	en esc*oo*dos

Car travel

ESSENTIAL INFORMATION

- Look for these signs:
  GASOLINA (gasoline)
  GASOLINERA (gas station)
  ESTACION DE SERVICIO (gas station)
- Grades of gasoline:
  NORMAL
  SUPER
  EXTRA
  GAS-OIL (diesel)
- 1 gallon is about 3¾ liters.
- Gasoline prices are standardized all over Spain, and a minimum sale of 5 liters is often imposed.
- For car repairs, look for signs with red, blue and white stripes or
  GARAJE
  TALLER DE REPARACIONES
- Most gas stations operate a 24-hour service, though some close late at night. Take care, however, as the stations themselves are few and far between.
- Garages will open at 8 or 9 a.m. and close between 7.30 and 8 p.m. Most will close lunchtime.

WHAT TO SAY

[*For numbers, see p. 424*]

(Nine) litres of . . .	**(Nueve) litros de . . .**
	(nweb-eh) litros deh . . .
(Five hundred) pesetas of . . .	**(Quinientas) pesetas de . . .**
	(kin-yentas) pes-et-as deh . . .
standard/premium/diesel	**normal/super/gas-oil**
	normal/soopair/gas-oil
Fill it up, please	**Lleno, por favor**
	yeno por fab-or

Can you check . . .
¿**Puede mirar . . .**
pwed-eh mee-rar . . .

the oil?
el aceite?
el athay-teh

the battery?
la batería?
la batteh-reea

the radiator?
el radiador?
el rad-yad-or

the tyres?
los neumáticos?
los neh-oomatticos

I've run out of petrol
Me he quedado sin gasolina
meh eh ked-ad-o sin gasoleena

Can you help me, please?
¿**Puede ayudarme, por favor**
pwed-eh a-yoodarmeh por fab-or

Do you do repairs?
¿**Hacen reparaciones?**
athen reparath-yon-es

I have a puncture
Tengo un neumático pinchado
tengo oon neh-oomattico pinchad-o

I have a broken windscreen
Tengo el parabrisas roto
tengo el parabrees-as rot-o

I think the problem is here
. . . [point]
Creo que el problema esta aquí . . .
creh-o keh el problem-ah esta
ak-ee . . .

LIKELY REACTIONS

We don't do repairs
No se hacen reparaciones
no seh athen reparath-yon-es

Where is your car?
¿**Dónde está su coche?**
dondeh esta soo coch-eh

What make is it?
¿**Qué tipo es?**
keh teepo es

Come back tomorrow/on
Monday
Vuelva mañana/el lunes
bwelba manyan-ah/el loon-es

[For days of the week, see p. 426]

Public transport

ESSENTIAL INFORMATION

- Finding the way to a bus station, bus stop, tram stop, railway station and taxi stand, see p. 379.
- Taxis are usually black sedans with a colored line painted along the side. They display a green light at night and during the day a sign on the windshield which says **LIBRE** (free) if they are available.
- These are the different types of trains, graded according to speed (slowest to fastest):
  TAF/FERROBUS/OMNIBUS
  TRANVIAS/AUTOMOTOR (all short distance local trains, not very reliable)
  EXPRESO/RAPIDO (do not be misled by their names; these are both *slow* trains the only difference being the first travels by night, the second by day)
  ELECTROTREN (fast and comfortable)
  TER (fast and comfortable – surcharge payable)
  TALGO (luxury train – surcharge payable)
- Key words on signs
  ANDEN (platform)
  BILLETES (tickets, ticket office)
  CONSIGNA/EQUIPAJES (left-luggage)
  DESPACHO DE BILLETES/TAQUILLA (ticket office)
  ENTRADA (entrance)
  HORARIO (timetable)
  LLEGADA (arrival)
  OFICINA DE INFORMACION (information office)
  PARADA (bus stop, taxi stop)
  PROHIBIDO (forbidden)
  RENFE (initials of Spanish railways)
  SALIDA (exit)
- Children travel free up to the age of three and pay half-price up to the age of seven. However, if you have an international ticket, children can travel free up to the age of four and travel half-price up to the age of twelve.
- On certain dates throughout the year known as **Días Azules** (Blue Days), numerous reductions are available on train travel;

check with the Spanish Tourist Office for dates and further information.

- On buses and subways there is a flat rate irrespective of distance and it is cheaper to buy a **taco** (book of tickets) for subway travel. Subways operate between 6 a.m. and 1 a.m.
- It is worth booking train and bus trips in advance.

WHAT TO SAY

Where does the train for (Madrid) leave from?	**¿De dónde sale el tren para (Madrid)?** deh dondeh sal-eh el tren para (madrid)
Is this the train for (Madrid)?	**¿Es éste el tren para (Madrid)?** es esteh el tren para (madrid)
Where does the bus for (Barcelona) leave from?	**¿De dónde sale el autobús para (Barcelona)?** deh dondeh sal-eh el ah-ooto-boos para (barthelona)
Is this the bus for (Barcelona)?	**¿Es éste el autobús para (Barcelona)?** es esteh el ah-ooto-boos para (barthelona)
Do I have to change?	**¿Tengo que cambiar?** tengo keh camb-yar
Can you put me off at the right stop, please?	**¿Puede avisarme en mi parada, por favor?** pwed-eh abee-sarmeh en mee parad-ah por fab-or
Can I book a seat?	**¿Puedo reservar un asiento?** pwed-o res-airbar oon as-yento
Where can I get a taxi?	**¿Dónde puedo tomar un taxi?** dondeh pwed-o tom-ar oon taxi
A single	**Un billete de ida solamente** oon bee-yet-eh deh eeda solamenteh
A return	**Un billete de ida y vuelta** oon bee-yet-eh deh eeda ee bwelta
First class	**Primera clase** prim-aira classeh
Second class	**Segunda clase** seg-oonda classeh

One adult	**Un adulto**
	oon ad*oo*lto
Two adults	**Dos adultos**
	dos ad*oo*ltos
and one child	**y un niño**
	ee *oo*n n*ee*n-yo
and two children	**y dos niños**
	ee d*o*s n*ee*n-yos
How much is it?	**¿Cuánto es?**
	cw*a*nto es

Reference

NUMBERS

0	**cero**	th*ai*ro
1	**uno**	*oo*no
2	**dos**	d*o*s
3	**tres**	tr*e*s
4	**cuatro**	cw*a*tro
5	**cinco**	th*i*nko
6	**seis**	se*y*s
7	**siete**	see-*e*t-eh
8	**ocho**	*o*cho
9	**nueve**	nw*e*b-eh
10	**diez**	dee-*e*th
11	**once**	*o*ntheh
12	**doce**	d*o*th-eh
13	**trece**	tr*e*th-eh
14	**catorce**	cat-*o*rtheh
15	**quince**	k*i*ntheh
16	**dieciséis**	dee-ethee-s*e*ys
17	**diecisiete**	dee-ethee-see-*e*t-eh
18	**dieciocho**	dee-ethee-*o*cho
19	**diecinueve**	dee-ethee-nw*e*b-eh
20	**veinte**	b*e*ynteh
21	**veintiuno**	beyntee-*oo*no
22	**veintidós**	beyntee-d*o*s

23	**veintitrés**	beyntee-tres
24	**veinticuatro**	beyntee-cwatro
25	**veinticinco**	beyntee-thinko
26	**veintiséis**	beyntee-seys
27	**veintisiete**	beyntee-see-et-eh
28	**veintiocho**	beyntee-ocho
29	**veintinueve**	beyntee-nweb-eh
30	**treinta**	treynta
31	**treinta y uno**	treynta ee oono
35	**treinta y cinco**	treynta ee thinko
38	**treinta y ocho**	treynta ee ocho
40	**cuarenta**	cwa-renta
41	**cuarenta y uno**	cwa-renta ee oono
45	**cuarenta y cinco**	cwa-renta ee thinko
48	**cuarenta y ocho**	cwa-renta ee ocho
50	**cincuenta**	thin-cwenta
55	**cincuenta y cinco**	thin-cwenta ee thinko
60	**sesenta**	ses-enta
65	**sesenta y cinco**	ses-enta ee thinko
70	**setenta**	set-enta
75	**setenta y cinco**	set-enta ee thinko
80	**ochenta**	ochenta
85	**ochenta y cinco**	ochenta ee thinko
90	**noventa**	nobenta
95	**noventa y cinco**	nobenta ee thinko
100	**cien**	thee-en
101	**ciento uno**	thee-ento oono
102	**ciento dos**	thee-ento dos
125	**ciento veinticinco**	thee-ento beyntee-thinko
150	**ciento cincuenta**	thee-ento thin-cwenta
175	**ciento setenta y cinco**	thee-ento set-enta ee thinko
200	**doscientos**	dos-thee-entos
300	**trescientos**	tres-thee-entos
400	**cuatrocientos**	cwatro-thee-entos
500	**quinientos**	kin-yentos
1000	**mil**	mil
1500	**mil quinientos**	mil kin-yentos
2000	**dos mil**	dos mil
5000	**cinco mil**	thinko mil
10,000	**diez mil**	dee-eth mil
100,000	**cien mil**	thee-en mil
1,000,000	**un millón**	oon mil-yon

TIME

What time is it?	**¿Qué hora es?**
	keh ora es
It's one o'clock	**Es la una**
	es la oona
It's . . .	**Son . . .**
	son . . .
two o'clock	**las dos**
	las dos
three o'clock	**las tres**
	las tres
a quarter past five	**las cinco y cuarto**
	las thinko ee cwarto
half past five	**las cinco y media**
	las thinko ee med-ya
quarter to six	**las seis menos cuarto**
	la seys men-os cwarto
It's . . .	**Es . . .**
	es . . .
noon	**mediodía**
	med-yo-deea
midnight	**medianoche**
	med-ya-noch-eh

DAYS AND MONTHS

Monday	**lunes**
	loon-es
Tuesday	**martes**
	mart-es
Wednesday	**miércoles**
	mee-aircol-es
Thursday	**jueves**
	hweb-es
Friday	**viernes**
	bee-airn-es
Saturday	**sábado**
	sabad-o
Sunday	**domingo**
	domingo

January	**enero**
	en-*air*o
February	**febrero**
	feb-r*air*o
March	**marzo**
	m*ar*tho
April	**abril**
	abr*i*l
May	**mayo**
	m*a*-yo
June	**junio**
	h*oo*n-yo
July	**julio**
	h*oo*l-yo
August	**agosto**
	a-g*o*sto
September	**septiembre**
	sept-y*e*mbreh
October	**octubre**
	oct*oo*breh
November	**noviembre**
	nob-y*e*mbreh
December	**diciembre**
	dith-y*e*mbreh

Index

CONVERSION TABLES

Read the center column of these tables from right to left to convert from metric to customary and from left to right to convert from customary to metric, e.g., 5 liters = 10.50 pints; 5 pints = 2.37 liters.

pints		litres	gallons		litres
2.10	1	0.47	0.26	1	3.79
4.20	2	0.95	0.53	2	7.57
6.30	3	1.42	0.79	3	11.36
8.40	4	1.89	1.06	4	15.14
10.50	5	2.37	1.32	5	18.93
12.60	6	2.84	1.58	6	22.71
14.70	7	3.31	1.85	7	26.50
16.80	8	3.79	2.11	8	30.28
18.90	9	4.26	2.38	9	34.07

ounces		grams	pounds		kilos
0.04	1	28.35	2.20	1	0.45
0.07	2	56.70	4.41	2	0.91
0.11	3	85.05	6.61	3	1.36
0.14	4	113.40	8.82	4	1.81
0.18	5	141.75	11.02	5	2.27
0.21	6	170.10	13.23	6	2.72
0.25	7	198.45	15.43	7	3.18
0.28	8	226.80	17.64	8	3.63
0.32	9	255.15	19.84	9	4.08

inches		centimetres	yards		metres
0.39	1	2.54	1.09	1	0.91
0.79	2	5.08	2.19	2	1.83
1.18	3	7.62	3.28	3	2.74
1.58	4	10.16	4.37	4	3.66
1.95	5	12.70	5.47	5	4.57
2.36	6	15.24	6.56	6	5.49
2.76	7	17.78	7.66	7	6.40
3.15	8	20.32	8.65	8	7.32
3.54	9	22.86	9.84	9	8.23

miles		kilometres
0.62	1	1.61
1.24	2	3.22
1.86	3	4.83
2.49	4	6.44
3.11	5	8.05
3.73	6	9.66
4.35	7	11.27
4.97	8	12.87
5.59	9	14.48

A quick way to convert kilometres to miles: divide by 8 and multiply by 5. To convert miles to kilometres: divide by 5 and multiply by 8.

fahrenheit (°F)	centigrade (°C)	lbs/ sq in	k/ sq cm
212°	100° boiling point	18	1.3
100°	38°	20	1.4
98.4°	36.9° body temperature	22	1.5
86°	30°	25	1.7
77°	25°	29	2.0
68°	20°	32	2.3
59°	15°	35	2.5
50°	10°	36	2.5
41°	5°	39	2.7
32°	0° freezing point	40	2.8
14°	−10°	43	3.0
−4°	−20°	45	3.2
		46	3.2
		50	3.5
		60	4.2

To convert °C to °F: divide by 5, multiply by 9 and add 32. To convert °F to °C: take away 32, divide by 9 and multiply by 5.

CLOTHING SIZES

Remember – always try on clothes before buying. Clothing sizes are usually unreliable.

women's dresses and suits

Europe	38	40	42	44	46	48
UK	32	34	36	38	40	42
USA	10	12	14	16	18	20

men's suits and coats

Europe	46	48	50	52	54	56
UK and USA	36	38	40	42	44	46

men's shirts

Europe	36	37	38	39	41	42	43
UK and USA	14	14½	15	15½	16	16½	17

socks

Europe	38–39	39–40	40–41	41–42	42–43
UK and USA	9½	10	10½	11	11½

shoes

Europe	34	35½	36½	38	39	41	42	43	44	45
UK	2	3	4	5	6	7	8	9	10	11
USA	3½	4½	5½	6½	7½	8½	9½	10½	11½	12½